Who's Who in Fashion

Who's Who in Fashion

Third Edition

Anne Stegemeyer

Fairchild Publications
New York

Library of Congress Catalog Card
Number: 95-61081

ISBN: 1-56365-040-2

GST R 133004424

Printed in the United States of
America

Contents

Preface

Who's Who in Fashion is designed to help students of fashion explore the history of their chosen field — to fill in the background, as it were.

The biographies trace the careers of gifted men and women who've contributed to fashion, not only legendary designers of the past and today's major figures, but also lesser-known performers and newcomers worth watching. There's also a sampling of interesting noncomformists, some of the free spirits who prefer to work off the main fashion routes.

The picture would be incomplete without the style makers — editors, artists, photographers — those with an eye and an instinct for fashion who interpret it for the public. They sketch clothes and photograph them, write about fashion and promote it. Often the first to recognize talent, they seek it out and encourage it. They may occasionally get carried away by their appetite for the new but without their support many a designer would go unrecognized and unappreciated.

It has been an absorbing project. I hope the book will prove useful — to students, to professionals, and to men and women everywhere who share my enthusiasm for this extraordinary, ever-changing business.

Acknowledgments

To the many people who've helped with this book, my warmest thanks. To the designers and their public relations representatives who returned questionnaires and supplied ancillary material, and to my friends and acquaintances in the fashion field who generously shared reminiscences and personal experiences, thanks to all. Some designers, alas, sent inadequate information, promised much but sent nothing, or ignored requests altogether. If a favorite name is not found here, that could be the reason.

Among those who made the book possible, Arlene Bienenfeld's tireless pursuit of the elusive PR person and the delinquent questionnaire was invaluable; without her the book would be much less complete. *Women's Wear Daily* offices in European fashion capitals gave valuable assistance in locating designers, and the librarians at the Fashion Libary of The Fashion Institute of Technology were invariably cooperative and helpful.

My gratitude, as always, goes to Merle Thomason of the *Women's Wear Daily* Library, always ready to supply the pertinent clipping, the missing fact. And from first to last, Olga Kontzias, my patient editor and sympathetic listener, quietly supplied the support I needed to get on with my main job of writing the book.

Thank you one and all. I could never have done it by myself.

Anne Stegemeyer
1995

Photo Credits

Unless otherwise noted, photographs and permission to reprint them in this text have been obtained from the archives of *W*, *Women's Wear Daily*, and *Daily News Record*, Fairchild Publications. The author wishes to especially thank Delcina Charles, in the Library Information Department at Fairchild, for her patience and persistence in gathering the contact files from our extensive list of designers.

Color Plates:
1 Gernreich, The Metropolitan Museum of Art, Gift of Rudi Gernreich Revocable Trust, 1985.
3 Pucci, Emilio Pucci, Italy.
5 Chanel, The Metropolitan Museum of Art, Purchase, Irene Lewisohn Bequest, Catherine Breyer Von Bomel Foundation Fund; Hoechst Fiber Industries Fund; Chauncey Stillman Fund, 1984.
7 Callot Soeurs, The Metropolitan Museum of Art, Gift of Isabel Shults, 1944.
9 Mainbocher, Photograph by Louise Dahl-Wolfe. Fashion Institute of Technology, New York.
10 Fortuny, The Metropolitan Museum of Art, Gift of C. J. Vincent Minetti, 1972.
13 James, Photograph by Louise Dahl-Wolfe. Fashion Institute of Technology, New York.
14 Beaton, The Kobal Collection.
15 Poiret, The Metropolitan Museum of Art, Gift of Mrs. Muriel Draper, 1943.
16 McCardell, The Metropolitan Museum of Art, Gift of Irving Drought Harris, in memory of Claire McCardell Harris, 1958.
20 Adrian, Norell, McCardell, The Metropolitan Museum of Art. Photograph by Sheldon Collins.
21 (Balenciaga, The Metropolitan Museum of Art, Gift of Louise Rorimer Dushkin, 1980.

A Amies, p. 13: AP/Wide World Photos.
B Balenciaga, p. 20: © Hearst Corporation, *Harper's Bazaar*, 1965. Banton, p. 22: The Kobal Collection. Brooks, p. 32: AP/Wide World Photos. Burrows, p. 33: Henri Bendel, New York.
C Cashin, pp. 41-42: Bonnie Cashin. Cesarani, p. 43: Photograph by Richard Reed. Cipullo, p. 46: Tiffany & Co. Cole, p. 48: Anne Cole. Cummings, p. 52: Photograph by Timothy Greenfield-Sanders.
D Dior, pp. 61-62 and front cover: © 1995 Artists Rights Society (ARS), New York / ADAGP, Paris. Photograph of Dior's New Look by Willy Maywald. Dweck, p. 65: Stephen Dweck.
E Emanuel, p. 71: UPI/Bettmann.
F Fath, p. 75: © Robert Capa, Magnum Photos, Inc. Ferragamo, p. 77: LOCCHI. Fogarty, p. 80: AP/Wide World Photo.
G Galanos, p. 84: James Galanos, California. Galliano, p. 86: Phillip Greenberg, NYT Pictures. Grès, p. 93: Photograph by Eve Arnold, Magnum Photos Inc.
H Hartnell, p. 99: AP/Wide World Photos. Head, p. 100 and back cover: The Kobal Collection. Helpern, p. 102-103: Joan and David.
J Javits, p. 111: Eric Javits.
K Kieselstein-Cord, p. 126: Barry Kieselstein-Cord. Kökin, p. 131: Kokin.
L Léger, p. 145: Hervé Léger, SA.
M Mackie, p. 160: UPI/Bettmann. Mainbocher, p. 161: © 1931 The Hearst Corporation, *Harper's Bazaar*. Maxwell, p. 165: NYT Pictures. McCardell, p. 166 (right): The Brooklyn Museum. Gift of Miss Sally Kirkland. Molyneux, p. 173: © 1931 The Hearst Corporation, *Harper's Bazaar*. Morlotti, p. 176: Dominique Morlotti. Morris, p. 177 (bottom left and right): Photographs by Teresa Misagal.
N Norell, p. 183 and back cover: AP/Wide World Photos; p. 184: The Brooklyn Museum. Gifts of Gustave Tassell (above) and Norman Norell, Inc. (right).
P Peretti, p. 195 and Picasso, p. 196: Tiffany & Co. Pipart, p. 197: Nina Ricci & Co.
Q Quant, p. 202: AP/Wide World Photos.
R Rabanne, p. 204 (both photos): AP/Wide World Photos. Rhodes, p. 206 and back cover: Photographs of designer and 1994 costume by Polly Estes, Zandra Rhodes Ltd.
S Schiaparelli, p. 222 (left) and front cover: © Robert Capa, Magnum Photos, Inc. Schlumberger, p. 223: Tiffany & Co. Sharaff, p. 225: The Kobal Collection. Per Spook, p. 229: Per Spook.
W Weitz, p. 255: J. Schoeneman Inc.

The Fashion Game: What's in a Name?

A business, an industry, the rag trade, a game — fashion's been called by many names, not always complimentary. With its stars and its convoluted financial arrangements it bears some resemblance to organized sports, but sports have rules and there the analogy breaks down. What sport or game could operate in the no-holds-barred, anything-goes state of chaos that is fashion's normal condition?

It was not always thus. Once upon a time, and not too long ago, there were rules of dress — hems so many inches from the floor, bags matched to shoes, gloves all year round, hats always, that sort of thing. Designers were hailed, or reviled as dictators who made women ridiculous by forcing them into bizarre styles. But designers as such are relative newcomers and even before they existed women and men followed certain dress conventions. These, back when royalty really reigned, began in the court and trickled down through the nobility and the rich. There were no designers as such; instead, there were dressmakers of greater or lesser renown, usually women. Not until the 18th century did one of these dressmakers become sufficiently influential for her name to be recorded. This was Rose Bertin, dressmaker and confidante to Queen Marie-Antoinette. Undoubtedly talented, she finally owes her place in history to her domineering personality and her relationship to her famous royal sponsor.

With the onset of the Revolution and the Terror, French fashion went underground. It still existed — even anti-fashion is a form of it — and profound changes in dress coincided with shifts in political structures, but we don't know the dressmakers' names. Perhaps wary of too high a profile (poor Mlle. Bertin, after all, had to flee to England to escape the guillotine), dressmakers kept their place, which was more tradesman than star, and it took over half a century for the next name to leave an imprint.

The year was 1858, and the Second Empire provided a suitable patron, the Empress Eugénie. In a departure from custom, the dressmaker was not only a man but not French; he was a transplanted Englishman.

Aside from sex and nationality, what distinguished this designer from a mere dressmaker? In his way he was a revolutionary. Instead of one dress at a time for individual clients, he designed entire collections; and instead of displaying his creations on dress forms or miniature dolls, he showed them on live mannequins. Perhaps more significantly, he no longer traipsed to his clients' homes but required them to wait on him in his salon. Charles Frederick Worth reshaped forever the way dressmakers did business and became the prototype for today's designers, truly the first *grand couturier*. He was also the first of a number of talented foreigners who have enriched the French couture. Think of the Spanish Balenciaga, the American Mainbocher, the English Molyneux, the German Lagerfeld, the Italian Ferré.

The end of the nineteenth century and the beginning of the twentieth ushered in a period of prosperity and conspicuous consumption, reflected in the elaborate fashions of the day and lasting until the first World War. Couture houses proliferated and we begin to know more designers by name. Paul Poiret was starting out and worked for several fashionable couturiers before setting up for himself in 1904. With a genius for publicity equalled only by his talent, he was the best known but by no means the only designer. Far from it. There were many, among them Lanvin, Callot Soeurs, and Chanel in her first appearance, and more of the English established themselves in Paris — Lucile and the tailors Redfern and Charles Creed.

As World War I ended and people resumed their daily concerns, a burst of creativity in the arts was matched in fashion by the emergence of fresh design talent, names familiar to us today: Vionnet, Chanel, Schiaparelli, Balmain, Nina Ricci, Rochas, Grès. And there were others, many others. Most had begun working before the war but came fully into their own in the heady days of peace. Many of the pre-war designers did not, could not, adjust their styles to the post-war woman and changing social patterns; their houses withered away and most are now obscure footnotes in fashion history.

Like the rest of the western world, America had relied on Paris for fashion direction and might have done so indefinitely if not cut off from its creative sources by two cataclysmic world wars. *Vogue* during the first war promoted the creations of American designers while luxury stores depended on American fashion for high-end glamour, but with peace Paris regained its customary position as fashion arbiter. So things remained between the two great conflicts.

Still, a burgeoning ready-to-wear industry was starting to recognize the worth of original talent and rely less on copyists. Most designers remained anonymous but a handful became known to the public and had their names on the labels. Notable among them were Claire McCardell, Vera Maxwell, and Clare Potter for sportswear, Norman Norell in luxury ready-to-wear, Sylvia Pedlar for lingerie. They were not alone but it took another war and another enforced separation from Europe to bring wider recognition to American designers and turn America into a major fashion force.

With World War II the flow of fashion ideas was again disrupted but at its end Paris again reclaimed its leadership — familiar names resurfaced and new ones appeared, memorably Christian Dior. Once more serious attention was paid to each French fashion edict as fine stores and the fashion press from across America made the twice-yearly pilgrimage to the couture showings.

Despite this business-as-usual atmosphere, there were premonitions of change. The increasing importance of ready-to-wear was so obvious that even the French couturiers had to recognize it. Tired of seeing their ideas exploited by others, they began to produce their own boutique or diffusion collections. Dior and Balmain, Fath and Saint Laurent, one by one they joined the ready-to-wear parade and the *prêt-à-porter* showings became another reason to make the Paris trip.

By the late 1950s and early 1960s the rule-makers may well have felt a chill. Revolutionary rumblings were clearly discernible, centered in London where young, uninhibited designers — the likes of Mary Quant and Zandra Rhodes — gained a following with their anti-establishment ideas. The London Youthquake was felt round the world and London joined the game as an on-again, off-again stop in the itineraries of fashion professionals. The cause of youth was taken up in Paris by Emmanuelle Khanh and the Japanese Kenzo (the first of his countrymen to make a name for himself in international fashion), in New York by Betsey Johnson.

Meanwhile, Italy entered the game on its home ground, both at the couture level and for luxury ready-to-wear and knits, and the Spanish couture was heard from. Even so, for nearly two decades after the war the French couture maintained its dominance and American retailers and manufacturers continued to look there for ideas. They still look to Paris, but now ready-to-wear designers everywhere propose the trends and ideas circulate in all directions. The emphasis has shifted so completely that some houses have dropped couture altogether.

In the 1970s the Japanese became major, major players, showing regularly in Paris. In the couture, there was Hanae Mori. In ready-to-wear, Issey Miyake was followed by Matsuda and Rei Kawakubo, all with highly individual styles, each applying ancient traditions to modern living. Their influence spilled over into the next decade and in the 1980s an influx of adventurous young designers, termed the deconstructionists, started taking a cool look at clothes and the entire business of fashion. As we near the end of this century, the design pool continues to widen, and influential points of view are generated in countries never before associated with fashion — Austria with Helmut Lang, Belgium with Martin Margiela, Ann Demeulemeester, and Dries Van Noten, Germany with Jil Sander and Joop — and on and on.

And what about America? Where do our designers fit in? At the couture level, we've produced a number of world-class players — Mainbocher worked in Paris between the two World Wars, Charles James was recognized there, and recently, Oscar de la Renta has designed for Balmain. It is through our ready-to-wear, however, that we've been most influential and where, in the final analysis we've made our most important contribution, which can be summed up in one word — ease. Think of sportswear, of separates, of denim, of jeans. The ideal of style wedded to comfort, an essentially American attitude, has crossed international boundaries and influenced designers everywhere.

Today, very few pay even lip service to rules of dress, and the wealthy women who once set the standards have been supplanted by newer role models. Still, the game goes on and so do the players — designers, manu-facturers, retailers, models and super-models, photographers, the fashion press. And, oh yes, do not forget the customers, though they, too, have changed. Knowledgeable and demanding, the traditional customer for advanced fashion played an important part in raising standards of design and workmanship to the highest level. She still exists, but increasingly the person interested in cutting-edge fashion is very young, fascinated by novelty, and either ignorant of or uninter-

ested in the finer points of dressmaking. However, a reassuring emphasis on quality from our younger designers gives hope for the future.

In all the fashion hoopla, what tends to be overlooked is that the tiny fraction of the population that cares passionately about clothes and about being in style has always been outnumbered by those intimidated by the entire process. The majority dislikes extremes and is wary of anything too attention-grabbing. Of course, women want their new clothes to look new, but most prefer things not too radically different from what they've been wearing. If these were the only customers, fashion would be nothing more than a trade and a business —and certainly not a lot of fun.

Fortunately, a core of dedicated fashion lovers persists, enthusiasts who recognize and appreciate creativity wherever they find it, and give the encouragement talented people need to survive and generate the ideas that keep fashion alive and move it ahead. These supporters are amused by fashion's whims and thrilled by its successes, and they treasure the variety and enrichment it brings to their lives. As long as they continue to care, it will be well worth every bit of effort, every ounce of skill and daring, every iota of artistry it takes to stay in the game.

A

Joseph Abboud
Adolfo
Adri
Adrian
Agnès B.
Alaïa
Victor Alfaro
Linda Allard
Hardy Amies
John Anthony
Maria Antonelli
Giorgio Armani
Laura Ashley

Abboud, Joseph

Born Boston, Massachusetts, May 5, 1950
Awards Cutty Sark Men's Fashion Award *Most Promising Menswear Designer*, 1988
• Woolmark Award for Distinguished Fashion, 1989 • Council of Fashion Designers of
America (CFDA) *Menswear Designer of the Year:* 1989, 1990

Abboud brings a fresh viewpoint to the conservative realm of men's clothing. Fusing a European aesthetic with American practicality, his clothes are classic but with a contemporary attitude, combining colors and textures to give classicism a modern edge. His women's collection, with the same attitude toward color, fabric, and texture, is based on tailored separates and extends through knits and flowing, body-conscious clothes. Emphasizing style over detail, everything for both men and women is very well made of beautiful fabrics.

Of Lebanese descent, Abboud came to designing with a strong retail background — twelve years in buying, merchandising, and sales promotion at Louis of Boston. He went to work there part time in 1968 during his freshman year at the University of Massachusetts, and full time after graduation. He also studied at the Sorbonne in Paris, where he fell in love with the European sense of style. He left Louis in 1981 for a job as sales rep at Polo/Ralph Lauren, joined the design team, and became associate director of men's wear. Following a year at

Joseph Abboud (above) and a design from his spring 1994 men's wear collection.

Barry Bricken, Abboud was ready to form his own company in 1986. In addition to his signature collection, there are women's clothes (1990) and J.O.E. casual sportswear (1992), as well as a less expensive line of tailored clothing and furnishings. Licenses include accessories, coats, and a fragrance for men, eyewear, women's shoes, a bed and bath collection. He has a retail store in Boston and is sold internationally from England to Australia, Japan to Saudi Arabia.

Adolfo

Born Adolfo Sardina; Havana, Cuba, February 13, 1933
Awards Coty American Fashion Critics' Award *Special Award (millinery):* 1955, 1969

When Adolfo announced his retirement in March 1993, he had been established in fashion for 25 years. First as a milliner, then with custom-made and ready-to-wear, he turned current trends into wearable, elegant clothes for countless socially prominent women and notables such as Nancy Reagan. His knitted dresses and especially his Chanel-inspired knit suits became daytime uniforms, while for evening he created extravagant gowns in luxurious fabrics and characteristically subtle color combinations.

Adolfo demonstrated an early interest in fashion, encouraged by an aunt, Maria Lopez. She took him to Paris to see the designer showings and introduced him to both CHANEL and BALENCIAGA, where he began his career as an apprentice. After a year's apprenticeship he came to New York in 1948 as designer for Danish-born milliner Bragaard. In 1953 he moved to the milliner Emme where he quickly gained recognition

Adolfo's designs from 1984 (left) and 1992 (above).

A

The designer adjusting his design in his studio, 1992.

and in 1956 his name on the label as Adolfo of Emme.

In 1962 he opened his own millinery firm with the help of a $10,000 loan from Bill Blass. Among his many successes were the Panama planter's hat in 1966 and the shaggy Cossack hat in 1967, plus huge fur berets and such non-hats as fur hoods, kidskin bandannas, and long braids entwined with flowers to be attached to the wearer's hair. His declining interest in hats coincided with their disappearance from the heads of fashionable women and Adolfo gradually added clothing, finally switching entirely into apparel. In addition to knits and the suit homages to Chanel, each collection included classic silk print dresses, often paired with the suit jackets, and one or two beautifully tailored coats and suits. His twice-a-year showings invariably brought out a large audience of faithful clients, usually with three or four women appearing in the same suit or dress.

Adolfo faithfully promoted his clothes with trips to stores around the country. In closing his apparel business, he looked forward to a less frenetic schedule, concentrating on his licenses. These include perfume, men's wear, luggage, handbags, sportswear, furs, and hats, and are sold variously in locations from fine specialty stores to J.C. Penney and the QVC television shopping network. Two years after closing his business he returned with a limited collection in his signature style in fall 1995, produced by Castleberry.

Adri

Born Adrienne Steckling; St. Joseph, Missouri, c. 1935
Awards Coty American Fashion Critics' Award *"Winnie,"* 1982

Adri specializes in soft, reality-based clothes combining simple, wearable shapes with unexpected fabrics in interesting mixes. She studied design at Washington University in St. Louis and was a guest editor at *Mademoiselle* magazine during her sophomore year. She continued her studies at Parsons School of Design in New York where CLAIRE MCCARDELL was her critic. McCardell, with her belief in functional, comfortable clothes, proved an important and lasting influence. In October 1971 Adri's clothes were included in a two-designer showing at the Smithsonian Institution in Washington, D.C. The theme was Innovative Contemporary Fashion; the other designer honored was Claire McCardell.

Adri worked at B.H. Wragge for eight years then went on her own. She had a succession of businesses, designing leisure wear as well as ready-to-wear. Deciding that the time had come for a smaller operation, she formed Adri Studio Ltd. in 1993 as a new way of marketing better-priced clothing. With this approach she designs a collection, which is then cut to order for private customers and a select group of retail stores. She has been a critic at Parsons since the early 1980s.

Adrian

Born Gilbert Adrian; Naugatuck, Connecticut, March 3, 1903
Died Los Angeles, California, September 13, 1959
Awards Neiman Marcus Award, 1943 • Coty American Fashion Critics' Award
"Winnie," 1945 • Parsons Medal for Distinguished Achievement, 1956

A top Hollywood studio designer of the 1920s and 1930s, Adrian was also successful at made-to-order and ready-to-wear. He attended the School of Fine and Applied Arts in New York in 1921 and in 1922 went to Paris to study. There he met Irving Berlin and soon was designing for the *Music Box Revues*, Greenwich Village *Follies*, and George White's *Scandals*.

In 1923 he went to Hollywood at the behest of Rudolph Valentino's wife, Natacha Rombova, to design her husband's costumes. There he began an association with Metro-Goldwyn-Mayer that lasted from 1925 until 1939. As the studio's chief designer, Adrian created costumes for such stars as Greta Garbo, Joan Crawford, Katharine Hepburn, Rosalind Russell, and Norma Shearer.

In general, the Adrian look was sleek and modern, a silhouette marked by exaggeratedly wide, padded shoulders tapering to a small waist. He was a master of intricate cut — stripes were worked in opposing directions on shapely, fitted suits, color patches and bold animal prints were set into sinuous black crepe evening gowns, diagonal closings, dolman sleeves, and floating tabs were recurring details. In addition, he did draped, swathed late-day dresses and romantic organdy evening gowns such as the "Letty Lynton" gown designed for Joan Crawford, which was widely copied. It is said that more than 500,000 were sold at Macy's alone.

In 1941 he opened Adrian Ltd. for couture and top-ticket ready-to-wear. He closed his Beverly Hills salon in 1948 but continued in wholesale until 1953. In addition to women's clothes, Adrian also designed stage costumes, produced several men's wear collections, and had two perfumes, *Saint* and *Sinner*.

After closing his business Adrian retired to Brazil with his wife, actress Janet Gaynor, to concentrate on landscape painting, a longtime avocation. He returned to Hollywood in 1958 and at the time of his death in 1959, was working on costumes for the 1960 stage production of *Camelot*.

Joan Crawford (left) wearing the "Letty Lynton Dress"; (right) a suit from Adrian's 1946 ready-to-wear collection. *Also see Color Plate 20.*

Agnès B.

Born Paris, France, 1942

Agnès B. is the inspiration for a generation of laid-back sportswear dressing. After an editorial stint at *Elle* magazine, she worked as assistant to a clothing designer before going into business for herself. She initiated her style in the early 1970s as a reaction to what she felt were the too-dressy clothes available at the time in Paris and it could be said that The Gap and stores like it owe a direct debt to her unforced, airy, low-key clothes, which are essentially sports separates and accessories. Her designs for men, women, and children are sold primarily in her own stores around the world, including the U.S. and Japan.

Alaïa

Born Azzedine Alaïa; Tunis, Tunisia

Until 1980 when he presented his first ready-to-wear collection, Alaïa worked in obscurity, known only to a select group of adventurous customers who also bought from the great couture houses. For the previous eighteen years he had worked out of his apartment, with a list of knowledgeable clients ranging from Paloma Picasso to Dyan Cannon and Raquel Welch.

Raised in Tunis by his grandmother, Alaïa studied sculpture at the Ecole des Beaux-Arts of Tunis and while in art school worked for several dressmakers. In 1957 he went to Paris where he had been promised a job with DIOR, arriving a few months before Dior's death. He did indeed get a job in the Dior cutting

---

Design from Alaia's 1992 collection.

room but lasted only five days. For the next few years he supported himself by working as an *au pair*, at the same time making clothes for his fashionable young employers and their friends. By 1984, he had become so commercially successful that he bought his own townhouse in the Marais section of Paris.

Alaïa's first international notice was for an accessory, black leather gauntlets studded with silver rivets. His original clothes, said to be the sexiest in Paris, were seamed, molded and draped to define and reveal every curve of a woman's body. Translating these techniques from woven cloth to knits is his greatest ready-to-wear achievement. At the heart of his style is his unique draping, inspired by the work of MADELEINE VIONNET.

Alfaro, Victor

Born Chihuahua, Mexico, May 26, 1963
Awards Vidal Sassoon, Excellence in New Design, 1993 • Omni-Mexican Award for Best Latin American Designer, 1994 • Dallas Fashion Award *Rising Star Award*, 1994 • Council of Fashion Designers of America (CFDA) *Perry Ellis Award for New Fashion Talent*, 1994

Alfaro takes his inspiration from the fabric, draping directly on the form. Working in a modern idiom without exaggeration or gimmicks, his work melds talent, intelligence, and technique, for sophistication with a contemporary edge. He attended the Fashion Institute of Technology from 1983 to 1986, got his first job with Mary Ann Restivo. After two years with Restivo he went to JOSEPH ABBOUD, remaining there until 1991 when he opened his own business. He specializes in designer sportswear and in evening clothes, where his strength is greatest.

Evening wear from Alfaro's spring 1993 collection.

Allard, Linda

Born Akron, Ohio, May 27, 1940
Awards Dallas Fashion Award: 1986, 1987, 1994

Linda Allard for Ellen Tracy is a label familiar to women who need career clothes that are up-to-the-minute but not over the top, excellent quality at prices that won't break the bank. Cut from fine fabrics, including precious fibers such as cashmere, the clothes reflect the designer's belief that what a woman

A design from Linda Allard, the fall 1994 collection for Ellen Tracy.

wears should be an extension of her own style and personality, helping her to look her best and conferring a feeling of confidence and power.

Allard has spent her entire career at Ellen Tracy, where she got her first job after leaving Kent State University in 1962 with a degree in Fine Arts. Starting out as assistant designer, she became design director in 1964, a position she's held ever

A

since. Her name went on the label in 1984. In addition to the signature collection, there is a separate dress division; a division of casual sportswear called Company was introduced in 1991. Licenses cover shoes, belts, eyewear, scarves, handbags, hosiery, and a fragrance produced by Revlon.

Actively involved with conservation, Allard turns for recreation to gardening, painting, and cooking. She has published a cookbook, introduced at Saks Fifth Avenue in 1994. Kent State has honored her with a Doctor of Humane Letters degree.

Amies, Sir Hardy

Born Edwin Hardy Aimes; Maida Vale, London, England, July 17, 1909
Awards KCVO (Knight Commander of The Royal Victorian Order), 1989

One of the favorite designers of Queen Elizabeth II, Hardy Amies has always specialized in tailored suits and coats, cocktail and evening dresses. The house also makes breezy, more contemporary women's clothes such as pantsuits and casual classics. Men's wear has become a major part of the business.

Amies succeeded in fashion without formal design training; his mother, however, worked for a London dressmaker and as a child he was sometimes taken there as a treat. After leaving school, he spent several years in France and Germany, becoming fluent in both languages, returning to England when he was twenty-one to work for a manufacturer of scales. In 1934 he became designer for Lachasse, a London couture house owned by his mother's former employer, and within a year was managing director. He left Lachasse in 1939 to serve in the British Army Intelligence Corps. During his Army career he gained the rank of lieutenant colonel and in 1944 was head of the Special Forces Commission to Belgium.

While in the service Amies was given two months' leave at the request of the Board of Trade to make a collection of clothes for South America. These, designed in his spare time at the War Office and made up by the House of WORTH, were his first steps toward his own business. In 1945 he was mustered out to take part in a multi-designer, government-sponsored collection designed in accordance with the rules of the wartime Utility Scheme; in 1946 he opened his own dressmaking business. He added a boutique line in 1950 and men's wear in 1959. Starting with ties and shirts, the men's wear business progressed to made-to-measure suits and soon extended to firms in the U.S., Canada, and Japan.

In 1984, at age seventy-five, Amies announced plans to leave his multi-million dollar fashion business to the members of his staff but denied any intention of an early departure. "I have tickets for Centre Court at Wimbledon up to 1990 and I plan to be there. Plus I'm working now on an outline of how I believe men will be dressing up to the year 2000." Ten years later Amies was still actively engaged in his businesses. Besides the men's wear, licensing agreements have included jewelry, small leathers, luggage, and bed linens. Among his publications are: *Just So Far*, 1954; *ABC of Men's Fashion*, 1964; *Still Here*, 1984.

Hardy Amies (facing page) photographs one of his creations, 1960.

Anthony, John

Born New York City, 1938
Awards Coty American Fashion Critics' Award *"Winnie,"* 1972; *Return Award,* 1976

Anthony's strength is in sophisticated, feminine clothes of refined elegance, marked by a feeling for asymmetry, a sensuous suppleness, and masterly tailoring. In each collection he has confined himself to a few lean, simple shapes in luxurious fabrics, a limited color palette, and a small group of key textures.

At the High School of Industrial Arts (now High School of Art and Design) Anthony won three European scholarships. He spent one year at the Academia d'Arte in Rome before returning to New York and two years at the Fashion Institute of Technology.

His first job was with Devonbrook, which lasted nine years, followed by three years with Adolph Zelinka. John Anthony, Inc. was established in January 1971, but closed in 1979. After a number of years spent in made-to-order fashion and in recovering the use of his own name, Anthony reopened for fall 1986, showing a small ready-to-wear collection out of his couture salon. Since then he has been in and out of ready-to-wear, concentrating mainly on custom work.

Antonelli, Maria

Born Tuscany, Italy, 1903
Died Rome, Italy, 1969

Starting as a dressmaker in 1924, Antonelli soon became known and respected for the exceptional tailoring of her coats and suits. One of the pioneers of Italian fashion as it came into prominence in the 1950s, she participated in the first showings at Florence in 1951. In 1958 she was made a Cavalier of the Republic by the Italian government in recognition of her contributions to Italian fashion. Antonelli Sport ready-to-wear was begun in 1961 with the assistance of her daughter Luciana.

Both ANDRÉ LAUG and Guy Douvier, who became successful designers on their own, trained with Antonelli. Her list of clients was international in scope and included many film and stage personalities.

Armani, Giorgio

Born Emilia-Romagna, Italy, July 1934
Awards Neiman Marcus Award, 1979 • Council of Fashion Designers of American (CFDA)
International Award, 1983

A selection of designs from two Armani collections, 1978 (left) and 1994 (below). *Also see Color Plate 8.*

After brief tries at medicine and photography, Armani became an assistant buyer of men's clothing for La Rinascente, a large Italian department store, where he spent seven years. During that time he developed his ideas on men's dress and a dislike for what he considered a stiff, formal look that disguised individuality. The next ten years were spent as a designer with a men's wear manufacturer of the Cerutti group where he became well versed in the practical and commercial aspects of the clothing business. He then freelanced for a number of Italian manufacturers.

Armani produced his first men's wear collection under his own label in 1974, incorporating the ideas he had developed while working for others.

A

An unconstructed blazer was his first attention-getter. He moved into the area of women's wear in 1975, bringing to it the same perfectionist tailoring and fashion attitude applied to his men's clothes. From day into evening Armani's emphasis is on easy, uncontrived shapes cut from exquisite Italian fabrics, tailored with absolute mastery. Color and fabric are primary considerations. His preference is for neutrals such as taupe, beige, black, and infinite tones of gray. He claims to have taught women to dress with the ease of a man but always with a feminine turn to even the most masculine cut. The word he uses most often is "modern."

Armani business interests now include perfumes and accessories for men and women sold in fine retail stores and free-standing shops in Italy and around the world. The Emporio label and shops were developed to bring Armani styles to young men and women who could not afford the regular line, and A/X: Armani Exchange, is younger and sportier still. He has also done film work.

Armani devotes himself to work singlemindedly, supervising every aspect of collections, which are shown in his own theater in the two adjoining buildings where he both lives and works. He insists on complete control, down to such details as the models' hairstyles and makeup.

Ashley, Laura

Born Merthyr Tydfil, Wales, 1926
Died Coventry, England, September 17, 1985

Romantic and innocent, the Laura Ashley look consists of dresses with long, soft skirts in small flower prints, sweetly trimmed with lace. It would appear to have little connection with life and fashion in the late 20th century yet its influence is to be seen today on city streets, worn in ways the designer would probably not have imagined — with backpacks, heavy socks, and work boots.

In 1953 Ashley and her husband began printing textiles on the kitchen table of their London flat. The couple began with towels, scarves, and place mats, which Bernard carried around to the major London stores and sold so successfully that the Ashleys formed their first company in 1954. As their business and family expanded, they moved from London to Wales, setting up a factory at Carno, Montgomeryshire. In the early 1980s the family moved into an 18th century chateau in Northern France, although the business remained centered in Wales.

Laura Ashley died in 1985 as a result of a fall, but the company has endured. Reaching its apogee in the 60s, 70s, and early 80s, it went public in 1985. At its height, there were Laura Ashley stores in cities as diverse as New York, Paris, Geneva, and San Francisco, dispensing the distinctive prints in decorative fabrics and clothes, bringing the cozy warmth of an English cottage into the harsh city environment.

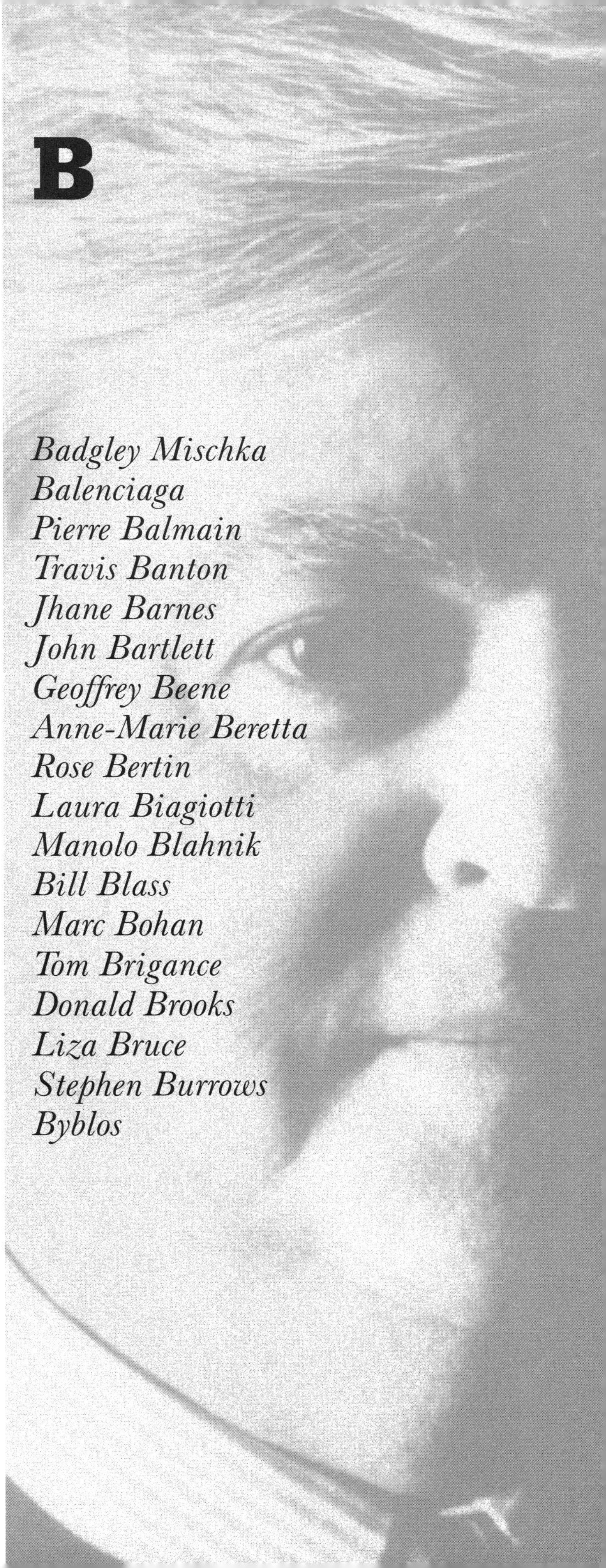

B

Badgley Mischka
Balenciaga
Pierre Balmain
Travis Banton
Jhane Barnes
John Bartlett
Geoffrey Beene
Anne-Marie Beretta
Rose Bertin
Laura Biagiotti
Manolo Blahnik
Bill Blass
Marc Bohan
Tom Brigance
Donald Brooks
Liza Bruce
Stephen Burrows
Byblos

Badgley Mischka

Born Mark Badgley; East St. Louis, Illinois, January 12, 1961
James Mischka; Burlington, Wisconsin, December 23, 1960
Awards Mouton Cadet Young Designer Award, 1989

Badgley attended UCLA and Mischka took a B.A. in Managerial Science at Rice University in Houston — they met at Parsons School of Design where both graduated with B.F.A. degrees in Fashion Design. After Parsons, their paths diverged, Mischka going to WilliWear from 1985 to 1987, Badgley successively to Jackie Rogers and DONNA KARAN. The two young designers teamed up in 1988 to form their own company. In January 1992 the firm was acquired by Escada, the large German fashion company, with the two designers retaining creative control and a financial stake in the business.

Right, designers Mark Badgley (right in photo) and James Mischka and an example from their spring 1994 collection (left).

Their designs, which they describe as "modern, sleek clothes for dinner, drinks, and dancing," are young and sophisticated with clean lines and a strong sense of luxury. For fall 1994 they broadened their focus, adding clothes for earlier in the day while maintaining an emphasis on evening.

Balenciaga

Born Cristobal Balenciaga; Guetaria, Spain, January 21, 1895
Died Valencia, Spain, March 24, 1972

Master tailor, master dressmaker, Balenciaga was a great originator, possibly the greatest couturier of all time. Of them all, only he could do everything — design, cut, fit, and sew an entire garment. He worked alone, using his own ideas, putting together with his own hands every model that later appeared in his collections. His clothes, so beautiful and elegant, were also so skillfully designed that a woman did not have to have a perfect figure to wear them. They moved with the body and were comfortable as well as fashionable.

The facts of Balenciaga's origins and early life are so obscured by legend that it is difficult to know where reality begins and myth ends. His father, for example, has been said to have been both captain of the Spanish royal yacht and captain of a fishing boat. It is known that after his father's death, the boy and his mother moved to San Sebastian where she became a seamstress. The son followed in her footsteps to become a skilled tailor. As the story goes, his career in fashion began when the Marquesa de Casa Torres allowed him to copy a DRÉCOLL suit he had admired on her, later sending him to Paris to meet the suit's designer. The Marquesa encouraged him to study design and in 1916 helped him set up his own shop in

These sketches illustrate the evolution of Balenciaga's designs from 1937 to 1957.

1947

1941

1947

1952

1950

1955

1956

1957

B

San Sebastian. This was the first of three houses named Eisa; the others were in Madrid and Barcelona.

Balenciaga moved to Paris in 1937, returning to Spain at the beginning of World War II. After the war he reopened in Paris on avenue George V, where he established himself as the preeminent designer of his time, one of the most imaginative and creative artists of the Paris couture.

A great student of art, he understood how to interpret his sources rather than merely copy them. The somber blacks and browns of the old Spanish masters were among his favorite colors and the influence of such early moderns as Monet and Manet can also be found in his work. His interest in the post cubists and abstract expressionists shows in his late designs.

His innovations, especially during the 1950s and 1960s, are still influential: the revolutionary semi-fitted suit jacket of 1951, the 1955 middy dress, which evolved into the chemise, the cocoon coat, the balloon skirt, the flamenco evening gown cut short in front, long in back. To achieve his sculptural effects he worked with the Swiss fabric house, Abraham, to develop a heavily sized silk called gazar, very light but with a capacity for holding a shape and floating away from the body.

In 1968 Balenciaga abruptly closed his house and retired to Spain. There has been speculation concerning his reasons but perhaps he was simply tired — he was 75 years old. He came out of retirement to design the wedding dress of Generalissimo Franco's granddaughter, whose marriage took place in 1972 just two weeks before Balenciaga died.

A shy and private man who loathed publicity, Balenciaga was seldom photographed, never appeared in his own salon, and, except for his perfumes, refused to have anything to do with commercial exploitation. Since his death he has been honored by a number of exhibitions: in New York in 1973 at the Metropolitan Museum of Art and in 1986 at the Fashion Institute of Technology; in France in 1985 at the Museum of Historic Textiles in Lyons, the center of the French silk industry. The Balenciaga name has been revived from time to time for ready-to-wear collections.

Balenciaga's sense of proportion and balance, his mastery of cut, his touches of wit, the architectural quality and essential rightness of his designs still inspire awe and admiration. He is rightly considered one of the giants of 20th-century couture.

Balmain, Pierre

Born St. Jean-de-Maurienne, France, May 18, 1914
Died Paris, France, June 29, 1982
Awards Neiman Marcus Award, 1955

Balmain claimed credit for beginning the New Look — critics and writers divided it between him, DIOR, FATH, and BALENCIAGA. It is true that his first collections accentuated the femininity of the figure with a small waist, high bust, rounded hips, and long, full skirts, all New Look characteristics. He continued making clothes of quiet elegance and at his death had just completed the sketches for his fall collection.

An only child, Balmain was only seven when his father died. He was raised by his mother, who later worked with him in his couture salon. In 1934, while studying architecture at the Ecole des Beaux Arts in Paris, he began sketching dresses and took his designs to Captain MOLYNEUX. The British-born designer allowed the twenty-year-old to work for him in the afternoons while continuing school in the mornings, finally advised him to devote himself to dress design. Molyneux then gave him a job and Balmain remained with the house until called into the Army in 1939. After the fall of France in 1940, Balmain returned to Paris to work for LUCIEN LELONG, where he

---

"Scotch" from Balmain's 1962-63 collection.

stayed until 1945 when he left to open his own house.

In 1946 he visited the U.S. and in 1951, opened a New York ready-to-wear operation, for which he designed special collections. He also did theater and film work. There were Balmain boutiques for women and men and over sixty licenses, including men's fashions, luggage, jewelry, glasses, belts. His first perfume was *Vent Vert*; his second and best-known fragrance, *Jolie Madame*, appeared in 1953. Revlon bought the fragrance business in 1960, launching *Ivoire* in 1981. A new fragrance called *Opera* was introduced in 1994.

After Balmain's death the business continued with Erik Mortensen as couture designer. When French financier Alain Chevalier acquired the house in January 1990, Mortensen, who had been with Balmain since 1948, was replaced by 25-year-old Hervé Pierre. Scottish-born Alistair Blair was placed in charge, first of ready-to-wear then with creative responsibility for the house, whose ownership changed once more. OSCAR DE LA RENTA took over design of the couture collection for Spring 1993 and has since been responsible for both couture and ready-to-wear.

Banton, Travis

Born Waco, Texas, 1894
Died Los Angeles, California, February 2, 1958

Banton was with Paramount Pictures for fourteen years, designing elegant, sophisticated clothes for some of the screen's most legendary actresses — Claudette Colbert, Marlene Dietrich, Carole Lombard, and Mae West among them. He favored glow and shimmer over sparkle and shine and was especially partial to the bias cut. With an extraordinarily long career, Banton is remembered particularly for what became known as "The Paramount look." He produced clothes of the highest quality, often cut on the bias, superb in fabric, workmanship, and fit. The effect was dreamy, elegant, understated.

His parents moved to New York City when Banton was two years old. He briefly attended Columbia University, transferred to the Art Student's League and then to the School of Fine and Applied Arts. His apprenticeship to Madame Frances, a successful New York custom dressmaker, was interrupted by naval service in World War I, but not before he established himself as a designer. On his return he worked for a number of custom houses, including LUCILE, training ground for Harold Greer and a number of other designers, then opened his own salon. There his designs included elaborate costumes for the Ziegfeld Follies.

At the instigation of Walter Wanger, he went to Hollywood in 1924 to design costumes for Leatrice Joy in Paramount Pictures' *The Dressmaker From Paris*. He stayed on at Paramount and in 1927, when Harold Greer left to open his own custom business, became the studio's head designer. At the expiration of his Paramount contract in 1938, Banton joined Harold Greer as a private couturier. A year later he went to 20th Century Fox, then worked off and on for Universal Studios. Meanwhile, he conducted his own dressmaking business, turning to ready-to-wear in the 1950s. He designed Rosalind Russell's wardrobe for the stage production of *Auntie Mame*, dressed Dinah Shore for both her television appearances and her private life.

Banton's designs for Marlene Dietrich in SHANGHAI EXPRESS, 1932.

Barnes, Jhane

Born 1954

Awards Coty American Fashion Critics Award *Men's Wear*, 1980; *Men's Apparel*, 1981; *Men's Wear Return Award*, 1984 • Council of Fashion Designers of America (CFDA) *Outstanding Menswear Designer*, 1981

Barnes established her own company in 1977 when she was twenty-three. While known mainly for men's sportswear, she has also made sportswear for women. Her designs are unconstructed, beautifully tailored in luxurious and original fabrics, many of which she designs herself. They are marked by innovative details, carefully thought out and carried through. She is original and creative, with architectural insight into clothing, now confined exclusively to men's wear, sold through a few fine stores such as Barney's New York.

Other design commitments include intricately-woven decorating fabrics for Knoll Textiles, and in 1995 a collection of tables, chairs, and upholstered furniture for Bernhardt Furniture, a North Carolina manufacturer.

From Jhane Barnes' men's wear collection, 1994.

Bartlett, John

Born Columbus, Ohio, March 22, 1963

Awards Woolmark "Cutting Edge" Award, 1992 • Fashion Institute of Technology Alumni Award, 1994 • Council of Fashion Designers of America (CFDA) *Perry Ellis Award for New Fashion Talent*, 1994

One of a new wave of designers putting a more relaxed spin on men's wear, Bartlett specializes in sportswear, giving the familiar pieces a fresh, younger look with altered scale and proportions, unconventional mixes of texture and pattern. Not for the timid or unimaginative, the clothes are thoroughly American in attitude, for free-thinking men with minds of their own.

Bartlett graduated from Harvard in 1985 with a B.A. in Sociology, went on to the Fashion Institute of Technology's men's wear program, graduating in 1988 with the Bill Robinson Award. He interned with WILLI SMITH, Bill Robinson, and RONALDUS SHAMASK, spent a year as men's designer for WilliWear from 1988 to 1989, was design director for Shamask from 1989 to 1991. He established his own label in 1992.

Beene, Geoffrey

Born Haynesville, Louisiana, August 30, 1927

Awards Coty American Fashion Critics Award *"Winnie,"* 1964; *Return Award,* 1966; *Hall of Fame,* 1974; *Hall of Fame Citation,* 1975; *Special Award (jewelry),* 1977; *Special Award (contribution to international status of American fashion),* 1979; *Special Award (women's fashions),* 1981; *Hall of Fame Citation,* 1982 • Neiman Marcus Award: 1964, 1965 • Council of Fashion Designers of America (CFDA) *Special Award,* 1985; *Special Award Designer of the Year,* 1986; *Special Award for fashion as art,* 1989

Widely considered the most original and creative designer in American fashion today, Beene is noted for his subtle cut, his imaginative use of color, and for the luxury of his fabrics. Making clothes that fit the life of the modern woman is a major preoccupation — he believes that clothes must not only look attractive but also must move well, be comfortable to wear, and easy to pack. Year by year he refines his style and continues to work toward greater simplicity, with increasing emphasis on cut and line and the lightest, most unusual fabrics.

The grandson and nephew of doctors, Beene came to fashion after three years in pre-med and medicine at Tulane University in New Orleans. Deciding that medicine was not for him, he went to California and while waiting to enroll at the University of Southern California, worked in window display at I. Magnin, Los Angeles. There his talent was recog-

Highlights from Beene's collection from 1981 (left) and 1982 (right).
Also see Color Plate 12.

----

nized by an executive who suggested he make a career of fashion.

He attended Traphagen School of Fashion in New York for one summer and in 1947 went to Paris to study at L'Ecole de la Chambre Syndicale and Académie Julian. While in Paris he apprenticed with a tailor who had worked for the couturier MOLYNEUX, a master of tailoring and the bias cut. Returning to New York in 1950, Beene designed for several small custom salons and for Samuel Winston and Harmay. In 1958 he joined Teal Traina and for the first time had his name on the label. He opened his own business in 1962.

Beene's first collection, shown in spring 1963, had elements characteristic of his work throughout the 1960s: looser fit, eased waistlines, bloused tops, flared skirts. Each collection included at least one tongue-in-cheek style to stir things up, such as a black coat of wood buttons and a tutu evening dress with sequined bodice and feather skirt.

Among the memorable Beene designs are long, sequined evening gowns cut like football jerseys and complete with numerals, tweed evening pants paired with jeweled or lamé jackets, a gray sweatshirt bathing suit, soft evening coats made of striped blankets from the Hudson's Bay Company.

He has at various times designed furs, swimwear, jewelry, scarves, men's wear, and Lynda Bird Johnson's wedding dress, had a boutique collection, and licensed his name for shoes, gloves, hosiery, eyeglasses, loungewear, bedding, and furniture. His fragrances are *Grey Flannel* for men and *Chance* for women. Beene has shown his clothes in Europe with great success — in Milan in 1975, and at the American Embassies in Rome, Paris, Brussels, and Vienna. In December 1989 he opened his first retail shop in the Sherry Netherland Hotel on Fifth Avenue.

In 1988 he was honored by a retrospective of his work at the National Academy of Design, "Geoffrey Beene: The First Twenty-Five Years," to celebrate the 25th anniversary of his business. In the fall of 1993, he commissioned a 30-minute film to mark his 30th year in his own business. In February 1994, The Fashion Institute of Technology mounted "Beene Unbound," a 30-year retrospective of his designs.

Beretta, Anne-Marie

Born Beziers, France, 1937

After taking a fashion course, Beretta began her career in 1955 at the age of eighteen when she joined Jacques Esterel as a designer. In 1965 she left him to design ready-to-wear for Pierre d'Alby and in 1975 opened her own boutique. She has designed for the Italian MaxMara organization, done sports clothes for Ramosport, leathers for MacDouglas, and coats for Abe Schrader.

Considered strongest in coats, Beretta works with sculptural shapes — rubberized and ciré raincoats are a specialty. She believes in the constant evolution of fashion and maintains that the first attraction in clothes is color, followed by fabric.

From Anne-Marie Beretta's 1987 collection.

Bertin, Rose

Born near Abbeville, France, July 2, 1747
Died Epinay, France, September 22, 1813

At sixteen Bertin became an apprentice in the Paris millinery shop of a Mlle. Pagelle. When sent to deliver hats to the royal princesses at the Conti palace, she was noticed by the Princesse de Conti, who became her sponsor. Nine years later in 1772, having become a partner in the shop, Bertin was appointed court milliner. She was introduced to Marie Antoinette and became her confidante.

With such connections her establishment, *Au Grand-Mogol*, became extremely successful, not only with the French court but with the diplomatic corps. She executed commissions for dresses and hats to be sent to foreign courts, thus becoming one of the early exporters of French fashion. She also produced fantastic headdresses reflecting current events, enormously costly and symbolic of the excesses that led to the French Revolution.

Bertin could be considered the first "name" designer. She was celebrated in contemporary memoirs and encyclopedias and has left behind a reputation for pride, arrogance, and ambition. So influential was she that she was dubbed "The Minister of Fashion." With the onset of the Revolution, she fled to England to escape the Terror but remained loyal to the Queen. She returned to France in 1800 and eked out her last impoverished years selling trinkets.

At her death, an obituary recognized her accomplishments: "Mlle. Bertin is justly famous for the

Marie Antoinette, patroness of Rose Bertin.

supremacy to which she has raised French fashions and for her services to the industries that made the material she used in her own creations and those that she inspired others to make."

Biagiotti, Laura

Born Rome, Italy, 1943

Biagiotti graduated from Rome University with a degree in archaeology, then went to work at her mother's clothing company and began producing clothes for other designers. Her first collection under her own label appeared in Florence in 1972. Soon afterwards she bought a cashmere firm and thus discovered her true métier.

She became known in Italy as the "Queen of Cashmere," producing beautiful sweaters in that precious fiber for both men and women. Exceptional in their colorings and quality, these were sold under the Macpherson label. Biagiotti also produces women's clothes in her own name, not on the leading edge of fashion but wearable, interestingly detailed, and of excellent workmanship.

B

Blahnik, Manolo

Born Santa Cruz, Canary Islands, November 28, 1943
Awards Council of Fashion Designers of America (CFDA) *Special Award (Outstanding Excellence in Accessory Design):* 1987, 1989

One of the world's most creative and influential shoe designers, Blahnik is based in London, where he turns out four collections a year of his fantastical, elegant shoes. His designs are sold through fine specialty stores worldwide and in his own boutiques to such celebrity customers as Bianca Jagger, PALOMA PICASSO, and Sigourney Weaver. They have frequently been chosen for runway presentations by designers as different in approach as ZANDRA RHODES and BILL BLASS. He has done collections for PERRY ELLIS, CALVIN KLEIN, and ANNE KLEIN, men's shoes for SAINT LAURENT.

Blahnik's father was Czech and his mother Spanish. He started sketching as a child and traveled with his parents to Paris and Madrid where his mother bought her clothes. He was exposed to and fascinated by the great designers of the time: DIOR, BALENCIAGA, and Spain's famous cobbler, Rius. Following a European education reading literature and studying art in Geneva, he moved to Paris in 1968 to become a theatrical designer. He studied art for two years at L'Ecole du Louvre and early in 1971 traveled to New York, where his portfolio of theatrical designs impressed fashion editors China Machado and DIANA VREELAND. They recommended that he go into shoe design and helped him connect with Italian manufacturers. He moved to London the same year, opened a shop there in the Chelsea district in 1973. He opened a New York shop in 1981, has since added shops in Hong Kong and Tokyo.

Filled with energy, Blahnik personally cuts eighty or more samples each season, a skill it took him seven years to acquire. As a hobby, he makes metal furniture, which he keeps in his house in Bath; he also maintains a house in the mountains of Spain and a London apartment. A movie buff, he uses his New York business trips to catch up, sometimes seeing as many as four movies in a day.

Blass, Bill

Born Fort Wayne, Indiana, June 22, 1922
Awards Coty American Fashion Critics' Award *"Winnie,"* 1961; *Return Award,* 1963; *First Coty Award for Men's Wear,* 1968; *Hall of Fame,* 1970; *Hall of Fame Citation,* 1971, 1982, 1983; *Special Award (furs for Revillon America),* 1975 • Neiman Marcus Award, 1969 • Council of Fashion Designers of America (CFDA) *Lifetime Achievement Award,* 1986

A leading member of the New York fashion establishment, Blass produces high-priced, high-quality, investment clothes, beautifully made from exquisite materials. He designs for a customer with an active social life and is especially admired for his glamorous, feminine evening clothes. His daytime fashions are elegant and simple, notable for refined cut and excellent tailoring. Interesting mixtures of patterns and textures are expertly coordinated for a polished, worldly look.

Blass graduated from Fort Wayne High School in 1939, then studied fashion in New York for six months. He got his first fashion job in 1940 as

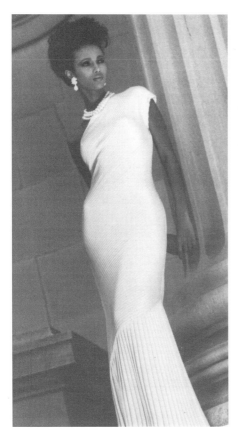

sketch artist for David Crystal, resigning to enlist in the Army in World War II. In 1946 he went to work as designer for Anna Miller & Co., which merged with Maurice Rentner in 1958. Blass stayed on as head designer, eventually becoming vice president, then owner. In 1970 the company was established as Bill Blass Ltd.

In addition to his designer clothes for women, the Blass design projects have included Blassport women's sportswear, rainwear, Vogue patterns, loungewear, scarves, and men's clothing. His name has also been licensed for automobiles, uniforms for American Airlines flight attendants, even chocolates. *Bill Blass* perfume for women was introduced in 1978.

Blass has given time and support to his industry and was an early vice president of the Council of Fashion Designers of America. He has also been a perceptive and generous supporter of design talent in others. In January 1994, he donated $10 million to the New York Public Library.

Bill Blass (below, right) at trunk showing in I. Magnin, San Francisco, 1993. Typical Blass designs for day and evening from 1986 (above, left) and 1994 (above, right).

B

Bohan, Marc

Born Paris, France, August 22, 1926

Chief designer and artistic director of CHRISTIAN DIOR from 1960 to 1989, Bohan was responsible for the couture and ready-to-wear collections, as well as accessories, men's wear, and bed linens. Refined and romantic, his clothes are also very wearable, notable for beautiful fabrics, and exquisite workmanship. He has always maintained that elegance consists of adapting dress for the place, the atmosphere, and the circumstances.

The son of a milliner who encouraged his early interest in sketching and fashion, Bohan had a solid background when he took over design direction at Dior. He was assistant to ROBERT PIGUET from 1945 to 1953, worked with Captain MOLYNEUX and MADELEINE DE RAUCH, had his own couture salon, which closed after one season due to undercapitalization. He was head designer at JEAN PATOU starting in 1954, after a few years left Patou to free-lance, working briefly in New York for Originala.

Designer Marc Bohan (top right) and (left) designs from his 1987 collection for Christian Dior.

In August 1958 Bohan went to work for Dior, designing the London, New York, and South American collections. When SAINT LAURENT was drafted into the army in September 1960 Bohan was chosen to design the January collection. In 1989, after twenty-nine years as chief designer, Bohan left Christian Dior and in September of the same year became fashion director for NORMAN HARTNELL, the British fashion house. His first collections were couture, followed by ready-to-wear in fall 1991. He left Hartnell when the house closed in 1992.

Brigance, Tom

Born Thomas Franklin Brigance; Waco, Texas, February 4, 1913
Died New York City, October 14, 1990
Awards Coty American Fashion Critics' Award *"Winnie" ("for revolutionizing the look of American women at the beach"),* 1953 • International Silk Citation, 1954 • National Cotton Fashion Award, 1955 • Italian Internazionale delle Arti (for foreign sportswear), 1956

Probably best known for his swimwear, Brigance designed everything from coats and suits to day and evening dresses and blouses, before finding his true calling in sportswear. His early beach outfits could be ultra-feminine with ruffles and frills or ultra-sophisticated in fabrics such as grey flannel and black velvet. At Brigance's death, the head of Gabar, where he worked for two years prior to his retirement, said that a Brigance-designed, skirted swimsuit was still one of his company's best-selling styles.

The son of an English mother and French father, Brigance studied at Parsons School of Design and the National Academy of Art in New York, and later at the Sorbonne in Paris. On his return to New York his talent was recognized by Dorothy Shaver, president of Lord & Taylor, and in 1939 he became the store's designer. He spent the war years in Air Corps Intelligence in the South Pacific, returning to Lord & Taylor in 1944. In 1949 he opened his own firm on Seventh Avenue. In the 1960s and 1970s he concentrated primarily on swimwear, designing for Sinclair, Water Clothes, and Gabar. He retired in the late 1970s but continued to lecture extensively on fashion throughout the U.S.

Brigance trained as a couturier in Paris and sold sketches to French and English designers but whatever he designed bore an unmistakable American viewpoint. In an interview in 1960, he said that "the secret of a woman being well dressed lies in her being appropriately dressed for her way of life."

Above, separates from 1941 and left, plaid swimsuit from 1946.

B

Brooks, Donald

Born New York City, January 10, 1928

Awards National Cotton Fashion Award, 1962 • Coty American Fashion Critics' Award *Special Award (influence on evening wear)*, 1958; *"Winnie,"* 1962; *Return Award*, 1967; *Special Award (lingerie design)*, 1974 • New York Drama Critics' Award for costumes (for *No Strings*), 1963 • International Silk Association Award, 1954 • Parsons Medal for Distinguished Achievement, 1974

Noted for romantic evening designs and uncluttered day clothes, Brooks has also designed extensively for theater and film. He is known for his use of clear colors in unexpected combinations, careful detailing, and dramatic prints of his own design.

Brooks studied at the School of Fine Arts of Syracuse University and at Parsons School of Design in New York City. He had his own company from 1964 to 1973 and has free-lanced extensively, specializing in better dresses. He has designed collections for Albert Nipon and exclusive designs for Lord & Taylor. He costumed Diahann Carroll in the Broadway musical, *No Strings*; his movie credits include wardrobes for Liza Minelli in *Flora the Red Menace*, and for Julie Andrews in *Star* and *Darling Lili*. He has also designed furs, bathing suits, men's wear, shoes, costume jewelry, wigs, and bed linens.

Donald Brooks with models in 1974 (below) and designs from his 1984 collection (right).

Bruce, Liza

Born New York City, September 21, 1954

Liza Bruce got into fashion without formal fashion training or art education. She gained her first recognition for swimwear, which she continues to design, has expanded her range to include contemporary women's wear.

The clothes are sometimes weird, sometimes beautiful, with an attitude that places them on the wilder side of fashion. She describes her professional experiences as "hell with occasional glimpses of heaven," her

design influences as Eileen Gray and Madame GRÈS, among others, and her ideal customer as anyone and everyone with imagination.

Burrows, Stephen

Born Newark, New Jersey, September 15, 1943
Awards Coty American Fashion Critics' Award *Special Award (lingerie),* 1974; *"Winnie,"* 1977

Burrows has always gone his own way in fashion, favoring soft, clinging fabrics such as chiffon and matte jersey, and with a partiality for the asymmetrical. He used patches of color for a mosaic effect in the early 1960s, top-stitched seams in contrasting thread, and stitched the edges of hems instead of hemming them, which resulted in a widely copied, fluted effect known as "lettuce hems."

He started making clothes as a young boy under the tutelage of his grandmother. He studied at the Philadelphia Museum College of Art and the Fashion Institute of Technology in New York. In 1968 he and an F.I.T. classmate, Roz Rubenstein, joined forces to open a boutique. The next year both went to work for Henri Bendel — Rubenstein

Stephen Burrows (right) with models in 1979 and a design from his 1994 collection (above).

as accessories buyer, Burrows as designer in residence. In 1973 they formed a partnership and a firm on Seventh Avenue and in November of the same year Burrows was one of five American designers to show in France at a benefit for the Versailles Palace. Burrows and Rubenstein returned to Bendel's in 1977.

Burrows resumed ready-to-wear design in 1989, after a seven-year absence during which he supported himself with work for private customers and the theater. He introduced a custom collection in January 1990, and in 1993 returned to Henri Bendel with a collection of evening dresses and separates. Among his dreams for the future are a men's collection and a couture collection to be shown in Paris.

Byblos

Established 1973

Part of Italy's Girombelli Group, Byblos was designed by an international group of stylists until 1975 when GIANNI VERSACE became its designer. Guy Paulin took over in 1977. Since 1981 the firm has developed a strong sportswear orientation under the direction of Donatella Girombelli and her team of two English designers, Alan Cleaver and Keith Varty. It is now noted for whimsical patterns, a young and affluent sportiness with a touch of British wit.

C

Callot Soeurs
Albert Capraro
Roberto Capucci
Pierre Cardin
Hattie Carnegie
Carven
Bonnie Cashin
Jean Charles de Castelbajac
Sal Cesarani
Gabrielle Chanel
Aldo Cipullo
Liz Claiborne
Robert Clergerie
Anne Cole
Sybil Connolly
Jasper Conran
André Courrèges
Jules-Francois Crahay
Charles Creed
Angela Cummings

Callot Soeurs

Founded 1895
Closed 1937

Founded by three sisters, the couture house, Callot Soeurs, was noted most particularly for formal eveningwear of intricate cut and rich color. It was famous for delicate lace blouses, the use of gold and silver lamé, of floating fabrics such as chiffon, georgette, and organdy, and for flower embroidery and embroidery in Chinese colors. The high standard of excellence maintained in collection after collection over many years built the Callot reputation and the world's most fashionable women went there to dress. Among them was the noted Spanish-American beauty, Mrs. Rita de Acosta Lydig, who was rumored to be a financial backer of the house.

The sisters were daughters of an antique dealer who specialized in fabrics and lace. He was also said to be a painter. All three were talented but it was Mme. Gerber, the eldest, who was the genius. Tall and gaunt, her hair dyed a brilliant red, she was usually dressed in a baglike costume covered with oriental jewelry and ropes of freshwater pearls. Mme. Gerber possessed great technical skill — she was also an artist of impeccable taste, an originator. Her two sisters eventually retired and she became the sole proprietor of the house, which at one time had branches in London and New York.

Henri Bendel was a great admirer of Mme. Gerber, referring to her as the backbone of the fashion world of Europe. She was an early influence on MADELEINE VIONNET, who worked for some time at Callot. During the 1920s the house produced every up-to-the-minute look, always with such taste, subtlety, and superb workmanship that the clothes had the timelessness and elegance of classics.

An evening gown in tulle with velvet bands by Callot Soeurs from 1931. *Also see Color Plate 7.*

Capraro, Albert

Born New York City, May 20, 1943

A graduate of Parsons School of Design, Capraro worked for LILLY DACHÉ as an associate and from 1966 to 1974 as associate to OSCAR DE LA RENTA. He established his own business for designer ready-to-wear in 1975. Capraro's first public notice came when Mrs. Gerald Ford, then First Lady, invited him to bring his collection to the White House. After closing the business in 1985, he continued to design for individual clients such as Mrs. Ford under the label Albert Capraro Couture. On the wholesale side, he designed exclusively for the specialty shop, Martha, since closed.

In June 1990 he joined ADELE SIMPSON as designer of a new collection while continuing to design his private collections, left in December of the same year when the future of the firm was uncertain. His couture business continues.

Capucci, Roberto

Born Rome, Italy, 1929

Scion of a wealthy Roman family, Capucci first studied art at the Accademia delle Belle Arti in Rome. In 1950, at the age of twenty-one, he opened a small fashion house in Rome and showed successfully in Florence the same year. He opened a house in Paris in 1962, moved back to Rome seven years later.

Considered a genius ranking with BALENCIAGA and CHARLES JAMES, Capucci experiments daringly with cut and fabric to achieve dramatic sculptural and architectural effects. Fittingly, because he raises dressmaking to the level of an art, his clothes are shown in total silence without histrionics. He does not use design assistants.

Two designs by Capucci from 1985.

Cardin, Pierre

Born Venice, Italy, 1922

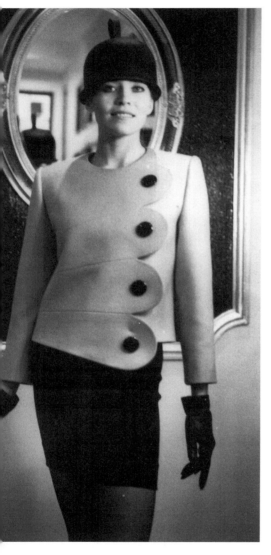

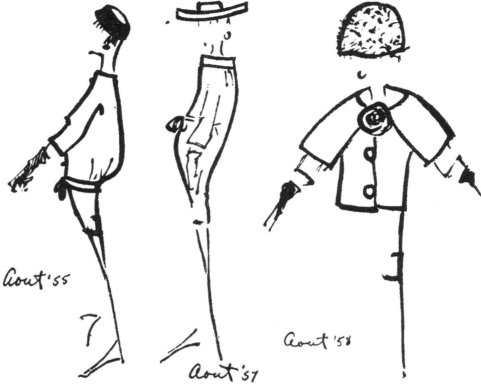

Aout '55
Aout '57
Aout '58

Above left, a Cardin design from his 1991 collection. Sketches (above right) of designs from 1955, 1957 and 1958 were drawn by Cardin exclusively for WOMEN'S WEAR DAILY.

Cardin is considered one of the most creative, intellectual, and avant-garde couturiers of the 1950s and 1960s. He showed the first nude look in 1966, followed by metal body jewelry, unisex astronaut suits, helmets, batwing jumpsuits, and other clothing suitable for space travel.

The son of Italian immigrants, Cardin grew up in St. Etienne, France, moved to Vichy at the age of seventeen. He worked there as a tailor, left Vichy for Paris at the end of World War II and went to work at PAQUIN. At Paquin he executed

costume designs based on sketches of Christian Bérard for Jean Cocteau's film, *La Belle et la Bête*, and was introduced by Cocteau to CHRISTIAN DIOR. He worked briefly for SCHIAPARELLI, then as assistant to Dior, where in 1947 he headed the coat and suit workroom. He left Dior to form his own business, showing his first collection in 1950.

Boutiques followed for men and women — men's ready-to-wear appeared in 1958, children's apparel ten years later. From there he went on to label the world with the Cardin name — more than 600 licenses extending from wines to bicycles, jewelry to bed sheets to food to toiletries. In 1970 he established his own theater, L'Espace Pierre Cardin. Cardin now owns the famous Paris restaurant, Maxim's. In 1979 he entered into a trade agreement with the Peoples Republic of China for production there of Cardin clothes. A Maxim's has been established in Beijing.

In July 1987 he named his long-time collaborator, ANDRÉ OLIVER, artistic director of the couture house, while continuing to share the design duties. In the wake of Oliver's death he reassumed artistic direction of the house.

Pierre Cardin in 1992.

Carnegie, Hattie

Born Vienna, Austria, 1889
Died New York City, February 22, 1956

Hattie Carnegie began as a milliner, opening her first shop when she was just twenty. By the end of her life, she had a multi-million dollar business, including two resort shops, made-to-order workrooms, ready-to-wear factories, millinery, jewelry, perfumes. She is said to have been the first American custom designer to go into ready-to-wear. Her knack for discovering design talent was legendary — JAMES GALANOS, NORMAN NORELL, PAULINE TRIGÈRE, and CLAIRE MCCARDELL all worked for her.

Carnegie's designs were youthful and sophisticated, never faddy, never extreme, eternally Carnegie whatever the current trends might be. Less than five feet tall, she was noted for suits with nipped waists and rounded hips that were especially becoming to smaller women, as well as embroidered, beaded evening suits, theater suits, at-home pajamas, and long wool dinner dresses. Beautiful fabrics and excellent workmanship were hallmarks and anything but the best was abhorrent to her.

Arriving in America when she was eleven, she started working in her early teens —first as a messenger at Macy's, then in a millinery workroom, later as a millinery model. In her spare time she designed hats for neighborhood women. She changed her name from Henrietta

Theater suit by Carnegie from 1950

c

Kanengeiser to Carnegie in emulation of Andrew Carnegie, "the richest man in the world." In 1909 she opened her own hat shop and in 1915, a custom dressmaking salon on West 86th Street near fashionable Riverside Drive. Her partner, Rose Roth, made dresses, Carnegie made hats and waited on customers. She did not know how to cut or sketch, and never learned. What she did have was great fashion flair and an acute business intelligence. In 1917 she bought out her partner.

Her first buying trip to Europe occurred in 1919, and from then on she went four times a year, bringing back quantities of Paris models, which she would adapt. She dressed society beauties, movie and stage stars such as Constance Bennett, Tallulah Bankhead, and Joan Crawford. In the early 1930s, recognizing the hard facts of the depression, she opened a ready-to-wear department in her shop where a good Vionnet copy could be had for as little as $50.

She was married briefly in 1918, again in 1922. In 1928 she married Major John Zanft, who survived her. Her clothing business continued for some years after her death.

Carven

Founded Paris, France, 1944

Carven (Madame Carven Mallet) built her success on attractive, wearable apparel for petite women like herself, specializing in imaginative sports, beach, and dress-up clothes, with accessories, too, kept in proportion to the small figure. An ardent traveler, she has been inspired by her travels, as shown in such silhouettes as the Greek amphora and a use of Egyptian pleats.

The daughter of an Italian father and a French mother, Carven had planned to study architecture and archaeology. It is said that she was diverted into dressmaking by the fact that her tiny size made it difficult to find beautiful clothes, which were always created for taller women. Following her retirement, the house has remained in business for couture, and, at one time or another, with Carven lines for children and teenagers and Monsieur Carven for men. Among her fragrances, *Ma Griffe* and *Monsieur Carven* have been especially successful.

Cashin, Bonnie

Born Oakland, California, 1915
Awards Coty American Fashion Critics' Award *"Winnie,"* 1950; *Special Award (for leather and fabric design),* 1961; *Return Award,* 1968; *Hall of Fame,* 1972 • Neiman Marcus Award, 1950

Cashin always worked in her own innovative idiom, uninfluenced by Paris. She especially believed in functional layers of clothing and showed this way of dressing long before it became an international fashion cliché. From the beginning she specialized in comfortable clothes for country and travel, using wool jersey, knits, canvas, leather, and tweeds in subtle, misty colors.

Some dominant Cashin themes were the toga cape, the kimono coat and the shell coat, a sleeveless leather jerkin, the poncho, the bubble top, the hooded jersey dress, and a long, fringed, mohair, plaid at-home skirt. Signature details included leather bindings and the use of toggles and similar hardware for closings. Clothes were coordinated with hoods, bags, boots, and belts of her own design. Her clothes are included in the costume collections of museums, colleges, and design schools around the country.

A third generation Californian, Cashin was raised in San Francisco where her father was an artist, photographer, and inventor; her mother a custom dressmaker. She played with fabrics from an early age and was taught to sew; her ideas were encouraged. She studied at the

Art Students League of New York, then returned to California where she designed costumes for the theater, ballet, and motion pictures. *Anna and the King of Siam* and *Laura* are among her sixty picture credits. She moved back to New York in 1949.

Bonnie Cashin in her studio (bottom left) and representative examples of her designs: plaid poncho (above left); right, an original sketch by Cashin.

From 1953 Cashin free-lanced, designing collections for sportswear houses Adler and Adler and Philip Sills, and bags for Coach Leatherware. In 1967 she started The Knittery, limited edition collections of hand knits and cashmeres from Scotland, also concentrating on coats and raincoats.

In the early 1980s she established The Innovative Design Fund, a public foundation, with herself as president. Its purpose is to nurture uncommon, directional ideas in design — clothing, textiles, home furnishings, or other utilitarian objects — with awards to be used solely for producing prototypes. Another fund, "The James Michelin Distinguished Lecturer Program," at the California Institute of Technology at Pasadena began operation in 1992. Its purpose is to bring the arts and sciences together. British playwright Tom Stoppard was the 1994 lecturer.

A 1968 version of "layering" by Cashin.

Castelbajac, Jean-Charles de

Born Casablanca, Morocco, 1950

Part of the ready-to-wear movement that burgeoned in France in the 1960s and came into full flower in the 1970s, Castelbajac is best known for the fashion flair he gives to survival looks — blanket plaids, canvas, quilting, rugged coats — and sportswear for both men and women. He has been called "the space age BONNIE CASHIN."

Castelbajac's parents moved to France when he was five. His mother started her own small clothes factory and he went to work for her when he was eighteen. He designed for Pierre d'Alby, joined a group of young designers in 1974, then opened his first retail shop. In addition to his own couture house he has a secondary line, Ko & Co. He has collaborated with COURRÈGES on ready-to-wear, designs for a number of manufacturers, including some in Italy, and has done theatrical costumes.

Cesarani, Sal

Born New York City, September 25, 1939

Awards Coty American Fashion Critics' Award *Special Award (men's wear)*, 1975; *Special Award (men's wear/neckwear)*, 1976; *Men's Wear Return Award*, 1982 • Fashion Group of Boston Award, 1977

The son of Italian immigrants who worked in the garment industry, Cesarani attended the High School of Fashion Industries, graduated from the Fashion Institute of Technology. He worked as fashion coordinator at the prestigious men's store, Paul Stuart (1964-1969), where he developed his knowledge of merchandising and sense of color. He was merchandise director of the men's and women's divisions of Polo by Ralph Lauren for two years, designer for Country Britches (1973-1975), and for Stanley Blacker until he left to form Cesarani Ltd. in 1976. Although he has produced women's clothes, he is currently involved only in dressing men. As of 1994, the Cesarani name is licensed in the U.S. for men's clothing, and in Japan for men's clothing, sportswear, ties, and accessories, as well as eyeglasses and children's wear.

Essentially a traditionalist, Cesarani handled modern trends in a classic way. Cut and tailoring are impeccable: pants break at precisely the right point, jackets fit exactly with contemporary ease. As befits a classicist, he favors natural fibers — fine woolens and tweeds for fall and winter, linens and cottons for the warm months.

Cesarani has taught men's wear at the Fashion Institute of Technology and serves there as a critic; he is also a member of the Advisory Board of the Fashion Crafts

Cesarani's 1994 collection.

Educational Commission of the High School of Fashion Industries. He is further involved with fashion education as a founding member of the New York Advisory Board of the Shannon Rodgers and Jerry Silverman School of Fashion Design and Merchandising at Kent State University in Ohio.

Chanel, Gabrielle "Coco"

Born Saumur, France, 1883
Died Paris, France, January 10, 1971
Awards Neiman Marcus Award, 1957

In evaluating Chanel, some place her alongside such giants as VIONNET and BALENCIAGA, while others see her as more personality than creator, with an innate knack for knowing what women would want a few seconds before they knew it themselves. Certainly her early designs exerted a liberating influence and even the evening clothes had a youthful quality that was all her own.

Very little is known of her early life. When she was six her mother died and Gabrielle was sent to live with her paternal grandmother in Moulins. She started in fashion making hats — first in a Paris apartment in 1910, later in a shop in Deauville. In 1914 she opened a shop in Paris, making her first dresses of wool jersey, a material that at the time was not considered suitable for fashionable clothes.

Her business was interrupted by World War I but she reopened in 1919, by which time she was famous in the fashionable world. Slender and vital, with a low, warm voice, she was a superb saleswoman and undoubtedly her personality and private life contributed to her success. Misia Sert, the wife of the Spanish painter, Jose Maria Sert, was a friend and introduced her to such leading figures of the 1920s art world as Diaghilev, Picasso, Cocteau, dancer Serge Lifar, and decorator/designer

Chanel suit, 1929. *Also see Color Plate 5.*

Leon Bakst. She was famous for feuds with other designers, notably SCHIAPARELLI. Although she never married, there were many love affairs. Grand Duke Dmitri, grandson of Czar Alexander II, was a frequent escort and a three-year liaison with the Duke of Westminster may have contributed to her long-standing use and appreciation of Scottish tweeds.

Chanel closed her couture house in September 1939 at the outset of World War 11. During and after the Occupation she shared her life with a German officer, for which many refused to forgive her. She managed to leave Paris for Switzerland in 1945, remaining there in exile for eight years.

At the age of seventy she decided to go back into business, presenting her first postwar collection on February 5, 1954. A continuation of her original themes of simplicity and wearability, it received a brutal reception from both the Paris and English press, still under the influence of the waist cinchers and pads of the New Look. By the end of the year, however, it was clear that once again Chanel had seized the moment when women were ready for change; the dresses from the reviled collection sold very well, especially in America but also in France. Her success continued into the 1960s when her refusal to change her basic style or raise hemlines led to a decline in her influence. Inevitably, the pendulum swung back and in 1969

Chanel (below) wearing her classic suit, 1972. Sketches of Chanel's suits from 1957, 1958, and 1960.

her life was the basis for *Coco*, a Broadway musical starring Katharine Hepburn.

Chanel's daytime palette was neutral — black, white, beige, red — with pastels introduced at night. Trademark looks included the little boy look, wool jersey dresses with white collars and cuffs, pea jackets, bell-bottom trousers, and her personal touches of suntanned skin, bobbed hair, and magnificent jewelry worn with sportswear.

In her second, post-World War II period, she is best remembered for her suits made of jersey or the finest, softest Scottish tweeds. Jackets were usually collarless and trimmed with braid, blouses soft and tied at the neckline, skirts at or just below the knee. Suits were shown with multiple strands of pearls and gold chains set with enormous fake stones. In her own case, these were mixed with real jewels. Other widely-copied signatures were quilted handbags with shoulder chains, beige sling-back pumps with black tips, flat black hair-bows, a single gardenia.

In addition to couture, Chanel's empire encompassed perfumes, a costume jewelry workshop, and for a time, a textile house. *Chanel No. 5* was created in 1922 and in 1924 Parfums Chanel was established to market the perfumes, which have continued to proliferate. A line of cosmetics was introduced after her death.

Chanel, "La Grande Mademoiselle," died on a Sunday night in January 1971, to the last working on a new collection. The House of Chanel has continued, directed by a succession of designers. Ready-to-wear was added in 1977 with PHILIPPE GUIBOURGÉ as designer. KARL LAGERFELD has since taken over design duties for both the couture and ready-to-wear and is credited with bringing the house into the modern era.

Chanel remains a legend for her taste, wit, personal style, and for her unfaltering dedication to perfection. Hers was a luxury based on the most refined simplicity of cut, superb materials, and workmanship of the highest order.

Cipullo, Aldo

Born Rome, Italy, November 18, 1936
Died New York City, January 31, 1984
Awards Coty American Fashion Critics' Award *Special Award (men's wear/jewelry),*
1974 • Diamonds Today Competition, 1977

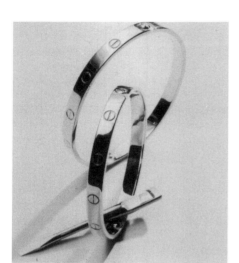

The Cartier love bracelet created by Cipullo in 1969.

Cipullo is probably best known for the gold "love bracelet" he designed while at Cartier in 1969. Coveted by both men and women, it fastened on the wrist with a screw, came with its own small vermeil screwdriver. He enlarged the scope of men's jewelry with the wraparound gold nail bracelet, lapel pins to replace the boutonniere for evening, and pendants. His work also included more conventional adornments: rings, cuff links, studs, and buttons.

Born into a family that owned a large costume jewelry firm in Italy, Cipullo studied at the University of Rome, came to New York in 1959 and attended the School of Visual Arts. He worked as a designer at David Webb, Tiffany, and Cartier, and in 1974 opened his own design studio. Cipullo's design projects extended from jewelry to silverware to textiles, included placemats, china, stationery, leather goods, and desk accessories. His design objectives were simplicity, elegance, function, and style.

Claiborne, Liz

Born Brussels, Belgium, 1929
Awards Council of Fashion Designers of America (CFDA) *Special Award,* 1985 • Dallas Fashion Award, 1985

Claiborne made her name in sportswear, where her strength lay in translating new trends into understandable and salable clothes. They were simple and uncomplicated with an easy, natural look and were in the moderate price range. She was known for sensitive use of color and for excellent technical knowledge of fabric. As her company expanded into other areas, such as dresses, men's wear, and children's clothes, she came to function largely as editor of the work of other designers.

The daughter of a banker, Claiborne spent her early childhood in New Orleans, went on to study painting in Belgium and France. Her career in fashion began in 1949 when she won a trip to Europe in a *Harper's Bazaar* design contest. On her return to the U.S., she worked as a model sketcher, as assistant to TINA LESER, Omar Khayam, and others. She was top designer at Youth Guild for sixteen years. In February 1976 she formed Liz Claiborne, Inc., with her husband, Arthur Ortenberg, as business manager.

She has served as critic at the Fashion Institute of Technology and has received numerous awards from retailers and industry associations. In 1989, she and her husband retired from the company to devote themselves to environmental issues.

Clergerie, Robert

Born Paris, France, July 18, 1934

Clergerie arrived in the shoe business by the unlikely route of Army service in Algeria and a job as salesman of concrete pipe for road construction. He was general manager of women's shoes for Xavier Danaud, a subsidiary of Charles Jourdan, before setting up his own company in 1978.

He derives inspiration from architecture, painting, the street, "everything but shoes." Never exaggerated or trendy, Clergerie shoes are elegant and refined with a strong element of architectural balance.

Robert Clergerie surrounded by his designs for men and women, 1990.

Cole, Anne

Born Los Angeles, California
Awards Dallas Fashion Award, 1987

The daughter of Fred Cole, one of swimwear's great innovators, Anne Cole was born into the beachwear business. She studied at UCLA and Holy Names College before joining the family firm, where she had to work her way up, moving from the mailroom to posting orders to taking trunk shows on the road.

Being drafted into the family business was a Cole tradition; Fred Cole was starring in silent movies when his mother decided it was time

he joined their firm, West Coast Knitting Mills. The factory made drop-seat underwear until Fred started them knitting women's swimsuits. Taking what had been a drab and shapeless garment, he lowered

the back and defined the bust and waistline; these became the first fashion swimsuits. He also introduced brilliant colors. He continued to innovate, working with Margit Fellegi, a Hollywood costume designer. They introduced the cotton suit puckered with rubber threads, and during World War II when rubber was restricted, originated the two-piece "swoon suit" that laced up the sides of the trunks and had a tie bra. The name of the company was changed to Cole of California in 1941. After the war came plunging necklines, cut-outs, bare midriffs, suits in sequins, gold lamé jersey, and water-resistant velvets.

After her father sold Cole of California to Kayser-Roth in 1960, Anne Cole left the company but was lured back to establish Cole's New York office and become stylist and company spokesperson. The firm was sold again in 1989; Anne Cole is now Cole's Executive Vice President. The Anne Cole Collection, launched in 1982, is the expression of her most advanced fashion ideas. She sees swimsuits as existing somewhere between fashion and beauty aids, reflecting current trends but with the prime function of enhancing the appearance of the wearer.

Anne Cole in 1994 and selections from her 1994 cruise collection.

Connolly, Sybil

Born Swansea, Wales, January 24, 1921

America discovered Connolly in the early 1950s, thanks to CARMEL SNOW of *Harper's Bazaar* and to the Fashion Group of Philadelphia who were visiting Dublin. In 1953 she took a collection to the U.S. where her one-of-a-kind designs and beautiful Irish fabrics made a strong impression. In 1957 she set up her own firm, with a special boutique for ready-to-wear. Her clothes were simple in cut, extremely wearable, notable for fabric and workmanship, especially the iridescent Donegal tweeds and the evening dresses made of gossamer Irish linen worked in fine horizontal pleats.

When she was fifteen years old, Connolly's father died and her mother moved the family to Waterford in southern Ireland. In 1938 she went to work for Bradley's, a London dressmaker, returning to Ireland at the outset of World War II as buyer for Richard Alan, a Dublin specialty shop. By the time she was twenty-two, she was a company director. She built the store's couture department into a thriving business and when their designer left in 1950 designed a small collection, the start of her designing career. Her clothes have been carried by fine specialty stores across the U.S.

Sybil Connolly design, 1957.

Conran, Jasper

Born London, England, 1959
Awards British Fashion Council Designer of the Year, 1986

Son of the founder of Conran's Habitat stores, Jasper Conran was educated at Bryanston School in England. In 1975, at the age of sixteen, he was accepted at New York's Parsons School of Design and studied there for eighteen months until 1977, when he went to work briefly for Fiorucci. The same year, he returned to London and in 1978 produced his first independent show; he became a member of London Designer Collections in 1979. His clothes are original in cut, sophisticated and elegant in feeling.

Courrèges, André

Born Pau, France, March 9, 1923

Courrèges emerged on the fashion scene as a brilliant tailor. Using woolens with considerable body, he cut his coats and suits with a triangular flare that disguised many figure defects, the balanced silhouettes defined by crisp welt seaming. His aim was to make functional, modern clothes. Among his successes — many of them widely copied — were all-white collections and tunics worn over narrow pants with flared bottoms that slanted from front to back. There were squared-off dresses ending above the knee, short, white baby boots, industrial zippers, and zany accessories such as sunglasses with slit "tennis ball" lenses. He was called the couturier of the space age.

Courrèges studied civil engineering before switching to textiles and fashion design. His first job was with Jeanne Lafaurie. From 1952 to 1960 he worked as a cutter for BALENCIAGA, whose influence showed clearly in his early designs. He opened his own house in August 1961 with the help of his wife, Coqueline, who had also spent three years with Balenciaga. Together they designed, cut, sewed, and presented their first collection in a small apartment in the avenue Kleber.

Courrèges was so widely plagiarized that he sold his business in 1965 and for two years did only custom work for private clients. He returned in 1967 with see-through dresses, cosmonaut suits, knitted "catsuits," flowers appliquéd on the

body, and knee socks. The Courrèges name also extended to accessories, luggage, perfumes, men's wear, and boutiques in the U.S. and other countries. These carried everything from sports separates to accessories to his Couture Future deluxe ready-to-wear. The name is still carried on a ready-to-wear line designed by Courrèges in collaboration with other designers, and is licensed worldwide.

Courrèges in 1984 and sketches (above) by the designer from WOMEN'S WEAR DAILY, 1965.

Crahay, Jules-Francois

Born Liege, Belgium, May 21, 1917
Died Monte Carlo, Monaco, January 5, 1988
Awards Neiman Marcus Award, 1962

Recognized for his thoughtful, interesting cuts, Crahay was deeply influenced by fabrics and liked to design his own. He was probably best known for his use of folkloric themes, admiring their rich mixture of color, materials, and embroidery.

Crahay literally grew up in the fashion business, starting to work at thirteen as a sketcher in his mother's couture house. After studying couture and painting in Paris (1934-1935), he returned to Liege to work for his mother (1936-1938). His army service during World War II ended in capture by the Germans and imprisonment in Germany from 1940 to 1944.

In 1951 he opened his own fashion house in Paris, which closed within a year. He then went as chief designer to NINA RICCI, receiving his first credit as sole designer in 1959. He stayed at Ricci until 1964 when he moved to the House of LANVIN, succeeding Antonio del Castillo as head designer. According to published reports, he was the highest paid couturier of his time. For twenty years he created and maintained a recognizable Lanvin look, civilized and wearable, with his own flair for original details. He retired from Lanvin in 1984 and the following year started a ready-to-wear collection under his own name in Japan.

Hard working and never satisfied, he is quoted as saying "I like ready-to-wear. I want to have fun making dresses. It is my love, it is my life." Shy and solitary, he had just a few close friends who served him as a surrogate family.

Creed, Charles

Born Paris, France, 1909
Died London, England, July 1966

Creed's family was established in London as men's tailors in 1710. His grandfather, Henry Creed, opened a Paris establishment in 1850, earning a reputation for the finest tailored riding habits for women in Europe. The client list included the actress Réjane, Empress Eugénie of France, England's Queen Victoria, opera singer Mary Garden, and the spy Mata Hari. Under the direction of Henry's son, the house expanded into tailored suits, sports clothes, even evening dresses.

Charles Creed entered the family business in Paris in 1930 after studies in France, Berlin, Vienna, Scotland, and the U.S. He opened his own London house in 1932, closed the Paris business a few years later with the advent of World War II. In the 1950s he designed wholesale lines for firms in London and the U.S., closed his couture house in March 1966 to concentrate on ready-to-wear. The house was distinguished for sound traditional tailoring and excellent fabrics, elegant suits for town, country, and evening, and bright printed blouses of sheer Rodier wool.

He was married in 1948 to Patricia Cunningham, a fashion editor of British *Vogue*, who later went to work for him. The house closed with his death.

Cummings, Angela

Cummings works in the classic tradition in 18 karat gold, platinum, or sterling silver, yet her work is far from conventional, often combining materials such as wood, gold, and diamonds. As thoroughly versed in gemology and goldsmithing as she is in jewelry design, Cummings has revived old techniques including *damascene*, the ancient art of inlaying iron with precious metal. Much of her inspiration comes from nature and organic forms, including silver jewelry derived from the leaf of a ginkgo tree and pieces influenced by the exotic orchids that she raises. She finds rings the most difficult to design because they must be entirely three dimensional, yet balanced, and must look good on the finger.

The daughter of a German diplomat, Cummings graduated from art school in Hanau, Germany, and studied at the Art Academy of Perugia, Italy. She joined Tiffany & Co. in 1967, remaining there until 1984 when she left to open her own business. The first Angela Cummings jewelry boutique was at Bergdorf Goodman, to be followed by others at stores such as Macy's San Francisco and Bloomingdale's in New York. Her design projects include flatware and tabletop accessories.

Angela Cummings (left). Earrings and necklace from her 1994 collection.

D

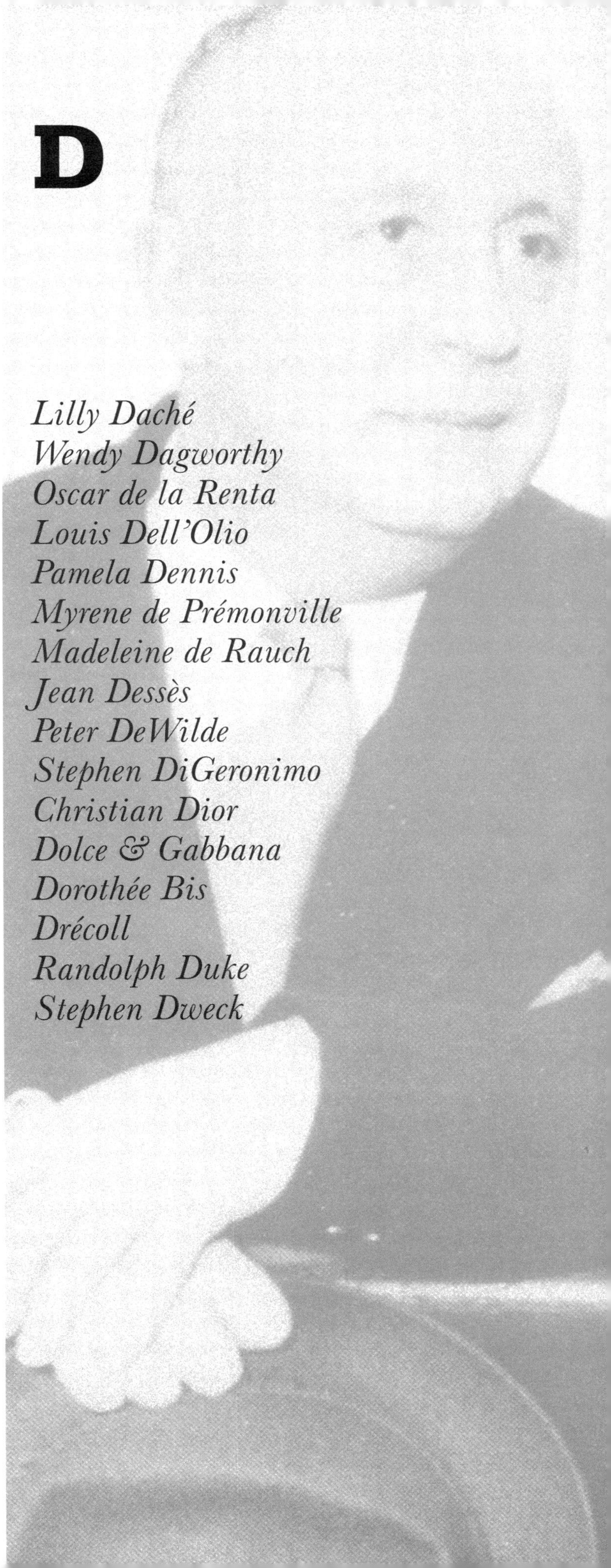

Lilly Daché
Wendy Dagworthy
Oscar de la Renta
Louis Dell'Olio
Pamela Dennis
Myrene de Prémonville
Madeleine de Rauch
Jean Dessès
Peter DeWilde
Stephen DiGeronimo
Christian Dior
Dolce & Gabbana
Dorothée Bis
Drécoll
Randolph Duke
Stephen Dweck

Daché, Lilly

Born Beigles, France, ca. 1904
Died Louvecienne, France, December 31, 1989
Awards Neiman Marcus Award, 1940 • Coty American Fashion Critics' Award *Special Award (millinery),* 1943

Vivacious and feminine, Daché brought an inimitable French flair to American fashion at a time when no woman was considered fully dressed without a hat. Born and raised in France, she left school at fourteen to apprentice with a milliner aunt, at fifteen was an apprentice in the workrooms of the famous Paris milliner Reboux, later worked at Maison Talbot. She came to the U.S. in 1924, spent one week behind the millinery counter at Macy's, then, with a partner, opened a millinery shop in the West Eighties. When her partner left, Daché moved to Broadway and 86th Street in the same neighborhood as HATTIE CARNEGIE.

Her next move was to Madison Avenue and, finally, to her own nine-story building on East 57th Street. This contained showrooms, workrooms, and a duplex apartment on the roof where she lived with her husband Jean Despres, executive vice president of Coty. By 1949 Daché was designing dresses to go with her hats. She also undertook lingerie, loungewear, gloves, hosiery, men's shirts and ties, even a wired strapless bra. The hairdresser Kenneth worked in her beauty salon before going into business for himself.

Her major design contributions were draped turbans, brimmed hats molded to the head, half hats, colored snoods, romantic massed flower shapes, also visored caps for war workers. She was considered America's foremost milliner and influenced many others in this country, including HALSTON. She closed her business in 1969 upon her husband's retirement.

Hats from Daché's spring 1940 collection inspired by late 1890s.

Dagworthy, Wendy

Born Gravesend, Kent, England, 1950

One of the second wave of young London fashion designers, Dagworthy's clothes are finely detailed and extremely wearable, successful both in the United Kingdom and abroad. She studied at Medway College of Art from 1966 to 1968, majored in fashion for three years at Hornsey College of Art. After graduating with honors, she designed for a wholesale firm for one year, opening her own company in 1972. In 1975 she joined the London Designer Collections, a cooperative of London designers. She feels a responsibility for the continuation of her craft and takes an active interest in fashion education.

de la Renta, Oscar

Born Santo Domingo, Dominican Republic, July 22, 1932
Awards Coty American Fashion Critics Award *"Winnie,"* 1967; *Return Award,* 1968; *Hall of Fame,* 1973 • Neiman Marcus Award, 1968 • Numerous awards from the Dominican Republic

De la Renta is known for sexy, extravagantly romantic evening clothes in opulent materials. His daytime clothes, sometimes overshadowed by the more spectacular evening designs, have a European flavor, sophisticated, feminine, and eminently wearable.

Educated in Santo Domingo and Madrid, de la Renta remained in Madrid after graduation to study art, intending to become a painter. His fashion career began when sketches he made for his own amusement were seen by the wife of the American ambassador to Spain, who

Designs from de la Renta's collections, 1979 (left) and 1994 (right).

D

asked him to design a gown for her daughter's debut. His first professional job was with BALENCIAGA's Madrid couture house, Eisa. In 1961 he went to Paris as assistant to Antonio de Castillo at Lanvin-Castillo, in 1963 went with Castillo to New York to design at Elizabeth Arden. He joined Jane Derby in 1965, was soon operating as Oscar de la Renta, Ltd., producing luxury ready-to-wear.

A signature perfume introduced in 1977 has been enormously successful; a second fragrance, *Ruffles*, appeared in 1983. He has also done boutique lines, bathing suits,

de la Renta and models, 1987.

- -

wedding dresses, furs, jewelry, bed linens, and loungewear. In 1992 he took over the design of the BALMAIN couture collection, then the ready-to-wear. He continues to design his own New York collection.

Dell'Olio, Louis

Born New York City, July 23, 1948
Awards Coty American Fashion Critics' Award *"Winnie" (with Donna Karan)*, 1977; *Hall of Fame (with Donna Karan)*, 1982; *Special Award (women's wear, with Donna Karan)*, 1984

Dell'Olio is best known for his years at ANNE KLEIN, first as co-designer with DONNA KARAN and then as sole designer when she left to open her own house. After her departure he continued the direction begun with Karan — a modern, sophisticated interpretation of the classic Anne Klein sportswear — clothes in the deluxe investment category marked by clean, sharp shapes in beautiful fabrics. His other design projects included furs for Michael Forrest.

In 1967 Dell'Olio received the Norman Norell Scholarship to Parsons School of Design, from which he graduated in 1969, winning the Gold Thimble Award for coats and suits. He assisted Dominic Rompollo at Teal Traina, was designer at the Giorgini and Ginori divisions of Originala. In 1974, he joined Karan, a friend from Parsons, as co-designer at Anne Klein & Co. Spring 1985 was their last joint collection. Dell'Olio continued as sole designer for Anne Klein until 1993, when he was replaced by RICHARD TYLER.

Dell'Olio with model for the 1993 Anne Klein collection.

Dennis, Pamela

Born Newark, New Jersey, August 24, 1960

Dennis has carved a distinctive niche for herself in the designer evening category. Without formal training, she came into design by chance when, invited to a wedding and with nothing to wear, she took a few yards of silk to a tailor and had him make it into a columnar dress. Another wedding guest, a photo stylist, asked to use the dress in a diamond commercial, which led to three more commercials and inspired Dennis to design her first collection.

Her clothes are distinguished by simple shapes in luxurious fabrics — silk crepe, chiffon, georgette, charmeuse, wool bouclé, stretch crepe — enhanced with crystals or hand-beaded lace. They are sold nationally and internationally to fine boutiques and specialty stores and are worn by celebrities ranging from Cindy Crawford to Joan Rivers, from Melanie Griffith and Jane Fonda to Whitney Houston.

de Prémonville, Myrene

Born France, 1950

A veteran of the French fashion industry, de Prémonville free-lanced for years before going into business with a partner in 1983. She first attracted attention with young, flirty, peplum suits in crisp, refined fabrics — subsequent collections included dresses for day and evening, and knits. Working exclusively with French fabrics and manufacturers, she has acquired a following among better retailers in the U.S.

The clothes blend a youthful spirit of innovation with conservative French chic, fastidious cut, and fine tailoring, and are favorites among well-dressed young Frenchwomen. De Prémonville has also continued to free-lance, her projects including children's clothes.

de Rauch, Madeleine

Starting in 1928 with a single worker, de Rauch grew and stayed in business for forty-five years. The house was known for beautiful, wearable, functional clothes. Soft fabrics were handled with great fluidity, draped close at the top of the figure. Wide necklines were often framed with folds or tucks. Plaids, checks, and stripes were treated with simplicity and precision, so perfectly done they seemed to have been assembled on a drawing board.

An accomplished sportswoman, de Rauch began in fashion in the 1920s designing her own clothes for active sports. When friends persuaded her to make clothes for them, she opened a business called the House of Friendship in 1928, employing a single worker. With the help of her two sisters, the business grew and in the 1930s evolved into the House of de Rauch overlooking the Cours de Reine. It closed in 1973.

Dessès, Jean

Born Alexandria, Egypt, August 6, 1904
Died Athens, Greece, August 2, 1970

Dessès is remembered primarily for draped evening gowns of chiffon and mousseline in beautiful colors, and for the subtlety with which he handled fur. Of Greek ancestry, he was as a child interested in beautiful clothes and designed a dress for his mother when he was only nine. He attended school in Alexandria, studied law in Paris, and in 1925 switched to fashion design. For twelve years he worked for Mme. Jane on the rue de la Paix and in 1937 opened his own establishment. Dessès visited the U.S. in 1949. He admired American women and in 1950 designed a lower-priced line for them called Jean Dessès Diffusion. This is seen as the beginning of French couture expansion into ready-to-wear.

A gentle man of refined and luxurious tastes, Dessès was inspired in his work by native costumes he saw in museums on his travels, especially in Greece and Egypt. He designed by draping fabrics directly on the form. Customers included Princess Margaret, the Duchess of Kent, and the Queen of Greece. He gave up his couture business in 1965 because of ill health and retired to Greece, continuing to free-lance until his death.

Sketch from WOMEN'S WEAR DAILY of gown by Jean Dessès, 1949.

DeWilde, Peter

Born Taplow, England, June 25, 1967
Died Setauket, New York, August 30, 1995

Before turning to fashion, Peter DeWilde attended business school and the Utrecht Academy of Fine Arts. He spent 1986 and 1987 as apprentice to Holland's foremost couturier, joined KOOS in the same capacity, became his assistant in 1988. In 1992 he bought the business and became president and co-designer; the firm's name was changed to Koos & DeWilde. DeWilde found inspiration just about anywhere: travel, movies, New York City, historical costume. He believed that clothes should be comfortable and simple but also elegant, feminine, and of good quality. He brought a lively, modern spirit to the signature Koos collage and patchwork effects.

From Koos and DeWilde resort 1994 collection.

D

DiGeronimo, Stephen

Born Clarks Green, Pennsylvania, January 4, 1960

DiGeronimo studied fine art at the Philadelphia College of Art and spent time at both Parsons School of Design and the Fashion Institute of Technology. In his own business since 1990, he had worked prior to that at a number of fashion houses: in 1981 with DIANE VON FURSTENBURG, CALVIN KLEIN in 1983, PERRY ELLIS in 1987, and MICHAEL KORS in 1989. During that time he worked on everything from furs to swimsuits, from eyeglasses to jeans, even interior design.

Working in the designer price range, DiGeronimo draws inspiration from painters and the art of different cultures, past and present. His objective is clean, playful sportswear with a sexy, modern, American attitude for a customer he visualizes as a career-minded woman of any age. He is a member of the Council of Fashion Designers of America.

Dior, Christian

Born Granville, France, January 31, 1905
Died Montecatini, Italy, October 24, 1957
Awards Neiman Marcus Award, 1947 • Parsons Medal for Distinguished Achievement, 1956

The name Dior is most associated with the New Look. This silhouette was, in essence, a polished continuation of the rounded line seen in the first postwar collections, appearing at the same time at a number of design houses. Dior's was a dream of flower-like women with rounded shoulders, feminine busts, tiny waists, enormous spreading skirts. Everything was exquisitely made of the best materials available.

Dior was the son of a well-to-do manufacturer of fertilizer and chemicals from Normandy. He wished to become an architect — his family wanted him to enter the diplomatic service. He studied political science at L'Ecole des Sciences Politiques, performed his obligatory military service, and in 1928 opened a small art gallery with a friend. This was soon wiped out by the Depression, which also ruined Dior's family. In 1931 he traveled to Russia, returned disillusioned with Soviet Communism, and for the next few years lived from hand to mouth, eating little and sleeping on the floor of friends' apartments.

He became seriously ill in 1934 and had to leave Paris. During an enforced rest in Spain and the south of France he learned tapestry weaving and developed a desire to create. He returned to Paris in 1935, thirty years old and without means of support. Unable to find any kind of job he started making design sketches and also did fashion illustrations for *Le Figaro*. That year he sold his first sketches — for twenty francs each.

His early hat designs were successful, his dresses less so. In 1937, after a two-year struggle to improve his dresses, he sold several sketches to ROBERT PIGUET and was asked to make a number of dresses for an upcoming collection. He was hired by Piguet in 1938 but in 1939 went into the Army. The fall of Paris

Left, Dior's New Look from 1947
and (above) a cowl-back jacket
with shift-dress from 1957.

in June 1940 found him stationed in the south of France. Asked by Piguet to come back to work, Dior delayed his return until the end of 1941, by which time another designer had been hired. He then went to work for LUCIEN LELONG, a much larger estab-lishment. At the end of 1946 he left Lelong to open his own house.

Dior was backed in his new project by Marcel Boussac, a French financier, race horse owner, and textile manufacturer, who originally was looking for someone to take over an ailing couture house he owned. Instead, Dior persuaded Boussac to back him, and in the spring of 1947, presented his wildly successful, first New Look collection.

He continued to produce beau-tiful clothes in collection after collec-tion, each evolving from the one before, continually refining and expanding his talent. In 1952, with the sensuous line, he began to loosen the waist, freed it even more with the H-line in 1954, the A- and Y-lines in 1955.

Dior described himself as a silent, slow Norman, shy and reticent by nature, strongly attached to his friends. He loved good food, and for relaxation and pleasure read history and archaeology and played cards. His chief passion was for architec-ture. Like many designers he was superstitious and believed in the importance of luck, consulting fortune tellers on the major decisions of his life.

Since his death, the House of Dior has continued under the direction of other designers: YVES SAINT LAURENT until 1960, MARC BOHAN until 1989, and since then GIANFRANCO FERRÉ. Christian Dior, Inc. has become a vast international merchandising operation with the Dior label on jewelry, scarves, men's ties, furs, stockings, gloves, ready-to-wear and, of course, perfume. Dior-Delman shoes were designed by ROGER VIVIER.

Dior in his studio, 1947.

Dolce & Gabbana

Born Domenico Dolce; Polizzi Generosa, Palermo, Italy, September 13, 1958
Stefano Gabbana; Venice, Italy, November 14, 1962

Members of the avant-garde of Italian fashion, Dolce and Gabbana came to their craft by disparate routes: Domenico Dolce, whose father had a small clothing factory in Sicily, attended fashion school, but Stefano Gabbana was totally lacking in fashion background, having studied graphics and worked in an advertising agency.

The two met in Milan in 1980, became assistants to a Milanese designer, and in 1982 joined forces in their own business, working as consultants to other companies while creating their own line. Their first international recognition came in 1985 when they were chosen by the Milano Collezioni as one of three young Italian talents to be given formal presentations. Their first knitwear collection appeared in 1987; they have since added men's wear and in 1994, a new, lower-priced collection called D & G.

Dolce & Gabbana continue to evolve along their own highly individual path. Their look, based on body clothes, seasons the modern with romantic historical references, the pieces designed to be worn in different ways in different situations. They have brought the same innovative, modern-romantic approach to their clothes for men.

Left, designers Dolce (right in photo) and Gabbana at the finale of their 1993 show; (right) designs from their 1994 collection.

Dorothée Bis

Dorothée Bis was begun in the 1960s as a chain of trend-setting Paris boutiques, with Jacqueline Jacobson as designer and her husband, Elie, as manufacturer. Among the pioneers of French ready-to-wear, the Jacobsons began in the fur business, branched out into manufacturing skirts, then into knits.

The clothes are sporty and casual; the firm is known for intarsia knits in imaginative patterns and for brilliant use of color, with collections totally color-keyed — knitted cap to knitted gloves to ribbed wool tights matched to shoes or boots. They were among the first in French ready-to-wear to sell a totally coordinated look.

Drécoll

Founded Paris, France, 1905
Closed 1929

The House of Drécoll was established in Vienna by a Belgian, Baron Christopher Drécoll. His designer bought the name and moved the business to Paris, where it survived the first World War only to perish like the dinosaur when it could not change with the times. Drécoll was never one of the top Paris houses but in the pre-war period of conspicuous display of wealth, its elaborate clothes fitted in and the house prospered. After the war, new attitudes and women's changed expectations demanded new clothes. Unable to change direction, the house was forced to close.

Duke, Randolph

Born Las Vegas, Nevada, January 14, 1958

Duke studied at the University of Southern California and at the Fashion Institute of Design and Merchandising in Los Angeles, from which he graduated in 1978 with the Bob Mackie and Peacock awards. From 1978 to 1984 he worked for various West Coast companies specializing in swimwear — Jantzen, Cole of California, the Anne Cole Collection — and until 1987 for Gottex. He continues as designer for the Anne Cole Collection. Duke briefly had a retail store on New York's Upper West Side, by 1989 was established in a wholesale business which closed in 1992. In 1993 he joined CMT, a private label concern, to produce exclusive signature collections for retail stores; he has sold the clothes successfully in personal appearances on the QVC TV shopping channel.

For his own collections, Duke starts with body clothes of stretch fabrics, then layers on freer, looser shapes. The clothes are young and full of energy, exuberant modern classics with a twist.

Dweck, Stephen

Born Brooklyn, New York, August 10, 1960

Necklace from Dweck's 1994 collection.

Graduating from New York's School of Visual Arts in 1980 with a gold medal in sculpture, Stephen Dweck went into business as a jewelry designer the same year in partnership with his brothers. Working with sterling silver, vermeil, and bronze, he combines the metals with natural minerals and semi-precious stones for jewelry that is modern with overtones of fantasy and hints of ancient cultures. He utilizes natural forms such as beetles and butterflies, leaves and vines, for his jewelry and for the collections for the home, which he creates for others. These include china for Sasaki and sterling silver gifts and accessories for Lunt Silversmiths. He also designs a belt collection.

D

Florence Eiseman
Mark Eisen
Perry Ellis
Elizabeth Emanuel

Eiseman, Florence

Born Minneapolis, Minnesota, September 27, 1899
Died Milwaukee, Wisconsin, January 8, 1988
Awards Neiman Marcus Award (the first children's designer recipient), 1955 • Swiss Fabrics Award, 1956 • Dallas Fashion Award, 1980

Two Florence Eiseman sayings are: "Children have bellies, not waists" and "You should see the child, and not the dress first." Ruled by these precepts and by her belief that children should not be dressed in small versions of adult clothing, Eiseman produced simple styles distinguished by fine fabrics and excellent workmanship, with prices to match. The clothes were so classic and so well made they were frequently handed down from one generation to another.

Florence Eiseman took up sewing as a hobby following the birth of her second son, Robert. As her children grew she turned out quilts and clothing for them and for her neighbors' children. In 1945, when family finances were pinched, her husband Laurence took samples of her organdy pinafores to Marshall Field & Co. in Chicago. The $3,000 order he came away with put them in business with her as designer, him as business manager/salesman.

Mrs. Eiseman first worked out of her home, enlisting other women to sew for her in theirs. Next, with two

----

Eiseman's all-time best-selling jumper and T-shirt from 1976-1979 (top); the sailor top and short culottes for resort 1982 (bottom left); the "hello" dress from the early fifties (bottom right).

sewing machines, she took over a corner of her husband's toy factory. Within a few years, Laurie Eiseman gave up his toy business to devote himself to the clothing firm, which in a short time grew into a large concern, with sales across the U.S. and abroad. Mrs. Eiseman functioned successively as vice president, president, and chairman.

She became known as the "NORMAN NORELL of children's clothes", making dresses and separates, swimsuits, playclothes, sleepwear, and boys' suits. In 1969 she added less expensive knits, brother-sister outfits, and for a short time, a limited group of women's clothes. In 1984, the company was asked by Neiman Marcus to do a luxury collection of dress-up clothes at prices beginning where the regular collection left off. The result was Florence Eiseman Couture, not custom-made but using rich fabrics and many hand touches. Its introduction in September 1984 coincided with Mrs. Eiseman's eighty-fifth birthday, finding her still actively involved in the company she founded. The same year, the Denver Art Museum presented a retrospective of her work. At her death she was praised for her role in raising the standards of fashion and quality in children's clothes and for encouraging manufacturers to trade up.

Eisen, Mark

Born Cape Town, South Africa, September 27, 1958

Mark Eisen earned a B.S. degree at the Business School of the University of Southern California in 1982 and in 1988 began his own design business in Los Angeles. In 1993 he moved to New York, bringing with him some of the freedom and relaxed feeling of California design. His chosen field is women's designer sportswear, both custom and ready-to-wear; his style is simple and spare. Other interests include a women's shoe collection and men's wear for Barney's New York and Mick Jagger's clothes for his 1994 Rolling Stones tour. He has been a critic in the Fashion Design Department of Otis Parsons School

in Los Angeles and was honored by USC Business School in 1988 as Alumni of the Year.

From Mark Eisen's fall 1994 collection.

Ellis, Perry

Born Portsmouth, Virginia, 1940
Died New York City, May 30, 1986
Awards Neiman Marcus Award, 1979 • Coty American Fashion Critics' Award *"Winnie,"* 1979; *Return Award,* 1980; *Hall of Fame,* 1981; *Special Award (men's wear),* 1981; *Hall of Fame Citation (women's wear),* 1983; *Men's Wear Return Award,* 1983; *Hall of Fame (men's wear),* 1984; *Hall of Fame Citation (women's wear),* 1984 • Council of Fashion Designers of America (CFDA) *Outstanding Designer in Women's Fashion,* 1981; *Outstanding Designer in Men's Fashion:* 1982, 1983 • Cutty Sark Men's Fashion Award *Outstanding Menswear Designer:* 1983, 1984

Ellis came to fashion design relatively late, having previously worked in retailing and merchandising. He took his B.A. at William and Mary College, his M.A. in retailing from New York University. He was sportswear buyer for Miller & Rhoads in Richmond leaving in 1967 to go as merchandiser to John Meyer of Norwich, a conservative sportswear firm. There he acquired three important design tools — sketching, pattern making, and fabric selection. In 1974 he joined the Vera Companies as merchandiser, the next

year became designer for the Portfolio division of Vera. Perry Ellis Sportswear, Inc. was established in 1978 with Ellis as designer and president; men's wear followed in 1980. Then came furs, shearling coats for both men and women, cloth coats, and for Japan, a complete sportswear line. There were shoes, legwear, scarves, Vogue patterns, and sheets, towels, and blankets. A fragrance collection was launched in 1985.

From the beginning, the clothes were distinguished by a young, adventurous spirit and the use of natural fibers: cotton, silk, linen, pure wool. Hand knitted sweaters of cotton, silk, and cashmere became a trademark. This use of fine fabrics and handwork soon drove the collection up into a higher price bracket. Hence, in 1984, the revival of the Portfolio name for a moderately priced collection with much the same relaxed classic look as the original.

Ellis believed that people should not take fashion too seriously or be overly concerned with what they wear, and following his own dictates, usually dressed informally for his rare public appearances. He was

----

The designer (above right); Perry Ellis design from 1979 (left). *Also see Color Plate 6.*

active in the Council of Fashion Designers of America and served two terms as president. He was elected to a third term the week before his death. In his honor, the organization established the Perry Ellis Award, to be given annually "for the greatest impact on an emerging new talent." David Cameron was the first recipient in 1986.

The company has continued in business under the direction of a number of designers. MARK JACOBS took over in 1989 and after several unprofitable seasons was dropped by the company in February 1993, when the designer and bridge sportswear collections were discontinued. The Perry Ellis name continues to licensed in up to 36 product categories.

Emanuel, Elizabeth

Born London, England, 1953

With her husband, David, Elizabeth Emanuel attended Harrow School of Art. Together, they took a postgraduate course in fashion at the Royal College of Art, the only married couple to be accepted there. They opened their own firm in 1977 with two wholesale collections a year, and in 1979 took the unusual step of closing their ready-to-wear business to concentrate on made-to-order. In June 1990 they announced the dissolution of their business and their marriage. Elizabeth has continued to use the Emanuel name for a ready-to-wear collection.

The Emanuels gained international attention for their wedding dress for Diana, the Princess of Wales. Their fantasy ball gowns and wedding dresses, afloat in lace, taffeta, organza, and tulle, evoked a romantic, bygone, never-never time. Licenses have included bed linens, sunglasses, perfume.

Lady Diana Spencer on arrival at St. Paul's Cathedral for her wedding to Prince Charles July 29, 1981.

F

Fabiani
Nicole Farhi
Jacques Fath
Fendi
Salvatore Ferragamo
Gianfranco Ferré
Alberta Ferretti
Anne Fogarty
Fontana
Fortuny

Fabiani, Alberto

Born Tivoli, Italy

Fabiani was introduced to fashion in Paris at the age of eighteen by a family friend, an Italian tailor. After three years, he returned to Italy and in 1952 emerged with his own distinctively Italian viewpoint, lively and elegant. A part of the burst of fashion creativity that occurred in Italy in the 1950s, he was married to SIMONETTA, also a designer. Together they moved to Paris, opening in 1961. After a successful beginning, their business failed and Fabiani returned alone to Rome where he rebuilt his business successfully with clients from Italy, Europe, and the U.S. He has since retired.

Farhi, Nicole

Born France, July 25, 1946
Awards British Fashion Award "British Classics," 1989

During 1965 and 1966, Farhi studied design at Studio Berçot, a Paris hotbed of creativity and independent thinking. She went on to free-lance, designing for women, men, and children, as well as creating accessories, textiles, knits, and underwear. Among others, her clients included Pierre D'Alby, and in Italy, Initial, Veste Bimbi, and the fabric house Bianchini Ferrier. She also did illustrations for the magazines *Elle* and *Marie Claire*.

In 1973, Farhi began a free-lance association in London with French Connection Ltd., designing for both the Stephen Marks and French Connection labels. In 1983, the Stephen Marks label was changed to Nicole Farhi to coincide with the opening of a Nicole Farhi boutique at Harvey Nichols, London. Free-standing shops opened in 1984 in both London and New York, other shops and boutiques followed. A complete professional, Farhi excels in well-cut separates, with simple, sexy dresses, strong coats and outerwear. She sees her customer as the "classic working woman."

Fath, Jacques

Born Lafitte, France, September 12, 1912
Died Paris, France, November 14, 1954
Awards Neiman Marcus Award, 1949

Fath's clothes were flattering, feminine, and sexy without slipping into vulgarity. They followed the lines of the body with hourglass shapes and swathed hips, often had full, pleated skirts and plunging necklines. He did not sew or sketch but draped material while his assistants made sketches.

Son of an Alsatian businessman, grandson of a painter, and great-grandson of a dressmaker, Fath attended both business school and drama school, acting briefly in films. He showed his design talent early on in costumes for the theater and films, opened his first couture house in Paris in 1937 with a small collection of twenty models. He went into the Army in 1940, was captured, and on his release reopened his house, which he managed to keep open during the war. After Liberation, he became enormously successful, eventually expanding his salon from the single wartime workroom with one fitter to an establishment with six hundred employees. In 1948 he signed with a U.S. manufacturer to produce two collections a year, one of the first French couturiers to venture into ready-to-wear. Other such agreements followed. The Fath name also went into perfume, scarves, stockings, millinery.

Handsome and personable, Fath had a flair for publicity and show-

Above, Fath attaching walnuts to a hat, 1951. Right, a sketch from 1947.

manship and became one of the most popular designers of his time. He loved parties and with his wife, actress Genevieve de Bruyere, gave elaborate entertainments at their Corbeville chateau. He was also an excellent businessman. After his death of leukemia at the age of forty-two, his wife continued the business for a few years, closed it in 1957.

Robe crêpe imprimé

J. Fath

9

Fendi

Founded 1918

Specializing in furs, handbags, luggage, and sportswear, Fendi is a family business founded in 1918 by Adele Fendi. After her husband's death in 1954, Signora Fendi called on her five daughters for help — Paola, Anna, Franca, Carla, and Alda were at that time aged 14 to 24. Working as a team, the sisters, with their husbands, have built the business and expanded the Fendi business, continuing to explore new areas. Their daughters, in turn, have also come into the firm. Adele Fendi died March 19, 1978, at the age of 81.

In 1962 the Fendis hired KARL LAGERFELD to design their furs, backing him with a dazzling array of new, unusual, or neglected pelts and the most inventive techniques. Their mother had made coats out of squirrel and had made it fashionable; the Fendis today still use squirrel, as well as badger, Persian lamb, fox, and sundry unpedigreed furs, often several in one garment. They are noted for such innovations as furs woven in strips and coats left unlined for lightness — the furs are always lighthearted and fun. Fendi styles have glamour, but their success is based on an understanding of what women need and want. The Fendi double F initials, designed by Lagerfeld, have become an international status symbol.

Fendi family (above right) and designs from fur and ready-to-wear collections, 1993.

Ferragamo, Salvatore

Born Bonito, Italy, June 1898
Died Fiumetto, Italy, August 7, 1960
Awards Neiman Marcus Award, 1947

Ferragamo began working as a shoe-maker in Bonito when he was thirteen, emigrated to the U.S. in 1923. He studied mass shoemaking techniques then opened a shop in Hollywood, designing shoes and making them by hand for such film stars as Dolores Del Rio, Pola Negri, and Gloria Swanson. He also maintained a successful business in ready-made shoes.

He returned to Italy and in 1936 opened a business in Florence. By the time of his death in 1960 he had ten factories in Italy and Great Britain. Since then the business has been carried on by his daughters Fiamma and Giovanna, and his son Ferruccio. In addition to shoes, the Ferragamo name appears on handbags, scarves, and luxury ready-to-wear sold in free-standing boutiques and in major specialty stores.

Early Ferragamo designs are fantasies of shape, color, and fabric. He is said to have originated the wedge heel and the platform sole, also the Lucite heel. In recent years, while still elegant, the emphasis has been on ladylike, conservative styling and comfortable fit.

Salvatore Ferragamo with Paulette Goddard in 1959.

Ferré, Gianfranco

Born Legnano, Italy, ca. 1945

Ferré's day clothes are exceptional, with a strong sculptural beauty, yet they are fluid, clean-lined, and comfortable. A fine tailor and leading exponent of architectural design, Ferré is now accepted as one of Europe's top designers.

Ferré originally intended to be an architect — he studied in Milan and qualified in 1967. After a period working for a furniture maker and time off for travel, he began designing jewelry, by 1970 had made a name for himself as an accessories designer. He sold his shoes, scarves, and handbags to other designers, including LAGERFELD, designed striped T-shirts for Fiorucci. As a free-lancer he began designing sportswear and raincoats and by 1974 was showing under his own name.

In 1989 he joined CHRISTIAN DIOR, replacing MARC BOHAN as design director. At Dior his clothes have been marked by lush extravagance in the traditional couture mode. He continues to design a signature ready-to-wear collection in Milan.

Evening wear by Ferré for spring 1994.

Ferré (right) at the finale of his
show and a design for day (above),
for spring 1994.

Ferretti, Alberta

Born Gradara near Riccione, Italy, May 2, 1950

To the business born, Alberta Ferretti
began at an early age to collaborate
with her mother, who owned an
atelier; by the age of eighteen she
had her own boutique. Her first
collection appeared in 1974. From
1981, when she presented her first
prêt-à-porter collection, her business
has grown to include the signature

couture collection, diffusion sportswear, and a Japanese operation with
boutiques in Tokyo, Osaka, and
Yokohama. She is owner and
managing director of AEFFE, which
produces and distributes her clothes
as well as the collections of FRANCO
MOSCHINO and RIFAT OZBEK.

The Ferretti look is feminine and

elegant, soft shapes interpreted in
the finest Italian fabrics that range
from silk, damask, and velvet for
evening to cashmere and worsted
wool for day. Her other projects have
included glassware, ceramics, and a
perfume, *Femina*.

F

Fogarty, Anne

Born Pittsburgh, Pennsylvania, February 2, 1919
Died New York City, January 15, 1981
Awards Coty American Fashion Critics' Award *Special Award (dresses)*, 1951 • Neiman Marcus Award, 1952 • International Silk Association Award, 1955 • National Cotton Fashion Award, 1957

Fogarty is best known for her "paper doll" silhouette, for crinoline petticoats under full-skirted shirtdresses with tiny waists, for the camise, a chemise gathered onto a high yoke, and for lounging coveralls. In the early 1970s she showed a peasant look with ruffled shirts and hot pants under long quilted skirts. She also designed lingerie, jewelry, shoes, hats, coats, and suits.

Anne Fogarty wears an evening gown from her summer 1957 collection to accept annual National Cotton Fashion Award. The dress is white waffle piqué with red velvet threaded through the strapless top.

After study at Carnegie Tech, Fogarty moved to New York, where she worked as a model and stylist. Between 1948 and 1957 she designed junior-size dresses for Youth Guild and Margot, Inc., next spent five years at Saks Fifth Avenue. She established Anne Fogarty Inc. in 1962, closed it twelve years later. At the time of her death she had completed a collection of spring-summer dresses and sportswear for a Seventh Avenue firm.

In 1940 she married Tom Fogarty, with whom she had two children. They later divorced and she married twice again: Richard Kolmar who died in 1971, and Wade O'Hara, from whom she was divorced.

Fontana

Founded Parma, Italy, 1907

Originally a small dressmaking establishment founded in Parma by Amabile Fontana, the business was taken over by her three daughters, Micol and Zoe as designers, Giovanna in charge of sales. In 1936 they moved to Rome and after World War II made a name for themselves in the emerging Italian haute couture as *Sorelle Fontana* (Fontana Sisters). Their designs were marked by asymmetric lines and interesting necklines, and were noteworthy for delicate handwork. They were particularly admired for their evening gowns.

Fontana created Ava Gardner's costumes for *The Barefoot Contessa*, Margaret Truman's wedding gown, also clothes for Jacqueline Kennedy. The house was at its peak in the 1950s, when it contributed largely to Italian fashion. Fontana boutiques still exist in Italy and Switzerland.

Fortuny

Born Granada, Spain, 1871
Died Venice, Italy, 1949

Fortuny's father was a famous painter who died when his son was only three years old. After art studies — painting, drawing, and sculpture — Fortuny became interested in chemistry and dyes. At the turn of the 20th century he moved to Venice, where he experimented with every aspect of design, from dyeing and printing silks by methods and in patterns of his own invention, to shaping clothes to his own aesthetic standards.

His silk tea gowns in rich and subtle colors have been widely collected, both by museums and by women who are, of necessity, both rich and slender. The most famous design is the *Delphos* gown, which first appeared in 1907 and which he patented. This is a simple column of many narrow, irregular, vertical pleats permanently set in the silk by a secret process. Slipped over the head and tied at the waist by thin silk cords, it clings to the figure and spills over the feet. It may have sleeves or be sleeveless. There is also a two-piece version called *Peplos*, with a hip-length overblouse or longer, unpleated tunic. These dresses are both beautiful and amazingly practical. For storage, each is simply twisted into a rope and coiled into a figure eight, then slipped into its own small box. Status symbols at the time they were made, the dresses have become so once again, bringing such high prices at auction they are almost too costly to wear. He also designed tunics, capes, scarves and kimono-shaped wraps to be worn over the *Delphos*.

Fortuny invented a process for printing color and metals on fabric to achieve an effect of brocade or tapestry. Velvets were dyed in many layers and sometimes printed with metallics, gold or silver. Fortuny fabrics are still used in interior design, still manufactured in Venice.

Painter, photographer, set and lighting designer, inventor, Fortuny has in recent years been recognized again for his originality and wide-ranging creativity. An exhibition of more than 100 examples of his work opened in Lyons, France, in May 1980. From there it travelled to New York's Fashion Institute of Technology and on to the Art Institute of Chicago. Included were dresses, robes, textiles, and clocks.

For an evening cape designed by Fortuny see Color Plate 10.

G

James Galanos
Irene Galitzine
John Galliano
Jean-Paul Gaultier
Jennifer George
Rudi Gernreich
Romeo Gigli
Marithé & François Girbaud
Hubert de Givenchy
Alix Grès
Philippe Guibourgé

Galanos, James

Born Philadelphia, Pennsylvania, September 20, 1925
Awards Neiman Marcus Award, 1954 • Coty American Fashion Critics' Award *"Winnie,"* 1954; *Return Award,* 1956; *Hall of Fame,* 1959 • National Cotton Fashion Award, 1958 • Council of Fashion Designers of America (CFDA) *Lifetime Achievement Award,* 1984

One of the greatest, most independent designers working in America today, Galanos is widely considered the equal of the great European couturiers. His ready-to-wear has become a symbol of luxury, both for its extraordinary quality and for stratospheric prices comparable to those of the couture.

This son of Greek immigrants left Philadelphia for New York to study at Traphagen School of Fashion and after only a few months began selling sketches to manufacturers. He worked for HATTIE CARNEGIE in 1944, went to Paris where he worked with ROBERT PIGUET (1947-1948). He returned to New York and designed for Davidow, moved to Los Angeles and worked at Columbia Pictures as assistant to Jean Louis. In 1951, with two assistants and a $500 loan from Jean Louis, he started his own business; he gave his first New York showing in 1952 in a private apartment.

In an age where hems are left unfinished, linings banished, and seams worn inside-out, Galanos believes a garment should be as luxurious inside as out and still insists on lining his clothes. Intricate construction, flawless workmanship, and magnificent imported fabrics are his

James Galanos (top right) and examples of his designs for 1962 (left) and 1987 (bottom right).

84

hallmarks, as well as detailing rarely found in ready-to-wear. Impeccably precise matching of plaids and the delicate cross pleating of his legendary chiffons are just two examples. Long admired by connoisseurs of fashion, he achieved wider recognition as one of Nancy Reagan's favorite designers. She chose a white satin Galanos gown for the first Inaugural Ball in 1981, and for the second in 1985, a slim, jeweled dress with bolero top.

Because he likes the climate and relaxed living style, Galanos lives and works in Los Angeles, where he has assembled a workroom of near-miraculous proficiency and skill, still housed in the same studio in which he started his business. He does not give large, public showings, preferring to exhibit his clothes to the press and retailers in the more intimate settings of hotel suites. In 1976, New York's Fashion Institute of Technology presented "Galanos — 25 Years," a special fashion show and exhibition celebrating his twenty-fifth year in business.

Galitzine, Princess Irene

Born Tiflis, Russia, ca. 1916

Galitzine made her name in the 1960s with silk palazzo pajamas as a sophisticated evening look. Cut with wide legs from fluid silks, they were an instant sensation, often fringed with beads, sometimes with attached necklaces. She was also known for at-home togas, evening suits, tunic-top dresses, evening gowns with bare backs or open sides.

Raised in Rome after her family fled the Russian Revolution, Galitzine studied art and design in Rome, where she worked three years for the FONTANA sisters. She opened an import business in Rome in 1948, first showed her own designs in 1949. She closed her business in 1968, continuing to design for various companies — cosmetics, furs, household linens. She revived her couture house in 1970 and showed sporadically for several years.

Galliano, John

Born Gibralter, 1960
Awards British Fashion Council Designer of the Year, 1987

The son of a Spanish mother and an English father, Galliano was not permitted by his parents to study art until he reached college. At London's prestigious St. Martin's School of Art, he studied textiles, learning about fabric, color, and the way cloth drapes, before switching to design. His graduation collection, called "Les Incroyables" after the group of French revolutionaries of the same name, used the same design method he still employs: researching a period in museums then creating his own design on the model.

Galliano started his career as part of the wildly uninhibited avant-garde London design scene. His designs were twisted and artfully torn, weird and also beautiful. By the end of the 1980s his style had evolved and matured into a smoother, more sophisticated manner based on flawless technique and complete command of craft, a synthesis of the original and the salable. In 1990 he joined the ranks of international designers participating in the Paris ready-to-wear showings. He continued to show there despite

---

John Galliano (right) with two of his bias-cut dresses; (left) gown from his 1994 collection.

difficulties in obtaining financial backing and has also shown in New York. His work, primarily evening clothes, is worldly and assured, in the forefront of fashion.

In July 1995 he was named to succeed HUBERT DE GIVENCHY as designer of both Givenchy couture and ready-to-wear, with his first collections for the house to appear in January and March of 1996. He was to continue to design a signature collection under his own name.

Gaultier, Jean-Paul

Born Paris, France, 1952

At age fourteen Gaultier was presenting minicollections of clothes to his mother and grandmother, and at fifteen had invented a coat with bookbag closures, an idea he was to use in a later collection. When he was seventeen he sent some design sketches to CARDIN, for whom he worked as a design assistant for two years. Other stints followed at Esterel and PATOU, after which he turned to free-lancing in 1976.

Once on his own Gaultier rejected the attitudes of his couture training, reflecting much more the spirit of London street dressing. He has become the bad boy of Parisian fashion, using his considerable dress-making and tailoring skills to produce irreverent send-ups of the fashion establishment. His juxtapositions of fabrics, scale, and shapes are unexpected and often witty, such as gray lace layered over voluminous gray wool knits and overscaled coats over tiny vests cropped above the waist. Madonna has worn his designs and modeled in his showings. His perfume, in a corseted bottle packaged in a beverage can, was introduced in 1994.

Gaultier in 1993 (bottom left) and examples from 1985 (top left) and spring 1995 (right).

George, Jennifer

Born Los Angeles, California, May 29, 1959

One of a number of talented younger designers making names for themselves in the difficult New York fashion arena, Jennifer George has established herself in the field of luxury sportswear. Softly tailored, with an emphasis on knits, her clothes are designed for a young, sophisticated, urban woman with a taste and need for simple, understated basics and the wit to enliven them with whimsical pieces.

Raised in New York and London, George graduated from Sarah Lawrence College with a major in English. While still in high school, she attended a summer program at the Fashion Institute of Technology — a year at Le Stylist, a Paris design school, and another year at Parsons School of Design completed her design training. In 1982 she established Jennifer George Inc., in partnership with David Rubin, whom she met in summer camp when she was fourteen. They started with hand-knit sweaters, went on to add knits, and in 1985, presented a complete sportswear collection, coats as well as day and evening separates. She has also produced maternity clothes under the Mother George label. George is a member of the CFDA and serves as a guest critic at F.I.T.

Gernreich, Rudi

Born Vienna, Austria, August 8, 1922
Died Los Angeles, California, April 21, 1985
Awards Coty American Fashion Critics' Award *Special Award (innovative body clothes),* 1960; *"Winnie,"* 1963; *Return Award,* 1966; *Hall of Fame,* 1967 • Knitted Textile Association Crystal Ball Award, 1975 • Council of Fashion Designers of America (CFDA) *Special Tribute,* 1985

Probably the most original and prophetic American designer of the 1950s and 1960s, Gernreich was the only child of an Austrian hosiery manufacturer who died when his son was eight years old. He was first exposed to fashion in his aunt's couture salon, where he made sketches and learned about fabrics and dressmaking. In 1938 he left Austria with his mother and settled in Los Angeles where he attended Los Angeles City College and Art Center School. In 1942 he joined the Lester Horton Modern Dance Theater as dancer and costume designer. He became a U.S. citizen in 1943.

After five years with Horton, Gernreich decided he was not sufficiently talented as a dancer and left the company. For the next few years he sold fabrics. When he designed a series of dresses to demonstrate his wares the dresses aroused so much interest that in 1951 he formed a partnership with William Bass, a young Los Angeles garment manufacturer, and began developing his personal view of fashion. He established his own firm in 1959, and in addition, designed a collection for Harmon Knitwear, a Wisconsin manufacturer.

Gernreich specialized in dramatic sport clothes of stark cut, enriched by bold graphic patterns and striking color combinations. Always interested in liberating the

body, he introduced a knit maillot without an inner bra in 1954, the era of constructed bathing suits. He favored halter necklines and cut-back shoulders to allow free movement, designed the soft "no-bra" bra in skin-toned nylon net, as well as "Swiss cheese" swimsuits with multiple cutouts, see-through blouses, knee-high hosiery patterned to match tunic tops and tights. His favorite shifts kept getting shorter until they were little more than tunics, which he showed over tights in bright colors or strong patterns.

Gernreich's innovations often caused a commotion, the see-through blouse, for example, and the topless bathing suit he showed in 1964. He was never interested in looking back, disdaining revivals of past eras. In 1968, at the height of his career, he announced he was taking a sabbatical from fashion. He never again worked at it full time, although he did return in 1971 with predictions for a future of bald heads, bare bosoms with pasties, and unisex caftans. He also free-lanced in the fields of furniture, ballet costume, and professional dance and exercise clothes.

Quiet and cultivated in his tastes, Gernreich lived in the Hollywood Hills in a house furnished with modern classics by Charles Eames and Mies van der Rohe.

Rudi Gernreich fitting a design from his 1968 collection on his model, Peggy Moffitt. *Also see Color Plate 1.*

Gigli, Romeo

Born 1950

Gigli's father and grandfather were antiquarian booksellers, and he grew up in an aura of antiquity. This background is in some contrast to the simplicity and modernity of his clothing designs, which nevertheless have something about them romantically rich and strange. Trained as an architect, he began designing in 1979, giving his first show in March 1982.

His approach to clothes is low key and minus frills, and has been compared to that of the Japanese — the pieces mean little on the hanger but take shape on the body. Using rich and luxurious fabrics in sun-dried colors, he achieves a kind of throwaway chic, and except for the romanticism of his designs could be considered one of the minimalists. Although his collections cover day into evening, he specializes in soft sportswear, gentle and unassertive, out of the mainstream of Italian fashion. The total effect is quiet and poetic.

Top right, Romeo Gigli and designs from 1987 (top left) and fall 1993 (bottom left).

Girbaud, Marithé & François

Born Marithé; Lyons, France, 1942
François; Mazamet, France, 1945

Champions of relaxed sportswear, the Girbauds established their business in 1965. The clothes, for both men and women, seem totally unconstructed but are more complex than they appear, and entirely functional. Jackets are often double, with one layer that buttons on for warmth; sweaters may be wool on the outside, cotton inside. This same thinking goes into their clothes for children. In the U.S. they are best known for their jeans and fatigue pants of soft, stonewashed denim.

Givenchy, Hubert de

Born Beauvais, France, February 20, 1927

Givenchy studied at the Ecole des Beaux Arts in Paris, and at age seventeen went to work in the couture at LELONG. He later worked at PIGUET and FATH, and spent four years at SCHIAPARELLI, where he designed for the boutique. In February 1952 he opened his own house near BALENCIAGA, whom he admired greatly and by whom he was much influenced.

His youthful separates brought early recognition, especially the "Bettina" blouse, a peasant shape named for the famous French model who worked with him when he first opened. When Balenciaga closed his house, Givenchy took over many of the workroom people, assuming as well much of the older designer's reputation for super-refined couture with clothes noted for masterly cut, exceptional workmanship, and beautiful fabrics. Those for day remained

Givenchy with his bridal creation in 1994.

within a framework of quiet elegance while the late-day and evening segments of the collection were more exuberantly glamorous to fit the lives of his extensive and conservative clientele.

In 1988 Givenchy sold his business to LVMH Moët Hennessy-Louis Vuitton, with a seven-year contract to remain as designer. He announced his retirement in July 1995, following the presentation of his final haute couture collections; the British designer, JOHN GALLIANO, was named to succeed him.

In addition to couture, the Givenchy interests include the Nouvelle Boutique ready-to-wear distributed worldwide, perfumes, men's toiletries. Fragrances include *Ysatis* and *Amarige* for women, *Xerius* and *Insensé* for men. Licensing commitments extend from sportswear and shirts for men and women to small leathers, hosiery, furs, eyeglasses, and home furnishings.

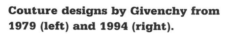

Couture designs by Givenchy from 1979 (left) and 1994 (right).

Grès, Alix

Born Paris, France, November 30, 1903
Died November 24, 1993
Awards Légion d'Honneur, 1947 • Chambre Syndicale de la Couture Parisienne *Golden Thimble Award,* 1976

Considered one of the most talented, imaginative, and independent designers of the couture, Madame Grès is ranked by many with VIONNET, although very different. She was born Germaine Emilie Krebs and first wanted to be a sculptor, but the combination of family disapproval and lack of money turned her to

dressmaking. Under the name Germaine Barton she apprenticed at the House of Premet and in the early 1930s was making and selling muslin *toiles,* copied from the couture. In 1933, with anonymous financial backing, she opened a salon, Alix, where she was not a principal but a salaried employee, obtaining a half

interest in the house in 1938. As Grès refused to take German clients and had a tendency to defy Nazi edicts, the house closed in 1940. A few years later, having lost the right to the name Alix, she reopened briefly as Grès, the first name of her artist husband, Serge Czerefkow, spelled backward, but was forced to close after only six months. After the war she reopened under the same name.

Her background as a sculptor showed in her mastery of draping, especially in the evening dresses of chiffon or the fine, silk jersey (called Alix after her use of it) she had encouraged the mills to make. Working directly with the fabric on a live model, Grès molded it to the figure, often baring some portion of the midriff; a gown could take two to three months to complete. Other recurring themes were jersey day dresses with cowl necklines, deep-cut or dolman sleeves, kimono-shaped coats, asymmetric draping. She travelled widely and brought back ideas that inspired her in her own work. Her influence has been felt by many designers and continues into the present time.

Small, serious, and intensely private, Madame Grès was always shy of publicity and details of her life are scarce. It is known that her husband was a painter and sculptor who left Paris for Tahiti soon after the birth of their one daughter, Anne, in 1939. Professionally, she went her own way; she resisted doing ready-to-wear until 1980, the last of the couture designers to make the move. Perhaps symbolically, her perfume is named *Cabochard*, which means an obstinate or pigheaded person. She was elected chairman of the Chambre Syndicale de la Haute Couture in 1973, and continued as honorary president throughout the 1980s. A retrospective exhibition of her work was mounted by the Metropolitan Museum of Art in 1994. On December 13, 1994 the fashion world was shocked to learn from a story in the French newspaper, *Le Monde*, that Madame Grès was dead, indeed had died more than a year before in a retirement home in the Var region of France. The fact had been kept secret by her daughter, who

Above, Mme Grès adjusting a design from 1979 and right, a Grès design from 1974.

----

as recently as a month prior to the appearance of the article had replied to queries with quotations in her mother's name.

Madame Grès sold her house to a French industrialist in 1984; it was resold in 1986, went bankrupt and closed in 1987. In 1988 the name was sold to a Japanese company and the business continues, primarily in Japan in *prêt-à-porter* and with numerous licenses in France and overseas. In 1994 the creative director and designer was Lloyd David Klein, twenty-six years old.

Guibourgé, Philippe

Born Paris, France, 1931
Died Paris, France, March 7, 1986

Guibourgé studied at the Ecole des Beaux-Arts in Paris, met JACQUES FATH during their Army service and went to work for him after leaving the Army. He stayed three years with Fath, training in all departments, and assisted with couture as well as ready-to-wear. In 1960 Guibourgé went to CHRISTIAN DIOR.

For twelve years at Dior as assistant to MARC BOHAN, he was responsible variously for the English ready-to-wear, fashion accessories for the boutiques, Miss Dior ready-to-wear. He also collaborated on the couture. From 1975 to 1982 he was director of CHANEL ready-to-wear, a post taken over by KARL LAGERFELD in 1983.

Guibourgé worked briefly for LANVIN and after Lagerfeld's departure, for Chloë. At the time of his death, he was planning a line of his own.

H

Halston
Katharine Hamnett
Cathy Hardwick
Holly Harp
Norman Hartnell
Edith Head
Daniel Hechter
Jacques Heim
Sylvia Heisel
Joan Helpern
Gordon Henderson
Stan Herman
Carolina Herrera
Carol Horn

Halston

Born Des Moines, Iowa, April 23, 1932
Died San Francisco, California, March 26, 1990
Awards Coty American Fashion Critics' Award *Special Award (millinery):* 1962, 1969;
"Winnie," 1971; *Return Award,* 1972; *Hall of Fame,* 1974

Halston grew up in Evansville, Indiana, attended Indiana University and the Chicago Art Institute. While still in school he designed and sold hats. He moved to New York in 1957, worked for LILLY DACHÉ, and in 1959 joined Bergdorf Goodman as a milliner. There he gained a name and a fashionable clientele. His fashion influence was immediate: he originated the scarf hat and designed the pillbox hat Jacqueline Kennedy wore for her husband's inaugural. In the late 1960s he started designing ready-to-wear.

In 1968 Halston opened his own firm for private clients and immediately established himself with a pure, ungimmicky, all-American look. His clothes were elegant and well made, with the casual appeal of sportswear. His formula of luxurious fabrics in extremely simple, classic shapes made him one of the top status designers of the 1970s. He has been quoted as saying, "I calmed fashion down!"

Among his successes were the long cashmere dress with a sweater tied over the shoulders, the combination of wrap skirt and turtleneck, evening caftans, and long, slinky, haltered jerseys. He pioneered in the use of Ultrasuede®. Halston worked closely with ELSA PERETTI, first using her as a model then showing her

Halston with models in his show-room, 1982

accessories and jewelry with his clothes. She also designed the containers for his immensely successful signature fragrance.

Halston expanded into knitwear and accessories in 1970, then into ready-to-wear. In 1973 he sold the business to a conglomerate. In 1983 when he signed with J.C. Penney for a cheaper line, a number of his accounts decided to drop his regular line. He attempted to regain ownership of his custom business and designer ready-to-wear in late 1984 but was unable to do so and went out of business.

Halston design from fall 1982.

Hamnett, Katharine

Born Gravesend, Kent, England, 1948

Both a feminist and a supporter of the peace movement, Hamnett often carries her political concerns into her work. Her oversize T-shirts printed with such statements as "Worldwide Nuclear Ban Now" and "Stop Acid Rain," were inspired by the women's anti-nuclear protests in England.

She was born into a diplomatic family, educated at Cheltenham Ladies College, studied art in Stockholm before enrolling at St. Martin's School of Art in London to study fashion. While still in school she worked as a free-lance designer and after graduation in 1970 opened a sportswear firm, Tuttabanken, with a school friend. After its demise, she designed for a number of firms in England, France, Italy, and Hong Kong before establishing Katharine Hamnett Ltd. in 1979.

Her clothes are relaxed and easy-going, often based on work clothes.

Katharine Hamnett (above) and an outfit from her 1994 collection (right).

Men's wear with the same feeling as her women's clothes appeared in 1982. Hamnett has shown in Paris and Milan and has been widely copied, especially in Italy.

Hardwick, Cathy

Born Seoul, Korea, December 30, 1933

Hardwick is known for clean-cut, fluid, sensuous clothes — advanced fashion at a price. She wants her clothes to be comfortable and useful as well as fashionable.

After music studies in Korea and Japan, Hardwick came to the U.S. and at the age of twenty-one opened a boutique in San Francisco.

Although she had no design training, she designed much of the merchandise for the shop and began to freelance. She moved to New York in the late 1960s.

In New York she did work for a number of ready-to-wear manufacturers and for Warner's Lingerie, opened her own design studio in 1972. She later established Cathy Hardwick & Friends, a manufacturing firm. She has designed home furnishings collections as well as ready-to-wear, and since 1980 has licensed her designs to various manufacturers. She has also sold them in England and Japan.

Harp, Holly

Born Buffalo, New York, October 24, 1939
Died Los Angeles, California, April 24, 1995

The daughter of a machinery designer, Harp dropped out of Radcliffe in her sophomore year and went to Acapulco, where she designed sandals and clothes to go with them. She returned to school at North Texas State University to study art and fashion design, married Jim Harp, an English instructor, later moved to Los Angeles. In 1968, with a loan from her father, she opened a boutique on Sunset Strip, which she called Holly's Harp. Henri Bendel gave her a boutique in 1972; she

started her wholesale line in 1973, and her clothes were soon sold in fine specialty stores around the U.S. Other design commitments have included Simplicity Patterns and Fieldcrest bed linens.

Holly Harp's early designs were off-beat evening clothes, popular with entertainment figures and rock stars. She soon switched from feathers and fringe to subtler, sophisticated cuts, often on the bias, usually two-piece and in one size. Essentially very simple and wearable, the clothes

were elegantly conceived in matte jersey or chiffon, frequently decorated with hand-painted or airbrushed designs. They were also imaginative, unconventional, and expensive, making her customer a free-thinking woman with money. Harp's design philosophy leaned to risk-taking: "Whenever I'm trying to make an aesthetic decision, I always go in the direction of taking chances."

Hartnell, Norman

Born London, England, June 12, 1901
Died Windsor, England, June 8, 1979
Awards Neiman Marcus Award, 1947

Educated at Cambridge University, where he designed costumes and performed in undergraduate plays, Hartnell was expected to become an architect but instead turned to dress design. After working briefly for a court designer and selling sketches to LUCILE, he opened a business with his sister in 1923. At the time a French name or reputation was indispensable to success in London so in 1927 he took his collection to Paris. In 1930 he again showed in Paris, resulting in many orders, particularly from American and Canadian buyers. The Hartnell couture house became the largest in London. He was dressmaker by appointment to H.M. the Queen, whose coronation gown he designed, and to H.M. the Queen Mother. He was knighted in 1977.

Hartnell is most identified with elaborate evening gowns, lavishly embroidered and sprinkled with sequins, particularly the bouffant gowns designed for the Queen Mother and for Queen Elizabeth II. He also made well-tailored suits and coats in British and French woolens and tweeds. By the 1970s he was making clothes in leather, designing furs and men's fashions. In September 1990, the house was revived with MARC BOHAN as fashion director. The first collections were couture; ready-to-wear followed in fall 1991. The firm has since gone out of business.

Norman Hartnell flanked by his models wearing creations from his 1954 collection.

Head, Edith

Born San Bernardino, California, 1907
Died Los Angeles, California, 1981
Awards Motion Picture Academy Awards: *The Heiress*, 1949 (black and white); *Samson and Delilah*, 1950 (color); *All About Eve*, 1950 (black and white); *A Place in the Sun*, 1951 (black and white); *Roman Holiday*, 1953 (black and white); *Sabrina*, 1954 (black and white); *The Facts of Life*, 1969 (black and white); *The Sting*, 1973 (color)

Edith Head had a long and illustrious career of over fifty years, starting at Paramount Pictures where she was chief designer for twenty-nine years. Hired as a junior designer by Howard Greer sometime in the 1920s, she became the studio's number one designer in 1938 when the then department head, TRAVIS BANTON, left Paramount for Universal Studios.

The dates are somewhat ambiguous but she graduated from the University of California at Berkeley where she majored in languages, and went on to Stanford for a master's degree in French. She taught French at private schools for girls, studied art at night at Otis and Chouinard, married and divorced, before answering a want ad for an artist, which led to her first job at Paramount. When Greer left Paramount to open his own salon, he was succeeded by Banton, who made Head his assistant.

As Banton's assistant and later as head designer, she designed for stars as diverse as Mae West, Dorothy Lamour (the sarong!), Barbara Stanwyck, and Audrey Hepburn, and for every type of film from Westerns to drawing room comedies, from musical comedies to monster movies. Given the variety of movies and the sheer quantity of her production, it is not surprising that she did not establish an "Edith Head look." When Paramount was acquired by Gulf+Western in 1966, Head was out of a job but soon moved to Universal to become resident costume designer. Over the years, she won eight Oscars for her work, starting in 1949 with *The Heiress*, and received thirty-three

Edith Head design for Grace Kelly in TO CATCH A THIEF, 1955 (right); and for Robert Redford and Paul Newman in THE STING, 1973 (left).

nominations. She also free-lanced at MGM, Warner's, Columbia, and Fox.

In addition to her film work, she did opera costumes, women's uniforms for the Coast Guard and Pan American Airlines, and designed printed fabrics. She also taught a course at UCLA, wrote articles and books, appeared on television and radio talk shows, and lectured to clubs around the country. Unlike many of her colleagues, she did not do custom work and was not interested in dressing women for the world outside of movies.

Hechter, Daniel

Born Paris, France, 1938

Hechter started his career designing for Pierre D'Alby. In business for himself since 1962, his first designs were for women, followed in 1965 by children's wear, with men's sportswear appearing in 1970.

The clothes embody sportswear ease, function, and dash. Wearable and affordable, they are comfortable fashion for young, active people who are both career oriented and imaginative. Hechter strives for a sense of reality and a continuity of line and color from season to season so that one collection adds to and is compatible with the one before. He has also designed active sportswear including tennis and ski clothes. He distributes and licenses around the world.

Heim, Jacques

Born Paris, France, 1899
Died Paris, France, 1967

Although not now a household name, Jacques Heim was in his time an important and influential designer. He introduced cotton beachwear to the haute couture in 1937, was the first to recognize the younger customer with his Heim-Jeunes Filles collection. He helped popularize the bikini, and beginning in 1946, opened his own chain of boutiques. He was President of the Chambre Syndicale de la Couture from 1958 to 1962.

Heim's parents were fashionable furriers and it was in their firm that he started his design career when he was twenty-six. Sometime in the 1930s he opened his own salon in the avenue Matignon with his wife as *directrice*. His clothes were elegant and refined, very much in the haute couture tradition. After his death, direction of the firm was taken over by his son, Philippe.

Heisel, Sylvia

Born June 22, 1962

Heisel specializes in designer dresses and dressy sportswear. She has attracted attention with her soft, feminine dresses and bias cuts — her aim is an elegant minimalism, dressy clothes with sportswear fit and attitude for the sophisticated woman. She has also designed men's wear and film costumes.

After graduation from high school in Wallingford, Connecticut, Heisel went to Barnard College in New York City for one and a half years, leaving in December 1981. During 1981 and 1982 she designed and sold costume jewelry, and used the money to start making clothes. Her first break came in 1982 when a Bendel's buyer admired the coat she was wearing and offered to buy it if she would make more. The coats sold and in 1983 she established her own company, Postmodern Productions, Inc., with herself as designer and president, using the Sylvia Heisel label. She recognizes that it takes more than ideas to succeed: "Fashion is not art, it's a business...You have to learn business to get anywhere."

Helpern, Joan

Born New York City

Awards Coty American Fashion Critics' Award *Special Award (footwear)*, 1978 • Cutty Sark Men's Fashion Award *Men's Footwear Design*, 1986 • Fairchild Publications and *Footwear News Footwear Designer Award*, 1988; *Hall of Fame*, 1990 • Golden Slipper, Florence, 1988 • Scarpe d'Oro, "The Golden Shoe Award" in Italy, 1989 • American Footwear Industry, "Ffany Award," 1990 • Silver Trophy, Florence, 1992 • Italian Trade Commission *Michelangelo Award for design (first designer award to an American for footwear)*, 1993

Joan and David, the family firm established in 1967 by David and Joan Helpern, is primarily known for imaginative, fashionable shoes for women and men. The firm is involved in every aspect of the shoemaking process — designing, manufacturing in Italy, distribution, and retailing. Starting in 1986, other fashion categories have been added: bags, belts, socks, scarves, sportswear, knitwear, jewelry, sunglasses, shawls, umbrellas, hats.

Joan Helpern, the design half of the team, believes that the design of a product should be relevant to its use. In approaching her work she matches a fresh, inventive approach to the desires and needs of her customer, whom she sees as highly intelligent and motivated, with a clear sense of self and personal style.

Ms. Helpern has been widely recognized for her accomplishments,

Joan and David Helpern, 1994.

both in her own field with citations from industry publications, and by such magazines as *Savvy* and *Working Woman* for her business success. She is a member of the Council of Fashion Designers of America and of the Committee of 200, an international organization of leading businesswomen.

An assortment of boots by Joan and David, 1995.

Henderson, Gordon

Born Berkeley, California, March 19, 1957
Awards Council of Fashion Designers of America (CFDA) *Perry Ellis Award for New Fashion Talent,* 1989

Henderson grew up in California and studied pre-med at the University of California, Davis. He came East in 1981 to attend Parsons School of Design, graduating in 1983. He worked first as chief designer for a sportswear firm that folded, was assistant designer at Calvin Klein in 1984, formed his own company in 1985. Since 1988 he has had a number of financial arrangements and has been in and out of business. He has also worked as a consultant.

Henderson's strength has always been in his mix of comfort and style at accessible prices, innovative and youthful sportswear in elegant fabrics, a designer look that's also affordable.

He is a designing critic at Parsons School of Design.

Herman, Stan

Born New York, New York, September 17, 1930
Awards Coty American Fashion Critics Award *Special Award (young contemporaries design)*, 1965; *"Winnie,"* 1969; *Special Award (loungewear)*, 1975 • Store Awards: *Burdine's*, 1965; *Hess*, 1967; *Joseph Horne*, 1968

Hard working and versatile, Herman has turned his designing hand variously to hats, dresses, sportswear, lingerie and loungewear, and uniforms. He has also done a stint as a nightclub entertainer. After earning a B.A. from the University of Cincinnati, he worked in the New York garment industry while attending Traphagen School of Fashion. By 1954 he was designing hats at John-Frederics. He went on to work at a number of firms before arriving at Mr. Mort in 1961, leaving in 1971. He has continued to design for many other companies, often concurrently, including Henri Bendel, Youthcraft-Charmfit, Slumbertogs, and multiple uniform houses, always in the affordable range.

Herman believes that fashion is one of life's nourishments, which, like all good food, must be grown each season to remain fresh. That is why he prefers to free-lance. He recharges his creative energies through painting, singing, sailing, tennis, opera, and community activism. A member of the Council of Fashion Designers of America since 1967, he served as Vice President from 1982, and since 1991 as President.

Herrera, Carolina

Born Caracas, Venezuela, January 8, 1939
Awards Dallas Fashion Award *Fashion Excellence Award*

Herrera came to fashion from a background where couture clothes and private dressmakers were the norm — she grew up and was educated in Caracas among women who appreciated and wore beautiful clothes. In 1980 she moved to New York with her husband and family, and encouraged by DIANA VREELAND among others, established her own firm in April 1981 with the backing of a South American publisher. Going into the dress business seemed a natural step as she had worked closely with her Caracas couturiers, often designing her clothes herself. She quickly made a name and developed a following.

Best known for her designer ready-to-wear — elegant clothes with a couture feeling and feminine details — she also makes clothes to order for private clients, many of whom are her friends. Estée Lauder, the late Jacqueline Onassis, and Nancy Reagan have all worn her designs and she made Caroline Kennedy's wedding dress. She has had licensing agreements in Japan and designed furs for Revillon; a lower-priced line of ready-to-wear called CH was introduced in 1986.

Herrera recognizes BALENCIAGA as her greatest influence. His example can be seen in her emphasis on a clear, dramatic line and her insistence that women can be feminine, chic, elegant, and at the same time comfortable.

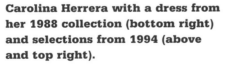

Carolina Herrera with a dress from her 1988 collection (bottom right) and selections from 1994 (above and top right).

Horn, Carol

Born New York, June 12, 1936
Awards Coty American Fashion Critics' Award *"Winnie,"* 1975

Horn studied fine arts at Boston and Columbia Universities, began her career working as a fashion coordinator in retailing. She designed junior sportswear for Bryant 9, was sole designer for Benson & Partners for four years, then designer-director of the Carol Horn division of Malcolm Starr International. In 1983, after a number of years with licensees, she opened her own company, Carol Horn Sportswear, to which Carol Horn Knitwear has been added.

Her trademarks are easy, uncontrived shapes in muted tones, preferably in natural fibers. The clothes are contemporary in feeling, comfortable and seasonless, at a moderate price.

I-J

Irene

Born Irene Lentz; Brookings, South Dakota, 1901
Died Los Angeles, California, 1962

Irene designed in two worlds, one the world of film and the other of real women. She started by dressing many of Hollywood's brightest stars for their private lives and was more and more often commissioned to design their on-screen wardrobes. Her first screen credit was at RKO in 1932 and was shared with Harold Greer; in 1942 she became executive designer at MGM when Adrian left. Her MGM years were not happy — she had to deal with other executives, producers, directors, cameramen, and publicity people, and was more involved with administrative duties than with design — but she stayed out her seven-year contract. After she left, while she continued to design personal wardrobes for a number of stars, she rarely designed again for the screen.

Accomplished in custom and ready-to-wear as well as film, Irene came to design after a brief fling at acting. She studied music at the University of California at Los Angeles, then draping, drawing, and fashion design at the Wolfe School of Design. Around 1928, newly married and at the urging of her husband and friends, she opened a small dress shop on the UCLA campus. This quickly became a success, attracting affluent students and eventually, movie stars Lupe Velez and Dolores Del Rio. She closed her shop when her husband died suddenly and spent some time touring England and the Continent, living for several months in Paris. This period, which exposed her to the Paris couture, had a lasting influence on her work.

On her return from Europe, Irene reopened her salon, soon moved to larger quarters, and in 1935 was persuaded to become designer and head of the Custom Salon at Bullock's Wilshire. Her clothes were not only beautiful but very expensive, even more so than comparable Paris creations, marking their wearers as women of means as well as taste. Shortly before her contract with MGM expired, Irene was granted permission to design for a wholesale concern, a venture financed by twenty-five leading department stores who held exclusive rights to the designs. The project was a success from coast to coast.

Irene's personal life was often unhappy: her first husband died only two years after they were married, her second marriage was stormy, and she suffered from a perceived lack of success in films as compared to her commercial work. Overwhelmed by personal problems, she committed suicide in 1962.

Jackson, Betty

Born Bacup, Lancashire, England, 1949

After a three-year fashion course at Birmingham College of Art, Jackson worked in London as a free-lance illustrator for two years, in 1973 joined WENDY DAGWORTHY as an assistant designer. She moved to another firm in 1975, stayed four years then spent two years at still another. In 1981 she opened under her own name.

Jackson is well known for her imaginative use of prints. Her clothes are young, classic in feeling but updated with a fresh sense of scale. They have sold well in America and Italy. Her first men's wear appeared for fall 1986.

Jacobs, Marc

Born New York City, 1964

Awards Council of Fashion Designers of America (CFDA) *Perry Ellis Award for New Fashion Talent*, 1987

While still a student at Parsons School of Design, Jacobs was designing sweaters and also working as a stock boy at one of New York's Charivari stores. He was hailed as a "hot talent" on his graduation, and went to work for Ruben Thomas, Inc. under the Sketchbook label, where he was building a reputation as an original designer of young fashion with a flair for lighthearted, individualistic clothes when his firm went out of business in October 1985.

He reopened for fall 1986 with a new backer; in 1988 moved to Perry Ellis International as designer of their women's collection. While often well received by retailers and press, the collection was never profitable and was dropped in February 1993, leaving Jacobs without a backer. Since then he has been a design consultant for an Italian sportswear firm and a Japanese retailer, and in the spring of 1994, showed a fall collection under his own name, backed in part by the Perry Ellis organization. Small in scope, it was characteristically spirited and was well received.

Left, from the 1987 Marc Jacobs collection; (below) Jacobs at his 1992 showing for Perry Ellis.

James, Charles

Born Sandhurst, England, July 18, 1906
Died New York City, September 23, 1978
Awards Coty American Fashion Critics' Award *"Winnie,"* 1950; *Special Award (innovative cut),* 1954 • Neiman Marcus Award, 1953

Stormy and unpredictable, fiercely independent, James is considered by many students of fashion to be a genius, one of the greatest designers, ranking with BALENCIAGA. His father was a colonel in the British Army, his mother an American from a prominent Chicago family; Charles was educated in England and America.

Sketches by James for WOMEN'S WEAR DAILY from 1960. *Also see Color Plate 13.*

After a brief stay at the University of Bordeaux, he moved to Chicago where he began making hats. He moved to New York in 1928, went on to London where he produced a small dress collection, which he brought back to New York. He then traveled back and forth between the two cities before moving to Paris around 1934 to open his own couture business.

In Paris, James formed close friendships with many legendary couture figures, including CHRISTIAN DIOR, whose obituary he wrote for *The New York Post*, and PAUL POIRET. His exceptional ability was recognized and acknowledged by his design peers. While he admired SCHIAPARELLI in her unadorned period, MADAME GRÈS was his favorite designer because she thought as he did in terms of shape and sculptural movement.

He returned to New York around 1939 and established his custom house, Charles James, Inc. He

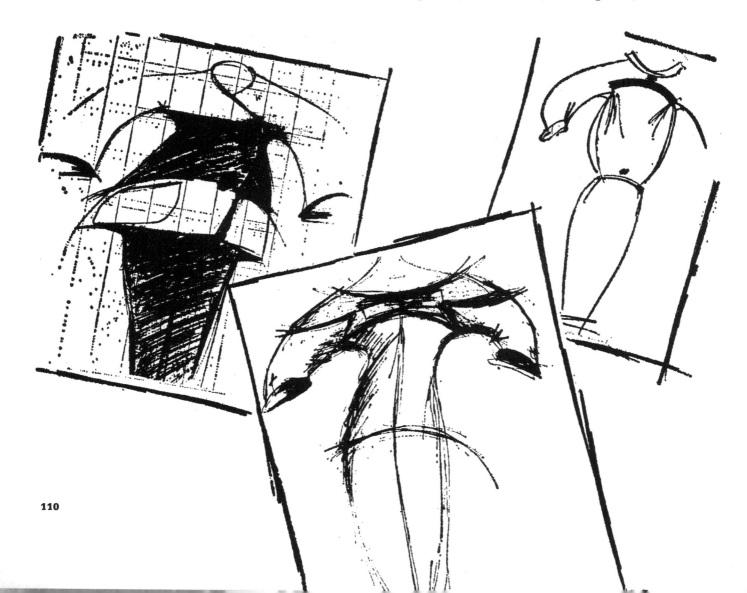

worked exclusively for Elizabeth Arden until 1945, continued to operate in New York and sometimes London until 1958, when he retired from couture to devote himself to painting and sculpture.

During the 1960s James conducted seminars and lectured at the Rhode Island School of Design and Pratt Institute. He designed a mass-produced line for E.J. Korvette in 1962, invented new techniques for dress patterns, created a dress form, jewelry designs, and even furniture, occupied himself with preparing his archives. For five years, usually at night, he worked with the illustrator ANTONIO, who made drawings of all his work to be kept as a permanent record.

James was a daring innovator, a sculptor with cloth. Each design began with a certain "shape," and hours were spent on the exact placement of a seam. Bold and imaginative, his designs depend on intricate cut and precise seaming rather than on trim. He was noted for his handling of heavy silks and fine cloths, for his batwing, oval cape coat, for bouffant ball gowns, for dolman wraps and asymmetrical shapes. In 1937, when his short, white satin evening coat filled with eiderdown appeared on the cover of *Harper's Bazaar*, Salvador Dali called it "the first soft sculpture."

Since he considered his designs works of art, it is only appropriate that they are in the costume collections of many museums, including the Metropolitan Museum of Art, the Brooklyn Museum, and the Smithsonian Institution, and also at the Fashion Institute of Technology. His ideas are still influential today.

Javits, Eric

Born New York City, May 24, 1956

Eric Javits came to millinery design through a succession of private schools and the Rhode Island School of Design, where he studied painting, sculpture, drawing, and photography, graduating in 1978 with a degree in fine arts. With Eliot Whittall he founded Whittall and Javits, Inc., producing hats in the bridge and better price ranges, and also sports separates and T-shirts for juniors and the contemporary market. He was bought out in 1985, then founded Eric Javits, Inc., specializing in women's hats, and from time to time, hair accessories.

Design by Javits, 1994.

His hats are romantic and flattering and have been worn in films, used in advertising promotions, shown in designers' runway presentations and on the covers of fashion magazines. He also has a large and diverse international clientele. Javits promotes his business with television guest appearances and is active in professional organizations, a member of the Council of Fashion Designers of America (CFDA) and the Millinery Institute of America. Outside of business, he pursues his interest in painting and is involved in community service and charitable activities.

Mr. John

Born Germany, March 13 or 14, ca. 1902
Died New York City, June 25, 1993
Awards Coty Fashion Critics Award *Special Award (millinery)*, 1943

Gloria Swanson, the Duchess of Windsor, Rosalind Russell — those are just a few of the fashionable women who wore Mr. John's hats in the 1940s and 1950s — and Greta Garbo, Marlene Dietrich, Marilyn Monroe were just a few of the stars who wore them on screen. An original and prolific designer, he made every style from close-fitting cloches to picture hats, relying on shape when other milliners were loading

hats with flowers and plumes. Wearable and flattering, his creations included such touches of wit as a face-hugging veil studded with a single rhinestone as beauty mark.

Born somewhere in Germany to Rose and Henry Harberger, Mr. John came to the U.S. with his parents. He worked briefly in his mother's Manhattan millinery shop then in 1928 formed a partnership with Frederic Hirst to make hats as John-

Frederics. He changed his name legally to John Frederics but in 1948, after breaking up with Hirst, opened the Mr. John salon on East 57th Street and again changed his name, this time to John P. John. He designed accessories, women's clothing, and furs but hats were his primary claim to fame. The business closed in 1970 although he continued to design for private clients until a year or so before his death.

Johnson, Betsey

Born Wethersfield, Connecticut, 1942
Awards Coty American Fashion Critics' Award *"Winnie,"* 1971

Johnson attended Pratt Institute for one year, then went to Syracuse University, graduating cum laude and a member of Phi Beta Kappa. In her senior year she was guest editor at *Mademoiselle* magazine where sweaters she made for editors earned her a job designing at the Paraphernalia boutiques. These collections, original and irreverent, established her at age twenty-two as a leader of the youth-oriented, anti-Seventh Avenue design movement of the 1960s.

In 1969, Johnson and two friends started the boutique Betsey, Bunky and Nini, which has several New York locations. She has designed for Alley Cat, Michael Milea, Butterick Patterns. In July 1978, she formed Betsey Johnson, Inc. to manufacture sportswear, bodywear, and dresses. She also operates a number of Betsey Johnson retail stores.

Johnson specializes in

Betsey Johnson in 1993.

body-conscious clothes, including everything from bathing suits to bodysuits, tight pants to dance dresses. Over the years, typical ideas have included: the Basic Betsey, a clinging T-shirt dress in mini, midi, or maxi lengths; a clear vinyl slip-dress complete with a kit of paste-on stars, fishes, and numbers; the Noise Dress with loose grommets at the hem. She has worked in a variety of fabrics, from cotton-and-spandex knits to rayon challis to heavyweight spandex in vibrant colors, designing her own fabrics and knits. Johnson is unique. Imaginative and uninhibited, she designs for spirited nonconformists like herself.

Above, Johnson's dress from 1993; (right) vinyl kit-dress from 1966.

Jones, Stephen

Born West Kirby, England, May 31, 1957

A Jones version of the newsboy cap, 1985.

In 1984 Stephen Jones became the first British milliner to work in Paris, designing hats for the collections of JEAN-PAUL GAULTIER, THIERRY MUGLER, and REI KAWAKUBO of Comme des Garçons. He has worked with ZANDRA RHODES, JOHN GALLIANO, and VIVIENNE WESTWOOD, among other English designers. Combining fantasy with confident style, his hats have been described as witty, outrageous, and daring; he continues to collaborate with designers around the world.

Educated at Liverpool College, Jones went on to study at St. Martin's School of Art, graduating in 1979. He immediately began to make hats for his friends in the pop world including Steve Strange, Boy George, and Duran Duran. In September 1980 he opened his first salon in a store called "PX" in Covent Garden, and soon established a burgeoning custom clientele. He was invited to represent Great Britain in fashion shows in New York, Montreal, Helsinki, and Tokyo, and his hats are in the permanent collections of the Victoria and Albert Museum in London, the Brooklyn Museum, and the Australian National Gallery in Canberra.

In addition to his signature line, he has added two diffusion lines and another under license in Japan. Other design projects have included scarves, handkerchiefs, gloves, kimonos, shoes, men's hats, cosmetics for Shiseido Cosmetics, interior design, and TV commercials.

Joop, Wolfgang

Born Potsdam, Germany

Joop studied both advertising and art, dual interests that have contributed to his success in fashion. He showed his first ready-to-wear collection in 1981, his first men's wear in 1985, and in 1994 brought his men's wear to the U.S. Well established in Europe with a flourishing jeans and men's underwear business, he entered the American market wholeheartedly, preceding his arrival with a sizable advertising campaign and the introduction of his *Joop! Femme* and *Joop! Homme* fragrances.

He considers that he and JIL SANDER are currently the only true designers in Germany, both known especially for technical knowledge, fabric research, and manufacturing, but now coming into their own for their design qualities. He uses the label Joop!, which he says stands for "quality and taste, but the ability to be a little bit tacky."

Joop (above) and a coat from 1994.

Jovine, Andrea

Born Closter, New Jersey, August 8, 1955

Following high school, Jovine studied in Switzerland for a year then attended the Fashion Institute of Technology in New York City, where she won an ILGWU "Next Great Designer" award. After graduation in 1977, she worked for Bill Kaiserman at Rafael for three years, then free-lanced for a year before going into business for herself. She designed belts and handbags for Omega, and in 1983, with Victor Coopersmith, formed Andrea Jovine, Inc. for better sportswear, with a first collection of knits.

Jovine's aim is to make modern, uncomplicated, sophisticated clothing for the busy woman who needs "clothes that are interesting and versatile without being overdesigned and impractical." She picks up the nuances of the latest happenings and translates them into her own idiom, feeling that clothing should be easy to wear, easy to care for, and affordable. Essentially contemporary sportswear, her clothes offer designer looks at reasonable prices. She has shown particular interest in special sizes, introducing a petite collection in 1992 and women's sizes in 1993. She sells internationally in Europe, Canada, and China.

Julian, Alexander

Born Chapel Hill, North Carolina, 1948
Awards Coty American Fashion Critics' Award *Men's Wear Award*, 1977; *Men's Wear Return Award*, 1979; *Men's Apparel*, 1981; *Special Award Citation*, 1983; *Special Award (men's wear)*, 1984 • Cutty Sark Men's Fashion Award *Outstanding Designer:* 1980, 1985 • Men's Woolknit Design Award, 1981 • Council of Fashion Designers of America (CFDA) *Designer of the Year*, 1981

Primarily known for men's wear, Julian has also designed for women and boys. Growing up in Chapel Hill where his father was a retailer, he designed his first shirt when he was twelve. At the age of eighteen he was managing his father's store and at twenty-one had his own shop. In 1975 he moved to New York.

A frustrated artist, Julian is an inspired colorist. He has studied weaving, and designs his own unusual and intricate fabrics, produced in Scotland and Italy. These can contain as many as sixteen colors, and he even designs the yarns that go into them if he finds it necessary. Because the fabrics are expensive, he uses them in traditional themes that do not go out of date quickly, leavening tradition with a lively dose of imagination and wit.

Julian licenses to manufacturers here and abroad, producing clothes and hosiery for men, home furnishings and decorative fabrics, small leather goods, and pocket accessories. Around 1990, Julian and his financial partner purchased his firm, Colours by Alexander Julian, from Cluett Peabody and formed Collection Clothing Corp. as the principal manufacturing arm.

K

Robin Kahn
Gemma Kahng
Norma Kamali
Donna Karan
Herbert Kasper
Rei Kawakubo
Patrick Kelly
Randy Kemper
Kenzo
Emmanuelle Khanh
Barry Kieselstein-Cord
Todd Killian
Anne Klein
Calvin Klein
Roland Klein
Kōkin
Koos van den Akker
Michael Kors

Kahn, Robin

Born: London, England, January 12, 1947

Awards Coty American Fashion Critics' Award *Menswear Special Award (belt and buckle designs),* 1984

Kahn arrived in the U.S. at the age of five. In New York, he graduated from the High School of Art and Design and Parsons School of Design, then studied at the Haystack Mountain School of Crafts, and trained with goldsmiths. He has designed accessories for KENNETH J. LANE, OSCAR DE LA RENTA, and PIERRE CARDIN, as well as one-of-a-kind pieces for Bloomingdale's. Robin Kahn, Inc. was established in April 1978.

Kahn describes himself as a "constructionist," forming his designs directly from the metal. He is known especially for working in three non-precious metals: brass, copper, and bronze. He has also employed ivory, ebony, turquoise, lapis, and such diverse materials as leather cording and taffeta. His jewelry, which has been described as futuristic Art Deco, is strong, bold, clean, elegant, and essentially classic in feeling.

Kahng, Gemma

Born Masan, South Korea, ca. 1955

One of a number of designers with a fresh point of view to emerge in the late 1980s, Gemma Kahng made her first impression with well-tailored suits and sexy little dresses in distinctive color combinations. Suit jackets were closely fitted and fastened with oversized, ornamental buttons. A graduate of the school of the Art Institute of Chicago, Kahng established her own business in New York in 1989. Specializing in designer ready-to-wear, she expresses her quirky point of view in ornaments and details. While her strength lies in simple shapes and excellent tailoring, she cannot resist embellishing them with pockets, buttons, lace. She has also expanded into accessories — handbags, belts, costume jewelry.

Gemma Kahng (above) and a design from her fall 1994 collection.

Kamali, Norma

Born New York City, June 27, 1945

Awards Coty American Fashion Critics' Award *"Winnie,"* 1981; *Return Award,* 1982; *Hall of Fame,* 1983 • Council of Fashion Designers of America (CFDA) *Outstanding Women's Fashions,* 1982; *Innovative Use of Video in Presentation and Promotion of Fashion,* 1985 • Fashion Institute of Design & Merchandising (Los Angeles) FIDM Award, 1984 • The Fashion Group "Night of the Stars" Award, 1986

Of Basque and Lebanese descent, Kamali grew up on New York's Upper East Side where her father owned a candy store. Her mother made most of her daughter's clothes, as well as costumes for neighborhood plays, dollhouse furniture, paper flowers, "anything and everything." Kamali studied fashion illustration at the Fashion Institute of Technology, graduating in 1964. Unable to find work in her field, she took an office job with an airline, using the travel opportunities to spend weekends in London.

In 1968 she married Eddie Kamali, an Iranian student, and in 1969 they opened a tiny basement shop in which they sold European imports, largely from England, and also Norma's own designs in the same funky spirit. They moved to a larger, second floor space on Madison Avenue in 1974 and Kamali moved away from funk, doing suits, lace dresses, delicate things. Divorced in 1977, she established a retail boutique and wholesale firm, OMO (which stands for On My Own) Norma Kamali, in 1978. In 1983 she bought a 99-year lease and moved her thriving business across the street into a multilevel, multiangled environment finished in concrete. Here, with video monitors showing film productions of her collection, she can display everything she designs, from accessories to couture.

Kamali coat from 1987 (above), and (right) jumpsuit made from silk parachute fabric, 1978.

Kamali was first recognized for adventurous, body-conscious clothes with giant, removable shoulder pads. Definitely not for the timid, her

IK

clothes were collected by such members of the fashion avant-garde as Donna Summer, Diana Ross, Barbra Streisand. A wider following developed for her swimsuits, cut daringly hip-high. She has designed a highly successful, moderately priced collection for the Jones Apparel Group using down-to-earth fabrics, notably cotton sweatshirting, and has also done children's clothes and lingerie. In 1978, her draped and shirred jumpsuits, using parachute fabric and drawstrings, were included in the "Vanity Fair" show at the Costume Institute of the Metropolitan Museum of Art.

Above, Norma Kamali in 1987 and (right) a design from 1993.

Karan, Donna

Born Forest Hills, New York, October 4, 1948
Awards Coty American Fashion Critics' Award *"Winnie"* (with Louis Dell'Olio), 1977; *Hall of Fame (with Louis Dell'Olio), 1982; Special Award (women's wear) (with Louis Dell'Olio), 1984* • Council of Fashion Designers of America (CFDA) *Special Award, 1985; Special Award, 1986; Womenswear Designer of the Year, 1990; Menswear Designer of the Year, 1992* • The Fashion Group "Night of the Stars" Award, 1986

Daughter of a fashion model and a haberdasher, Karan was steeped in fashion from childhood. After her second year at Parsons School of Design, she took a summer job with ANNE KLEIN and never returned to school. She was fired by Klein after nine months and went to work for another sportswear house, returning to Klein in 1968, becoming associate designer in 1971. When Anne Klein became ill in 1973, Karan became head designer and asked LOUIS

DELL'OLIO, a school friend, to join her as co-designer. While it is impossible to separate her designs at Anne Klein from Dell'Olio's, their hallmark was always wearability—terrific blazers, well-cut pants, strong coats, sarong skirts, easy dresses—classic sportswear looks with a stylish edge and an element of tough chic.

In 1984 Karan and her husband, Stephan Weiss, founded Donna Karan New York with the backing of Takihyo Corporation of Japan, Anne

Klein's parent company. Karan's first collection under her own label established her immediately as a new fashion star. It was based on a bodysuit over which went long or short skirts, blouses, or pants, to make a complete, integrated wardrobe. These pieces were combined with well-tailored coats and bold accessories, everything made of luxurious materials. As the clothes followed the body closely without excess detail or overt sexiness, the effect was both spare and sensuous. Her idea was to design only clothes and accessories she would wear herself — the best of everything for a woman who could be a mother, a traveller, perhaps a business owner, someone who doesn't have time to shop. The clothes are definitely in the status category.

Her initial company has grown into a giant of a thousand employees and myriad divisions: DKNY (Donna Karan New York) (1988), jeans and men's wear (1991), DKNY Men, and in 1992, Donna Karan fragrance and beauty. A collection of luxury lingerie, sleepwear, and loungewear is called Intimates; there is a full range of accessories — handbags, jewelry, scarves, rain hats and umbrellas, belts, hosiery, shoes, sunglasses. There was also, briefly, DKNY kids.

In May 1987 a bit of unfinished business was taken care of when Karan was awarded a Bachelor of Fine Arts degree by Parsons. She is on the board of directors of CFDA, as well as Design Industries Foundation For AIDS (DIFFA).

Donna Karan (below left) at the finale of her 1993 show; designs from 1993 (above left), 1994 (above right), and 1987 (below right).

K

Kasper, Herbert

Born New York City, December 12, 1926
Awards Coty American Fashion Critics' Award *"Winnie,"* 1955; *Return Award,* 1970; *Hall of Fame,* 1976

Kasper was majoring in English at New York University when World War II intervened. While serving in the Army, he designed costumes for Army shows; after the war he attended Parsons School of Design. He spent two years in Paris, where he worked for FATH and ROCHAS, and at *Elle* magazine. On his return to the U.S. he designed hats for John-Frederics and costumes for Broadway revues. From 1953, Kasper worked for several Seventh Avenue firms, joining Leslie Fay in 1963. Kasper for Joan Leslie Inc., a division of Leslie Fay, was established in 1967, then Kasper for JL Sport Ltd., and Kasper for Weatherscope. He resigned as vice president and designer in March 1985 to open his own company.

Noted for his well-tailored, sophisticated sportswear and dresses, Kasper has always designed for a specific American woman who does not like extremes but for whom dressing with style is an important part of life. Other design projects have included furs, handbags, bed linens.

Kawakubo, Rei

Born Tokyo, Japan, 1942
Awards Mainichi Newspaper Fashion Award, 1983 • The Fashion Group "Night of the Stars" Award, 1986

The most avant of the Tokyo avant-garde, Kawakubo was a literature major at Keio University in Tokyo, graduating in 1965. She came to fashion design after two years in the advertising department of a textile firm and three years as a free-lance stylist. She founded Comme des Garçons for women's clothes in 1973, since then has added men's wear and knits. She is president and designer of every part of her company. Her collections are shown in Tokyo and Paris.

Originally, Kawakubo designed almost exclusively in tones of gray and black, has since softened the severity of her view with subtle touches of color. She plays with asymmetrical shapes, drapes and wraps the body with cotton, canvas, or linen fabrics, often torn and slashed. In her early Paris showings, she emphasized the violence of her designs by making up her models with an extreme pallor and painted bruises and cuts.

She has been successful in the U.S. with in-store boutiques and her own free-standing shops. These are so minimalist that often nothing at all is on display. In spring 1987, the Fashion Institute of Technology included her clothes in an exhibition entitled, "Three Women: Kawakubo, Vionnet, McCardell."

Rei Kawakubo, 1992 (above); designs from her 1983 (center) and 1993 (left) collections.

Kelly, Patrick

Born Vicksburg, Mississippi, ca. 1950
Died Paris, France, January 1, 1990

An American who made his name in Europe, Kelly was the son of a seamstress. He grew up in Vicksburg and Atlanta, arrived in Paris in 1979 after a stopover in New York. In Paris, his first job was making stage costumes, which he produced in a tiny hotel room on a domestic Singer sewing machine. His first signature ready-to-wear collection was for fall 1985.

Kelly designed with a light, happy touch in an affordable price range. His specialty was sexy, clingy dresses in knits or stretch fabrics, the tops often covered with buttons or tiny black dolls. Models were the first to discover him, and his designs were so popular with them that they were known to work his shows for nothing more than some of the clothes. He sold to Bergdorf Goodman in New York and to shops in France and Italy, and did a special collection for Benetton.

K

Kemper, Randy

Born Philadelphia, Pennsylvania, August 22, 1959

Kemper graduated from Parsons School of Design, worked for a variety of firms including one-year stints at J.G. Hook in Philadelphia, GIVENCHY in Paris, HANAE MORI in New York. He then worked for BILL BLASS from 1984 to 1986 before forming Randy Kemper Corp. in 1987 with himself as president. His specialty is sportswear in the moderate price range, to which he brings a subtle distinction.

Kemper outfit for fall 1993.

Kenzo

Born Kyoto, Japan, February 28, 1940

Kenzo in 1990.

The son of hotelkeepers, Kenzo won top prizes in art school; he began his fashion career in Tokyo designing patterns for a magazine. He arrived in Paris in 1964, one of the first of his compatriots to make the move, and found work with a style bureau. He sold sketches to Féraud, free-lanced several collections, including Rodier.

In 1970 he opened his own boutique, decorated every inch with jungle patterns, and named it Jungle Jap. The clothes were an immediate success with models and other young fashion individualists. Money was scarce for his first ready-to-wear collection, so although designed for fall-winter, it was made entirely of cotton, much of it quilted. He showed it to the sound of rock music, using photographic mannequins rather than regular runway models. These were innovations and like many other Kenzo ideas, were the beginning of a trend. A prolific originator of fresh ideas, Kenzo is known for spirited combinations of textures and patterns. His clothes are young, always wearable, often copied, and have been widely distributed in the U.S. in both in-store boutiques and his own free-standing stores.

Kenzo designs from 1980 (left) and 1988 (far left) collections.

Khanh, Emmanuelle

Born Plain, France, September 7, 1937

Khanh started designing in 1959 with a job at Cacharel. Although she began her fashion career as a mannequin for BALENCIAGA and GIVENCHY, she rebelled against the couture in her own work and is credited with starting the young fashion movement in France. She was a revolutionary who is quoted as saying, "This is the century of sex. I want to make the sexiest clothes."

She first became known for The Droop, a very slim, soft, close-to-the-body dress, contrasting sharply with the structured couture clothes of the time. Her clothes had a lanky 1930s feeling with such signature details as dog's ear collars, droopy lapels on long, fitted jackets, dangling cufflink fastenings, half-moon moneybag pockets. Altogether, her work reflected an individual approach

symbolic of the 1960s. Khanh survived the era and has continued to produce soft and imaginative fashions.

She is married to Vietnamese engineer and furniture designer, Nyuen Manh (Quasar) Khanh, also prominent in avant-garde fashion circles of the 1960s.

K

Kieselstein-Cord, Barry

Born New York City, November 6, 1943
Awards Art Directors Club of New York, 1967 • Illustrators Society of New York, 1969 • Coty American Fashion Critics' Award *Outstanding Jewelry Design,* 1979; *Excellence in Women's Wear Design,* 1984 • Council of Fashion Designers of America (CFDA) *Excellence in Design,* 1981

Barry Kieselstein-Cord and a selection of his designs.

Kieselstein-Cord comes from a family of designers and architects, including his mother, father, and both grandfathers. His formal education included study at Parsons School of Design, New York University, and the American Craft League. He first attracted the attention of the fashion world with his jewelry, which was introduced at Georg Jensen around 1972. By the end of the decade, his designs included handbags and other accessories and were sold around the U.S. and exported abroad.

Working mainly in gold and platinum, Kieselstein-Cord starts with a sketch, moving from there directly into metal or wax, depending on whether the design will be reproduced by hand or from a mold. Each piece is finished by hand. His jewelry, widely featured in the press, has been praised for elegance, beauty, and superb craftsmanship, which is also true of his handbags and other accessories. While he aims at timeless design not tied to fashion, pieces such as the Winchester buckle and

palm cuffs are collected by fashion designers and celebrities everywhere.

In addition to his designing career, he has worked as art director/producer of commercial films at an advertising agency and as creative director for a helicopter support and maintenance company. He has served as vice president of the Council of Fashion Designers of America (CFDA) and as a director.

Killian, Todd

Born Fleetwood, Pennsylvania, April 29, 1963

Todd Killian got his start in men's wear in the Army, on a secondhand sewing machine he bought to make a tuxedo so he could take a girlfriend to her prom. This was the beginning of a small alterations business he pursued on the side while in basic training. After leaving the service, he attended the Fashion Institute of Technology on an academic scholarship, earning an Associate Degree in 1987. He then worked at Gail Blacker, Lou Levy, and Harper Industries before starting his own business in 1991.

Killian first concentrated on shirts, knitted and woven, for dress and sports. He has added vests, jackets, and trousers, working toward his objective of a full designer sportswear collection. Basing his designs on classic silhouettes, he adds his own energy and a softer, easier direction to achieve his desired goals of simplicity and ease. The clothes are in the designer price range.

Klein, Anne

Born Brooklyn, New York, August 3, 1923
Died New York City, March 19, 1974
Awards Coty American Fashion Critics' Award *"Winnie,"* 1955; *Return Award,* 1969; *Hall of Fame,* 1971 • Neiman Marcus Award: 1959, 1969

Anne Klein was just fifteen when she got her first job on Seventh Avenue as a sketcher; the next year she joined Varden Petites. In 1948, she and her first husband, Ben Klein, formed Junior Sophisticates. She designed for Mallory Leathers in 1965; operated Anne Klein Studio on West 57th Street in New York. In 1968, with Sanford Smith and her second husband, Chip Rubenstein, she formed Anne Klein & Co., now wholly owned by Takihyo Corporation of Japan.

Early in her career, Klein became known for her pioneering work in taking junior-size clothes out of little-girl cuteness and into adult sophisti-cation. At Junior Sophisticates there was the skimmer dress with its own jacket, long, pleated plaid skirts with blazers, gray flannel used with white satin. At Anne Klein & Co. the emphasis was on investment sportswear, an interrelated wardrobe of blazers, skirts, pants, sweaters, with slinky jersey dresses for evening. Klein was also a pioneer in recognizing the value of sportswear as a way of dressing uniquely suited to the American woman's way of life. In 1973, she was among five American and five French designers invited to show at the *Grand Divertissement* at the

Anne Klein in her studio, 1962.

Anne Klein designs from 1971 (left) and 1974 (right).

Palace of Versailles. The other Americans were BILL BLASS, STEPHEN BURROWS, HALSTON, and OSCAR DE LA RENTA.

After Anne Klein's death, the firm continued with DONNA KARAN and LOUIS DELL'OLIO as co-designers. Other divisions have been added: in 1982, Anne Klein II, a less expensive collection designed by Maurice Antaya, and in 1993 the younger, sporty-casual A-Line. When Karan left to establish her own label in 1984, Dell'Olio became sole designer; he resigned in May 1993 and was replaced by RICHARD TYLER. In December of 1994, the company announced that Tyler was leaving, to be replaced by Patrick Robinson, previously with the Giorgio Armani Le Collezione lower-priced label.

128

Klein, Calvin

Born New York City, November 19, 1942

Awards Coty American Fashion Critics' Award *"Winnie,"* 1973; *Return Award, 1974; Hall of Fame,* 1975; *Special Award (fur design for Alixandre),* 1975; *Special Award (contribution to international status of American fashion),* 1979; *Women's Apparel,* 1981 • Council of Fashion Designers of America (CFDA) *Best American Collection:* 1981, 1983, 1987; *Womenswear Designer of the Year,* 1993; *Menswear Designer of the Year,* 1993

Klein attended New York's High School of Industrial Art (now the High School of Art and Design) and the Fashion Institute of Technology, from which he graduated in 1962. He spent five years at three large firms as apprentice and designer; his first recognition came for his coats.

In 1968, with long-time friend Barry Schwartz, he formed Calvin Klein Ltd., which has developed into an extensive design empire. Besides women's ready-to-wear and sportswear, and men's wear, it has included everything from blue jeans to furs to shoes to women's underthings modeled on traditional men's undershirts and briefs; from bed linens to cosmetics, skin care, fragrances, and pantyhose. Calvin Klein Home, a new luxury home furnishings collection was introduced in April 1995. He has promoted his products with provocative, sexy, often controversial advertising, notably the jeans and *Obsession,* the first of his women's fragrances, which now include *Eternity* and *Escape.* All three exist also in versions for men. They were joined in the fall of 1994 by *CK One,* a shared fragrance for women and men, inspired by Klein's daughter Marci.

Considered the foremost exponent of spare, intrinsically American style, Klein presents a full wardrobe, day into evening. He has said, "It's important not to confuse simplicity with uninteresting," and executes his

Calvin Klein, 1992 (bottom left); designs from 1979 (top left) and 1994 (top right).

simplified, refined, sportswear-based shapes in luxurious natural fibers, such as cashmere, linen, and silk, as well as leather and suede. His color preferences are for earth tones and neutrals — his hallmark is a lean, supple elegance, an offhand, understated luxury.

In June 1993, as part of a benefit in the Hollywood Bowl for AIDS Project Los Angeles, the designer presented a 20-minute showing of his current collection, which also marked his 25th anniversary in his own business.

Calvin Klein gown from 1994 (left) and coat 1984 (right).

Klein, Roland

Born Rouen, France, 1938

A Frenchman who moved to London in 1965 to learn English then decided to stay, Roland Klein studied from 1955 to 1957 at l'Ecole de la Chambre Syndicale de la Couture Parisienne. From 1960 to 1962 he worked in the tailoring department at CHRISTIAN DIOR, from Dior went to PATOU as assistant to KARL LAGERFELD, whom he considers his greatest influence. Klein's clothes demonstrate his sound training — they are well cut, simple, elegant, and extremely well made.

In London he worked at Marcel Fenz, where in 1973 he became managing director with his own label. He opened his own ready-to-wear business in 1979. In addition to his own label, Klein designs a woman's line in Italy for MaxMara and is design consultant to several retail chains. His men's wear and women's wear are sold under license in Japan, where he also creates fabrics and wedding dresses specifically for that market.

Kōkin

Born Buffalo, New York, August 29, 1959

Kokin studied at the State University of New York at Buffalo, moved to New York, and in 1980 began what he planned as an acting career. For fun, he took a millinery course at Fashion Institute of Technology and in 1983 found himself in business making hats. His creative output now includes hair accessories, scarves and wraps, and of course, hats.

Early on he was strongly influenced by theater and film fashions from his growing-up years. Later, as he studied the great designers, such as CHARLES JAMES, BALENCIAGA, DIOR, and SCHIAPARELLI, they exerted a powerful effect on his thinking. His sense of theater is a continuing trait and his hats have an edge of drama and wit — they are not for women who want to avoid notice. Kokin has

Kokin and design, 1994.

done hats for films and music videos and has been honored by his own trade organization as designer of the year in 1991, 1992, and 1994, and in 1993 by the National Kidney Foundation.

K

Koos

Born Koos Van Den Akker; Holland, ca. 1932
Awards American Printed Fabrics Council "Tommy" Award for his unique use of prints, 1983

Koos started making dresses when just eleven years old. He studied at the Netherlands Royal Academy of Art, worked in department stores in The Hague and in Paris, whizzed through a two-year fashion program at L'Ecole Guerre Lavigne in Paris in seven months. After an apprenticeship at CHRISTIAN DIOR, he returned to The Hague and spent six years

Koos van den Akker, 1987 (below); sketch of his signature collage-look from 1976 (left).

there selling custom-made dresses in his own boutique.

In August 1968, with a portable sewing machine and very little money, he came to New York. He first set up his "office" by the fountain at Lincoln Center, taking commissions from passers-by; after this, he designed lingerie for Eve Stillman and eventually opened his own boutique, at the same time running a limited wholesale operation. Men's wear followed. In 1992, he joined forces with PETER DEWILDE to form Koos & DeWilde. In addition to the men's wear, design projects include furs, home furnishings, theater costumes.

For his women's clothes Koos has always specialized in simple shapes in beautiful fabrics, enriched with his signature "collages" of colorful prints and lace. They are considered collectors' items and have been on display in the Museum of Contemporary Crafts, New York. Customers have included Cher, Madeleine Kahn, Elizabeth Taylor, Gloria Vanderbilt.

Kors, Michael

Born Long Island, New York, August 9, 1959

Kors attended the Fashion Institute of Technology for one semester in 1977. He then worked for three years as designer, buyer, and display director for a New York boutique before starting his own business in 1981. His first collection of sixteen pieces, entirely in brown and black, sold to eight accounts. By 1986 the list had grown to over seventy-five specialty stores. He has also designed a lower-priced clothing collection called Kors, approximately half the price of the regular collection, has done cashmere knits for the Scottish firm of Lyle & Scott, and has had licensing agreements for shoes and swimwear.

Kors designs individual pieces then combines them into outfits. His aim is a flexible, versatile way of dressing by which a woman can put pieces together in different ways to achieve any desired effect, from the most casual to the dressiest. The clothes belong in the designer sportswear category — dresses and separates in luxurious fibers and fabrics, clean and understated in cut and line. They are meant for a sophisticated, modern, affluent woman who dresses to please herself.

Michael Kors (below) and designs from fall 1994.

L

Christian Lacroix
Karl Lagerfeld
Kenneth Jay Lane
Helmut Lang
Jeanne Lanvin
Guy Laroche
Byron Lars
André Laug
Ralph Lauren
Hervé Léger
Judith Leiber
Lucien Lelong
Tina Leser
Michael Leva
Lucile

Lacroix, Christian

Born France, 1951

Lacroix is given credit by some critics for revitalizing the Paris couture at a time when it had grown stale, and with his irreverent wit and sense of humor returning an element of adventure to fashion.

A native of Provence in the South of France, he grew up surrounded by women, developing an early interest in fashion and accessories. After studies in art history and classic Greek and Latin at Montpellier University, he went to Paris in 1972 to attend L'Ecole du Louvre. A stint as a museum curator followed, then in 1978 Lacroix turned to fashion, first as a design assistant at Hermès, next for two years at Guy Paulin. He went to Japan for a year as an assistant to a Japanese designer, returned to Paris and joined JEAN PATOU in 1982 as chief designer of haute couture.

At Patou he produced collection after idea-filled collection of theatrical, witty clothes and fantastic accessories. Imaginative and elegant, not all were wearable by any but the most daring, but many would appeal to an adventurous woman with flair and confidence in her own style. After five years with Patou, Lacroix left in 1987 to establish his own couture house backed by the French conglomerate that also owns Dior. The arrangement includes ready-to-wear. Under his own name, he has continued to show the same irrepressible instinct for drama, with the ready-to-wear somewhat less extreme that the couture.

Christian Lacroix in his workroom, 1987 (near right); another design from this same collection (right); coat from fall 1994 (above). *Also see Color Plate 19.*

Lagerfeld, Karl

Born Hamburg, Germany, September 10, 1939
Awards Neiman Marcus Award, 1980 • Council of Fashion Designers of America (CFDA) *Special Award,* 1982

The son of a Swedish father and German mother, Lagerfeld arrived in Paris in 1953, at fourteen already determined to become a clothes designer. The same year he won an award for the best coat in the same International Wool Secretariat design competition in which SAINT LAURENT won for the best dress. In 1954 he was working for BALMAIN, three and a half years later went to work for PATOU.

He left Patou, again tried school, and after two years at loose ends began free-lancing. In 1963 he went to work for the upscale ready-to-wear house, Chloë, as one of a team of four designers. The team of four became two, Lagerfeld and the Italian GRAZIELLA FONTANA. They continued to design the collection together until 1972 when Lagerfeld became sole designer.

In 1982 he became design director for Chanel, but continued with Chloë until 1984 when he severed the connection to work for Chanel and to inaugurate his first collection under his own label. Enormously hard-working and prolific, he has had a sportswear collection under his own name designed specifically for the U.S., designed gloves, done shoes for Mario Valentino and Charles Jourdan, sweaters for Ballantyne. He does both furs and sportswear for FENDI, and has resumed designing for Chloë. He has a number of successful fragrances for women and men.

Karl Lagerfeld for Chloë, 1994.

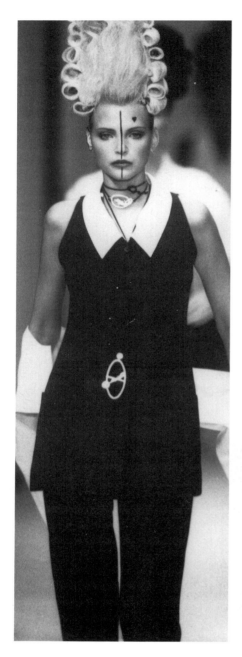

These include *Chloé* (1970) and *Sun Moon Stars* (1994) for women, and for men, *Lagerfeld* (1978) and *Lagerfeld Photo* (1990).

Lagerfeld is an unpredictable, original designer, highly professional and a master of his craft. At his best he mixes inventiveness and wearability, spicing the blend with a dash of wit. He likes to remove clothes from their usual contexts — he's used elaborate embroidery on cotton instead of the usual silk, made dresses that could be worn upside down, showed *crepe de chine* dresses with tennis shoes long before it was a styling cliché. He is credited with bringing Chanel into the present while retaining its distinctive character, although nowadays the house appears to be more Lagerfeld than Mlle. Coco.

Karl Lagerfeld, 1994 (below) and designs from his collections of 1987 (right) and spring 1994 (left).

Lane, Kenneth Jay

Born Detroit, Michigan, April 22, 1932
Awards Coty American Fashion Critics' Award *Special Award for "Outstanding Contribution to Fashion,"* 1966 • Neiman Marcus Award, 1968

Lane attended the University of Michigan for two years, went on to the Rhode Island School of Design, from which he graduated in 1954 with a degree in advertising. He worked on the promotion art staff at *Vogue* and there met French shoe designer ROGER VIVIER. Through him, Lane became an assistant designer for Delman Shoes, then associate designer of Christian Dior Shoes, spending part of each year in Paris working with Vivier.

In 1963, still designing shoes, Lane made a few pieces of jewelry that were photographed by the fashion magazines and bought by a few stores. Working nights and weekends, he continued to design jewelry, using his initials K.J.L. By June 1964 he was able to make jewelry design a full-time career. Kenneth Jay Lane, Inc., which became part of Kenton Corporation in 1969, was repurchased by Lane in 1972. The less expensive KJL line is licensed to the Costume Jewelry Company and he has appeared on its behalf with great success on QVC, the televised home shopping channel. His jewelry is sold in fine department and specialty stores and in his own shops throughout the world.

Like a designer of precious jewels, Lane first makes his designs in wax or by carving or twisting metal. He says, "I want to make real jewelry with not-real materials," and he sees plastic as the modern

Kenneth Jay Lane pins, 1991.

medium, lightweight, available in every color, perfect for simulating real gems. He likes to see his jewelry intermixed with the real gems worn by his international roster of celebrity customers.

Lang, Helmut

Born Vienna, Austria, 1956

Lang was raised in the Austrian Alps, at eighteen moved to Vienna to study business. He worked behind a bar, became involved with artists and "night people," and was encouraged by his friends to do something creative. He got into fashion when he met someone who could make up the things he had in his mind, as at that time he had no idea how to put them together himself. His vision of fashion developed gradually until in 1984 he opened a shop in Vienna. By 1987 he had a contract with an Italian textile firm and a licensing agreement with Mitsubishi in Japan, where he now has numerous

Helmut Lang (below) and (left) sheer top and vinyl pants for spring 1994.

boutiques. While he shows in Paris, Lang maintains his personal viewpoint by continuing to live and design in Vienna.

Variously dubbed a deconstructionist, a minimalist, a follower of the Japanese avant-garde, Helmut Lang is really none of the above but very much his own man. An anomaly simply by being Austrian, he exhibited his distinctive view of fashion and clothes fully formed with his first Paris showing in 1986, when he sent out waif-like models with scrubbed faces in simple silhouettes and somber colors. His personal stamp — experimentation with fabric technology, including PVC, nylon, Lurex, stretch synthetics, shiny cellophane-like effects, and his rumpled looks and subtle layerings — were there from the beginning and have been enormously influential. One wing of fashion sees him as a prophet, the other sees him as the antithesis of fashion. He believes that fashion has to do with attitude, appearance, and character, and that it defines the spirit of the time. His clothes express his view of how modern men and women want to dress: without affectation and with the understanding that perfect cut, comfort, and ease of movement are among fashion's great luxuries.

Lanvin, Jeanne

Born Brittany, France, 1867
Died Paris, France, July 6, 1946
Awards Légion d'Honneur

The eldest of a journalist's ten children, Lanvin was apprenticed to a dressmaker at the age of thirteen, became a milliner when she was twenty-three. The dresses she designed for her young daughter, Marie-Blanche, were admired and bought by her hat customers for their children, and this business in children's clothes evolved into the couture house of Lanvin, Faubourg St. Honoré.

Lanvin's designs were noted for a youthful quality, often reflecting the influence of the costumes of her native Brittany. She collected costume books, daguerreotypes, historical plates, and drew inspiration from them, notably for the *robes de style* for which she was famous, and for her wedding gowns. She took plain fabrics and decorated them in her own workrooms, maintaining a department for machine embroidery under the direction of her brother. The house also produced women's sport clothes and furs, children's wear, and lingerie. In 1926 she opened a men's wear boutique, the first in the couture, directed by her nephew, Maurice Lanvin.

She was famous for her use of quilting and stitching, for her embroideries, for the discreet use of sequins. She introduced the

chemise during World War I; fantasy evening gowns in metallic embroideries were a signature. She was one of the first couturiers to establish a perfume business, with *Arpège* and *My*

Jeanne Lanvin gown from 1931.

Sin among the most notable fragrances.

Mme. Lanvin was an accomplished businesswoman and was elected President of the Haute Couture committee of the Paris International Exhibition in 1937. She represented France and the couture at the 1939 New York World's Fair. After her death the House of Lanvin continued under the direction of her daughter, the Comtesse de Polignac.

The couture was designed by Antonio del Castillo from 1950 to 1963, and from 1963 until 1984, by JULES-FRANCOIS CRAHAY. Control of the firm passed from the Lanvin family in 1989. Maryll Lanvin, who had taken over design direction of ready-to-wear, and after Crahay's retirement of the couture, was replaced by CLAUDE MONTANA for couture, Eric Bergère for ready-to-wear. The couture operation was discontinued in 1992 and design of ready-to-wear was taken over by DOMINIQUE MORLOTTI, also responsible for the men's collections. In July 1995, responsibility for the women's collection was given to Ocimar Versolato, a 34-year old Brazilian; Morlotti was to continue with the men's wear.

Laroche, Guy

Born La Rochelle (near Bordeaux), France, ca. 1923
Died February 16, 1990

Laroche arrived in Paris at age twenty-five with no immediate goals and no interest in clothes. Through a cousin working at JEAN PATOU, he toured several couture houses and fell in love with the business. He got a job as assistant to JEAN DESSÈS and stayed with him five years. From 1950 to 1955 he free-lanced in New York, then returned to Paris and opened a couture establishment in his apartment. His first collection was for fall 1957. In 1961 he expanded and moved to the Avenue Montaigne, where the house is still located.

In the beginning influenced by BALENCIAGA, Laroche soon developed a younger, livelier, less formal look. "It was very, very conservative when I started. I gave it color...youth, suppleness and informality." His evening pants were worn by the most fashionable women in Paris.

Laroche had his greatest fame during the early 1960s. At the time of his death he presided over an extensive company producing both Laroche couture and ready-to-wear and with boutiques around the world. Other licensed ready-to-wear labels in the group included Christian Aujard, Lolita Lempicka, ANGELO TARLAZZI, and a lower-priced collection by THIERRY MUGLER. His name has been on products ranging from intimate apparel, furs, luggage, sportswear, rainwear, dresses, and blouses, to sunglasses, accessories, footwear, and of course, fragrances. Michel Klein became couture designer in 1993, with Jean-Pierre Marty in charge of ready-to-wear.

Lars, Byron

Born Oakland, California, January 19, 1965
Awards Cecil Beaton Award for Illustration (in *British Vogue*), 1990

Byron Lars exploded onto the fashion scene in 1991 with a small collection that established him as a fresh, young talent with professional skills and commercial savvy, enlivened by a whimsical sense of humor. His first hits were based on men's shirts draped into saucy little dresses; his tailoring, draping, and creativity have continued to develop.

After graduation from high school in 1983, Lars attended the Brooks Fashion Institute in Long Beach, California for two years and the Fashion Institute of Technology in New York in 1986. The next few years brought him a number of honors: he was chosen to represent the U.S. at the International Concours des Jeunes Créateurs de Mode in Paris, and took first place awards in various international

Byron Lars (above) at the end of his 1994 show; (right) from his 1993 collection.

competitions. Press response to his debut was immediate and favorable and he has enjoyed a steady growth of commercial success.

Laug, André

Born Alsace, France, 1932
Died December, 1984

Laug worked briefly for NINA RICCI and ANDRÉ COURRÈGES before moving to Italy. He designed for MARIA ANTONELLI for five years, and in 1968 opened a couture house in Rome. He also produced ready-to-wear, which

he showed in Milan.

Laug's strength was in translating young ideas into chic, wearable clothes for a conservative international clientele. Both the couture and deluxe ready-to-wear were refined in

cut and attitude, and beautifully made. The house continued for several years after his death through the efforts of a devoted staff but is now closed.

Lauren, Ralph

Born New York City, October 14, 1939
Awards Coty American Fashion Critics' Award *Men's Wear,* 1970; *Return Award (men's wear),* 1973; *"Winnie,"* 1974; *Return Award,* 1976; *Hall of Fame (men's wear),* 1976; *Hall of Fame (women's wear),* 1977; *Men's Apparel,* 1981; *Special Award (women's wear),* 1984 • Council of Fashion Designers of America (CFDA) *Special Award,* 1981; *Retailer of the Year,* 1986

A gifted stylist, Ralph Lauren has taken his dream of a mythic American past of athletic grace and discreet elegance and transformed it into a fashion empire. He chose the name Polo as a symbol of men who wear expensive, classic clothes and wear them with style; he extends the same blend of classic silhouettes, superb fabrics, and fine workmanship to his women's apparel. For both women and men, the attitude is well-bred and confident, with an offhand luxury. He has projected his romantic view in his advertising, which features a large cast of models in upper-crust situations, and to his flagship New York stores. Definitely investment caliber, the clothes are known for excellent quality and high prices.

The son of an artist, Lauren took night courses in business while working days as a stock boy at Alexander's, arrived in the fashion world without formal design training. After college he sold at Brooks Brothers, was variously an assistant buyer at Allied Stores, a glove company salesman, and New York representative for a Boston necktie manufacturer. He started designing neckties, and in 1967 persuaded Beau Brummel, a men's wear firm, to form the Polo neckwear division. The ties were unique, exceptionally wide and made by hand of opulent silks. They

Ralph Lauren, 1994 (above); (right) hunting jacket for fall 1994.

quickly attracted attention to the designer and brought him a contract to design the Polo line of men's clothing for Norman Hilton, with whom he established Polo in 1968 as a separate company producing a total wardrobe for men.

In 1971 Lauren introduced finely tailored shirts for women and the next year a total ready-to-wear collection. The women's wear now includes Ralph, a younger look, and Polo Sport for active sports such as riding, skiing, and golf. Other lines include Polo for Boys, Polo University Club, Double RL men's jeans and rugged apparel. Other collections are distributed only outside the U.S. in countries such as Japan and Canada. His licensing has expanded world-wide to include men's robes and underwear, swimwear for men and women, hosiery, small leathers, luggage and handbags, jewelry, eyewear, and scarves. Other involvements are cosmetics and skin care, and in 1983, a total home environment. His men's fragrances include *Polo*, *Safari for Men*, and *Polo Sport*; for women there is *Lauren* and *Safari*. In addition, Lauren has done film work, designing for the leading men in *The Great Gatsby* in 1973, and in 1977, the clothing for *Annie Hall*.

Lauren's soigné dress from 1986 (left) and western-influenced separates (right) from 1978.

Léger, Hervé

Born Bapaume (Pas de Calais), France, May 30, 1957

Hervé Léger's preparation for a fashion career was an education in art history and theater. In 1975 he began designing hats and accessories for designers such as Dick Brandsma and Tan Giudicelli. Two years later he started his serious apprenticeship, first as assistant to Giudicelli, then assisting KARL LAGERFELD at FENDI and CHANEL. He spent two years designing for the Italian firm Cadette, then in 1985 joined LANVIN, working with Maryll Lanvin on the ready-to-wear and couture collections. Lanvin gave him a boutique under his name in the same year. He also collaborated with DIANE VON FURSTENBERG in that year. He has designed furs for Chloé, ready-to-wear for Charles Jourdan, and costumes for theater and advertising campaigns.

Léger's first collection under his own label appeared in 1992 with both couture and deluxe ready-to-wear. These were frankly sensuous clothes that wrapped the body closely with bands and tucks, at their best both seductive and beautiful. He acknowledges CHARLES JAMES as his major influence, followed by Lagerfeld.

Léger design from 1994.

Leiber, Judith

Born Budapest, Hungary, January 11, 1921

Awards Coty American Fashion Critics Award *Special Award (handbags),* 1973 • Neiman Marcus Award, 1980 • Council of Fashion Designers of America (CFDA) *Lifetime Achievement Award,* 1994 • Dallas Fashion Award *Fashion Excellence Award.*

Renowned especially for her fantastic jeweled evening bags, Judith Leiber learned her craft in Budapest, starting as an apprentice at nineteen, the only woman in what was considered a man's trade. It was there she met her American husband at the end of World War II; they married and she came to the U.S. as a war bride in

1946. She worked in the handbag industry until 1963, gaining a diversified experience in every type of bag and every price range, then she and her husband went into business for themselves. The company was sold to a British conglomerate in 1993, resulting in expansion of the business and the addition of a retail presence.

Leiber does all the designing, from the small animal shapes encrusted with thousands of jewels to daytime bags in rare leathers, softened with pleats, braid, coins or charms, and stones. She lists her influences as the 20s, 30s, and oriental art, and wants her bags to be great to hold, beautiful to look at, and practical. She also makes some accessories, such as wallets, key chains, and belts, and plans to do a full line of accessories, from scarves to jewelry and eyewear, and possible luggage, shoes, and fragrance. The bags have become collector's items for women who wear real jewelry and designer clothes.

She has been much honored with innumerable awards from trade groups, colleges and universities, and charitable organizations. In late 1994, New York's Fashion Institute of Technology marked her 30th year in business with an exhibition of her work.

From Leiber's 1990 collection.

Lelong, Lucien

Born Paris, France, October 11, 1889
Died Anglet (near Biarritz), France, May 10, 1958

Lelong made his first designs at the age of fourteen for his father, a successful dressmaker. At first trained for business, he decided on a career in couture and designed his first collection; two days before its presentation in 1914, he was called into the Army. He was wounded in World War I, invalided out after a year in the hospital, and received the *Croix de Guerre*.

In 1918 he entered his father's business and took control soon after. By 1926, the year he established *Parfums Lelong*, the house was flourishing and continued to do so up until World War II. A farsighted businessman, he was one of the first to have a ready-to-wear line, established in 1934. Lelong was elected president of the Chambre Syndicale de la Couture Parisienne in 1937. He held the post for ten years, including the Occupation period when the Germans wanted to move the entire French dressmaking industry to Berlin and Vienna. Lelong managed to frustrate the plan and guided the couture safely through the war years. He reopened his own house in 1941, with DIOR and BALMAIN as designers. A serious illness in 1947 caused him to close his couture house, but he continued to direct his perfume business.

Lelong was considered a director of designers rather than a creator. PIERRE BALMAIN, CHRISTIAN DIOR, and HUBERT DE GIVENCHY all worked for him, and Dior particularly praised him as a good friend and a generous employer. From 1919 to 1948, his house produced distinguished collections of beautiful, ladylike clothes for a conservative clientele. Lelong believed strongly in honest workmanship and good needlework and it was his credo that a Lelong creation would hold together until its fabric wore out. He was also an accomplished painter, sculptor, composer, and sportsman.

Lucien Lelong (above left) and two fur-trimmed coats from 1938 (below left) and 1939 (below right).

Leser, Tina

Born Philadelphia, Pennsylvania, December 12, 1910
Died Sands Point, Long Island, January 24, 1986
Awards Neiman Marcus Award, 1945 • Coty American Fashion Critics' Award *"Winnie,"* 1945

Leser studied art in Philadelphia and Paris. In 1935 she opened a shop in Honolulu to sell her fashion designs; she returned to New York in 1942 after the outbreak of World War II and began to make the glamorous sportswear that became her trademark. For ten years she designed for a sportswear manufacturer, and in 1952 formed her own company, Tina Leser Inc. She retired in 1964, returned to fashion in 1966, then quit for good in 1982.

One of the group of innovative sportswear designers that included CLAIRE McCARDELL and TOM BRIGANCE, Leser always was distinguished by her romanticism and her use of exotic fabrics from the Orient and Hawaii. These she often enriched with embroidery and metallic threads. She used hand-painted prints, designed harem pajamas and toreador pants long before other designers who were later credited with them. She is also thought to have been the first to make dresses from cashmere.

She was married first to Curtin Leser, from whom she was divorced, then to James J. Howley, who survived her. They had one daughter.

Strapless dress by Tina Leser in exotic floral print, 1945.

Leva, Michael

Born Morristown, New Jersey, January 15, 1961

Michael Leva attended the Rhode Island School of Design from 1979 to 1983. He studied landscape architecture before switching to fashion design and was awarded RISD's Textron Fellowship, their highest honor for apparel design. Following graduation, he worked as assistant at BILL BLASS and WilliWear in New York, for France Andrévie in Paris, and Lapine Co. in Japan. He opened his own firm in 1986, which closed in 1991 for lack of capital. He regrouped and reopened in 1993.

Leva's initial successes were sculptural, monastic clothes that appealed to both the arty avant-garde and the socialite. He continues his emphasis on cut, adding dress-

maker details and a softer viewpoint. His aim is to make clean, simple clothes that are comfortable, versatile, and a bit out of the ordinary, for women of taste of any age.

From Leva's 1993 collection.

Lucile

Born London, England, 1862
Died London, England, 1935

Now known mainly for the designers who worked for her, including MOLYNEUX and TRAVIS BANTON, Lucile was the most successful London-based couturiere of her time. Born Lucy Kennedy, she was married at eighteen but soon divorced. Her fashion career began in the 1890s when she and her mother set up as dressmakers; as they became known and their business grew she started doing business under the name Lucile. Around the turn of the century she married Sir Cosmo Duff Gordon and as Lady Duff Gordon was soon dressing London's very grandest ladies. She opened a New York branch in 1909, a salon in Paris in 1911. Her business declined after World War I, when her floating chiffons were too exotic for the times. While her design viewpoint was romantic and theatrical, she was a tough and forward-thinking businesswoman with the vision to see the potential of the North American market and the ability to succeed there.

1 Gianni Versace for evening, 1992.

2 An Emilio Pucci print named "Menelik" on silk twill, 1966.

3 Three by Rudi Gernreich. Left: wool tweed mini-bloomer outfit, 1968. Center: patchwork double-knit wool bathing suit, ca. 1956. Right: peacock-print jersey minidress with peacock-feather hat.

4 Yves Saint Laurent interprets Turkish influences, 1991.

5 Classic Chanel evening coat of gold brocaded silk crepe, ca. 1927.

6 Perry Ellis spirited look at ethnic sources, 1982.

7 The pure shapes and exquisite embroideries of Callot Soeurs. Left, ca. 1924. Right, ca. 1926.

8 Jackets of jeweled embroidery with petal skirts, Giorgio Armani, 1994.

9

9 The grandeur of Mainbocher, 1949.

10 Pleated *Delphos* gown with silk velvet evening cape by Mariano Fortuny, ca. early 1930s.

11 Todd Oldham at play with pattern, 1994.

12 The inimitable colors of Geoffrey Beene, 1982.

13 Charles James sculptures ballgowns in silk satin, 1948.

10

11

12

13

14

15

16

17

14 Audrey Hepburn dressed by Cecil Beaton in *My Fair Lady*, 1964.

15 Paul Poiret's bold horizontals in silk faille, ca. 1922, 1923.

16 Wrapped column of silk damask pleats by Claire McCardell, 1950.

17 Valentino's theatrics, 1980.

18 Ballgown skirt meets skivvy top. Isaac Mizrahi finale, 1994.

19 The unabashed luxury of Christian Lacroix, couture, 1990.

20 Three American masters look at evening. Left: red wool jersey by Norman Norell for Traina-Norell, 1954. Center: black crepe dinner dress with red and white horse print, Adrian Original, 1945. Right: red-and-white striped velvet coat over black wool jersey dress, by Claire McCardell.

21 Balenciaga flamenco gown, fuchsia silk and linen gazar with feather underskirt, ca. 1959.

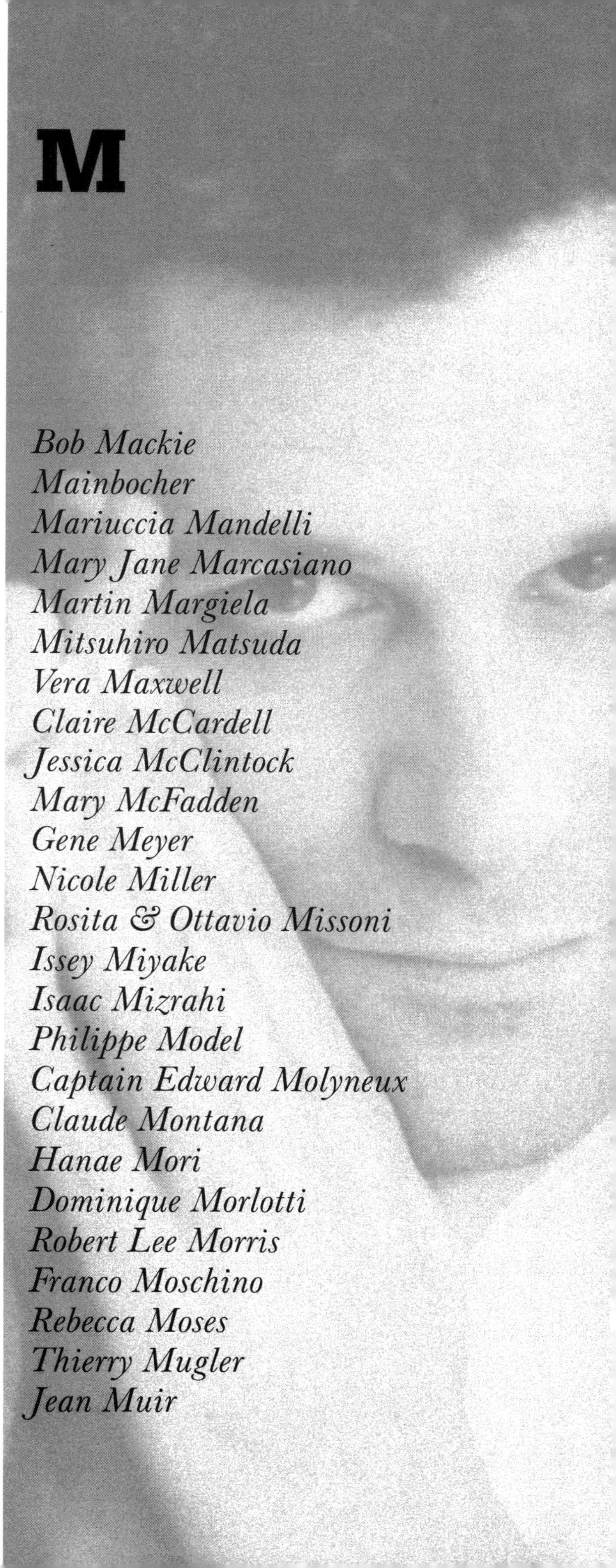

M

Bob Mackie
Mainbocher
Mariuccia Mandelli
Mary Jane Marcasiano
Martin Margiela
Mitsuhiro Matsuda
Vera Maxwell
Claire McCardell
Jessica McClintock
Mary McFadden
Gene Meyer
Nicole Miller
Rosita & Ottavio Missoni
Issey Miyake
Isaac Mizrahi
Philippe Model
Captain Edward Molyneux
Claude Montana
Hanae Mori
Dominique Morlotti
Robert Lee Morris
Franco Moschino
Rebecca Moses
Thierry Mugler
Jean Muir

Mackie, Bob

Born Los Angeles, California, March 24, 1940

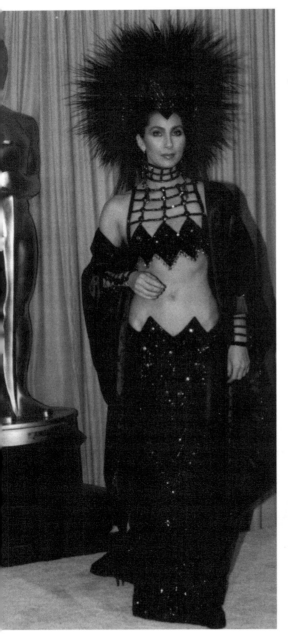

Mackie grew up in Los Angeles where he studied art and theater design. While still in art school he worked as a sketcher for designers Jean Louis and EDITH HEAD, and for Ray Aghayan, whose partner he became. The spectacular costume designs he and Aghayan, together and separately, have designed for nightclub performers and stars of TV and movies have established the two in the top rank of their field. Among the celebrities they have dressed are Marlene Dietrich, Carol Burnett, Mitzi Gaynor, Barbra Streisand, Raquel Welch, Carol Channing, and notably, Cher.

In addition to costumes, Mackie has been successful in ready-to-wear, not surprisingly with emphasis on glamorous evening clothes, as well as bathing suits and loungewear. In June 1993 he closed his ready-to-wear business but retained the couture and licensing operations.

Cher (far left) wearing a Bob Mackie creation at the 1986 Academy Awards ceremony; (left) the designer in 1982; (above) gown from the 1987 ready-to-wear collection.

Mainbocher

Born Main Rousseau Bocher; Chicago, Illinois, October 24, 1891
Died Munich, Germany, December 26, 1976

Noted for a nearly infallible sense of fashion, Mainbocher created high-priced clothes of quiet good taste, simplicity, and understatement. He was the first American designer to succeed in Paris and before that had a distinguished career as a fashion journalist.

Encouraged by his mother, he studied art at the Chicago Academy of Fine Arts and in New York, Paris, and Munich. In 1917 he went to France with an American ambulance unit and stayed on in Paris after the war to study singing. To support himself he worked as a fashion illustrator for *Harper's Bazaar* and *Vogue*. By 1922 he had abandoned singing and become a full-time fashion journalist, first as Paris fashion editor for *Vogue* then as editor of French *Vogue*. During his journalistic career, he invented the *"Vogue's Eye View"* column and discovered the artist, Eric, and the photographer, HOYNINGEN-HUENE. He resigned in 1929 to open his own Paris salon.

With his many influential contacts and sure fashion sense he made an immediate success. The Duchess of Windsor, whose wedding dress he made, and Lady Mendl were among his clients. It is said that in his first year in business he introduced the strapless evening gown and also persuaded French textile manufacturers to again set up double looms and weave the wide widths not produced since before World War I.

Mainbocher left Paris at the outbreak of World War II and in 1939 opened a couture house in New York. He became the designer with the most snob appeal, designing elegant and expensive clothes for elegant and expensive women, screening his clients according to his own stringent standards. He also designed uniforms for the American Red Cross, the WAVES, the SPARS, and the Girl Scouts.

In his work he was greatly influenced by VIONNET and used the bias cut with great mastery. Elegant evening clothes were his forte, from long ball gowns of lace or transparent fabrics to short evening dresses and beaded evening sweaters with jeweled buttons. He made dinner suits of tweed, combining them with blouses of delicate fabrics. Pastel gingham was a signature, accessorized with pearl chokers, short white kid gloves, and plain pumps. Mainbocher knew his own worth and insisted that in magazines his designs be shown on two facing pages, never mixed with those of other designers, no matter how great.

A skillful editor of others' work as well as a creator, Mainbocher has been ranked with MOLYNEUX, SCHIAPARELLI, and LELONG. His design philosophy, often quoted: "The responsibility and challenge...is to consider the design and the woman at the same time. Women should look beautiful, rather than just trendful."

Mainbocher design illustrated in HARPER'S BAZAAR, April 1931. *Also see Color Plate 9.*

M

Mandelli, Mariuccia

Born Near Milan, Italy, ca. 1933

Krizia, the firm headed by Mariuccia Mandelli and her husband, Aldo Pinto, was founded in Milan in 1954, the name of the company taken from Plato's dialogue on the vanity of women. Always interested in fashion, Mandelli was teaching school when she became frustrated by the clothes available to her in shops and, with a friend, made up some of her own designs and personally carried them around Italy to sell to retail outlets. The process gave her valuable insights into customer preferences and soon her business had grown from two workers to a *premiere* and six workers. The clothes were young and original with a sense of fantasy and her first show in 1957 won favorable press response and an award. As her business blossomed she persuaded her husband to become her business partner and to supervise her knitwear company, Kriziamaglia, which took off in the early 1970s. Further success led to boutiques, licenses, and highly successful fragrances.

Mandelli is a witty, fertile designer, each collection bursting with ideas, veering between classicism and craziness. Her animal sweaters — a different bird or beast for each collection — are famous and often have been copied; she is also known for fantastic evening designs, such as the tiered, fan-pleated cellophane dresses that looked like the Chrysler Building. Walter Albini was a design collaborator for three years and LAGERFELD has been a consultant.

An accomplished businesswoman with a sure grasp of company affairs, Mandelli is a hard worker, producing ten collections a year, including children's wear. She has devoted her considerable energy to various causes of the Milan design community and is considered responsible for moving the ready-to-wear showings from Florence to Milan.

Marcasiano, Mary Jane

Born New Jersey, September 23, 1955
Awards Cartier "Stargazer" Award, 1981 • Wool Knit Award, 1983 • Dupont Award *Most Promising Designer,* 1984 • Cutty Sark Mens Fashion Award *Most Promising Menswear Designer,* 1984

A 1978 graduate of the Parsons School of Design, Marcasiano designed her first collection in 1979, and has had her own label since that time. She added men's wear in 1982, began licensing in 1985 with a shoe collection, fine and semi-precious jewelry, and furs for Ben Kahn.

Her clothes — sportswear, dresses, outerwear — belong in that desirable category that combines elegance with comfort and ease. She sees her customer as a woman without age limits, a traveller active in business who appreciates subtle, luxurious clothes that enhance her individuality.

Margiela, Martin

Born Belgium, 1957

Margiela is one of the radical trend-setters — others are Dries van Noten, Ann Demeulemeester, and HELMUT LANG — who burst on the Paris scene in the late 1980s with their iconoclastic fashion approach. Well trained in classic techniques, they use their considerable skills to turn accepted ideas about clothes inside-out and upside-down as they dismantle conventional approaches to beauty and fashion.

From 1976 to 1980, Margiela studied at the Academy of Fine Arts in Antwerp, and in 1984 went to work in Paris as assistant to JEAN-PAUL GAULTIER. In 1988 he presented his first collection for spring-summer 1989. Reflecting his view of the times we live in, he makes clothes and objects of recycled materials: used linings turned into dresses, subway posters or broken china made into waistcoats, shirts constructed from

ripped-apart socks and hosiery, among other ideas. He thinks "it is beautiful to make new things out of rejects or worn stuff," and when he slashes down old or new clothes, it is not to destroy them but rather to bring them back to life in a different form. For his fifth anniversary in 1993, he recreated his favorite pieces from the previous five years.

Unconventional clothes are matched by off-beat showing venues: a children's playground, a parking lot, an abandoned subway station, the Salvation Army's flea market.

From Margiela's 1993 collection.

Matsuda, Mitsuhiro

Born Tokyo, Japan, 1934

Influenced by his father, who worked in the Japanese kimono industry, Matsuda became interested in the idea of applying traditional Japanese principles to the design of Western-style clothes. He graduated from Waseda University, studied at Tokyo's famous Bunka College of Fashion, where KENZO was a classmate. After graduation in 1962, Matsuda worked as a ready-to-wear designer and in 1965 travelled with Kenzo to Paris. After six months, he returned to Japan via the U.S. In 1967 he founded his own company, named "Nicole" after a model he admired in *Elle* magazine. It started poorly but took off when he began to make custom T-shirts. Today, Nicole, Ltd. produces ready-to-wear for women and men, plus a full range of accessories.

Matsuda's work shows a bold, offbeat sense of proportion. He sticks largely to black and tones of gray, balances layers and levels with complete mastery of scale and texture. His clothes are reminiscent of YAMAMOTO and KAWAKUBO but lighter, less severe, and more wearable. They are well tailored, with an edge of wit, and walk a fine line between East and West.

Maxwell, Vera

Born New York City, April 22, 1903
Died Rincon, Puerto Rico, January 14, 1995
Awards Coty American Fashion Critics' Award *Special Award (coats and suits)*, 1951 • Neiman Marcus Award, 1955

Maxwell was one of a small group of American craftsmen-designers of the 1930s and 1940s, true originals such as CASHIN and McCARDELL, who worked independently of Europe. She also represents an even smaller group of women who successfully ran their own businesses.

Born Vera Huppe, she was the daughter of Viennese parents with whom she traveled to Europe and who provided the core of her early education. She went to high school in Leonia, New Jersey, studied ballet, and danced with the Metropolitan Opera Ballet from 1919 until her marriage in 1924 to Raymond J. Maxwell. She was divorced from Maxwell in 1937, and a second marriage to architect Carlisle H. Johnson also ended in divorce.

Maxwell specialized in simple, timeless clothes, marked by the effortless good looks and ease of movement particularly valued by active American women. These were largely go-together separates in fine Scottish tweeds, wool jersey, raw silk, Indian embroideries, and Ultrasuede®. Among her numerous innovations were the weekend wardrobe of 1935, consisting of a collarless jacket in tweed and gray flannel, a short pleated flannel tennis skirt, a longer pleated tweed skirt, and cuffed flannel trousers. There were also a cotton coverall for war workers that could be considered the precursor of the jumpsuit, print dresses with coats lined in matching print, and the Speed Dress with stretch-nylon top, full skirt of polyester knit, and print stole — no zippers, no buttons, no hooks.

She was honored in 1970 with a retrospective at the Smithsonian Institution in Washington, D.C. In 1978, a party and show were given at the Museum of the City of New York to celebrate her 75th birthday and 50th year as a designer. She continued to work until early in 1985, when she abruptly closed her business. In 1986, at age eighty-three, she went back to work with a fall collection of sportswear, dresses, and coats but soon retired again to spend most of her time working on her memoirs.

Vera Maxwell in her showroom, 1964, with some early designs.

McCardell, Claire

Born Frederick, Maryland, May 24, 1905
Died New York City, March 23, 1958
Awards Coty American Fashion Critics' Award *"Winnie,"* 1944; *Hall of Fame (posthumous),* 1958 • Neiman Marcus Award, 1948 • National Women's Press Club, 1950 • Parsons Medal for Distinguished Achievement, 1956

Claire McCardell is credited with originating the "American Look," easy and unforced, a striking contrast to structured, European-inspired fashion. She had complete understanding of the needs of the American woman with her full schedule of work and play, and designed specifically for this customer. Her philosophy was simple: clothes should be clean-lined, functional, comfortable, and appropriate to the occasion. They should fit well, flow naturally with the body and, of course, be attractive to look at. Buttons had to button, sashes were

required to be long enough not only to tie, but to wrap around and around.

Her father was a banker and state senator, and McCardell grew up in comfortable circumstances. As a child, she showed her interest in clothes with paper dolls and as a teenager designed her own clothes. She attended Hood College for Women in Maryland, studied fashion illustration at Parsons School of Design and for a year in Paris. Returning to New York, she painted lampshades for B. Altman & Co., and modeled briefly, joining Robert Turk,

Inc. in 1929 as model and assistant designer. When Turk moved to Townley Frocks, Inc. McCardell moved with him, taking over as designer after his death. She stayed with Townley until 1938 when she moved to HATTIE CARNEGIE, returning to Townley in 1940, first as designer, then as designer-partner. She remained there until her death.

McCardell picked up details from men's clothing and work clothes, such as large pockets, blue-jeans topstitching, trouser pleats, rivets, gripper fastenings. Favorite fabrics were sturdy cotton denim, ticking,

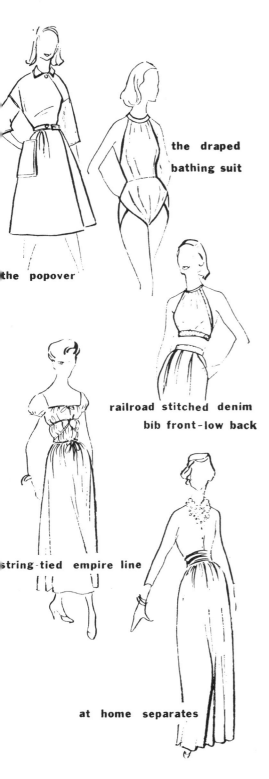

the draped
bathing suit

the popover

railroad stitched denim
bib front-low back

string-tied empire line

at home separates

gingham, and wool jersey. She used colored zippers in an ornamental way, was partial to spaghetti ties and surprise color juxtapositions. The result was sophisticated, wearable clothes, often with witty touches.

Among her many innovations were the diaper bathing suit, the monastic dress —waistless, bias-cut, dartless — the Popover, the kitchen dinner dress, and ballet slippers worn with day clothes. She also designed sunglasses, infants' and children's wear, children's shoes, and costume jewelry. Her designs were totally contemporary; the proof of her genius is that they still look contem-

porary today. As if in proof, Parsons School of Design honored her with an exhibition in 1994, one of the events celebrating the school's 100th anniversary. Entitled "Claire McCardell: Redefining Modernism," the show also included a section of clothes from contemporary American designers whose work might be considered in the McCardell tradition: DONNA KARAN, ISAAC MIZRAHI, ANNA SUI, ADRI, and MICHAEL KORS.

Stanley Marcus spoke of her as "...the master of the line, never the slave of the sequin. She is one of the few creative designers this country has ever produced."

Claire McCardell (below) and (left) McCardell classics from the WOMEN'S WEAR DAILY obituary, March 24, 1958. Right, evening dress and coat from the 1950s.
Also see Color Plates 16 and 20.

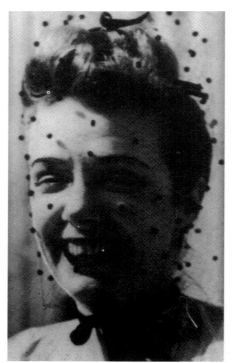

McClintock, Jessica

Born ca. 1931

Awards American Printed Fabrics Council "Tommy" Award, 1968 • Dallas Fashion Award: 1987, 1988, 1990, 1993

McClintock was raised in Maine by her mother, and as a child designed her own clothes and made patterns. Her training came from her grandmother, who was a pattern maker and seamstress. She married at nineteen, moved to California, and after her husband's death in an automobile accident in 1963, remarried, divorced, and taught school. In 1969, she invested $5,000 in a tiny company called Gunne Sax. From this small beginning she has built a company of more than 400 employees and carved a niche in the market with her highly personal blend of prettiness and old-fashioned allure.

Gunne Sax, with its formula of lace and country charm, is an unlikely success for the late 20th century, an American version of the LAURA ASHLEY aesthetic. A formidable businesswoman, McClintock has, from time to time, added various divisions, including the Jessica McClintock designer collection, Scott McClintock contemporary dresses and sportswear (named for her son), Gunne Sax for Girls (largely adapted from Gunne Sax), and a bridal collection. In addition, there are boutiques and a signature fragrance. She is a member of the Council of Fashion Designers of America (CFDA).

McFadden, Mary

Born New York City, October 1, 1938

Awards Coty American Fashion Critics' Award *"Winnie,"* 1976; *Return Award,* 1978; *Hall of Fame,* 1979 • American Printed Fabrics Council "Tommy" Award, 1984

Until she was ten, McFadden lived on a cotton plantation near Memphis, Tennessee, where her father was a cotton broker; after his death she returned north with her mother. She attended Foxcroft School in Virginia, Traphagen School of Fashion in New York, Ecole Lubec in Paris; she studied sociology at Columbia University and the New School for Social Research.

From 1962 to 1964, McFadden was director of public relations for Christian Dior-New York. She married an executive of the DeBeers diamond firm and moved to Africa in 1964. There she became editor of *Vogue* South Africa; when it closed she continued to contribute to both the French and American editions. She also wrote weekly columns on social and political life for *The Rand Daily Mail*. She divorced, remarried in 1968, and moved to Rhodesia, where she founded Vokutu, a sculpture workshop for native artists.

McFadden returned to New York in 1970 with her daughter, Justine, and went to work for *Vogue* as Special Projects Editor. While there she designed three tunics using unusual Chinese and African silks she had collected on her travels; these were shown in the magazine as a new direction and were bought by Henri Bendel, New York. The silks were handpainted using various resist techniques; the colorings were oriental in feeling with a use of calligraphy and negative spacing that became hallmarks of her future style. Mary McFadden, Inc. was established in 1976. In addition to the very high-priced luxury collection, a bridge collection, MMCF, was introduced in 1993. Other projects have included lingerie and at-home wear, Simplicity Patterns, scarves, eyewear, furs, shoes, bed and bath designs, and upholstery fabrics.

Unique fabrics have always been a preoccupation and prints have become a "full-time hobby." Exotic colorings, extensive use of fine pleating and quilting, ropes wrapping the figure — these are recurring themes. Her poetic evening designs are best known but all her work shares the same original viewpoint, refined and sophisticated. She is a past president of the Council of Fashion Designers of America.

Mary McFadden, 1994 (top left); design from 1987 (bottom left) and signature pleating from 1976 (far right).

Meyer, Gene

Born Louisville, Kentucky, May 2, 1954
Awards Council of Fashion Designers of America (CFDA) *Men's Accessory Award,* 1994

Interested from boyhood in drawing and fashion, Gene Meyer studied for one year at the Louisville School of Art, and from 1974 to 1976 at Parsons School of Design in New York. There he earned the J.C.

Penney's Children's Design Award and two Golden Thimble Awards. It was at Parsons that he became aware of the designers who were to influence him — the great figures of the French couture of the 1940s, '50s,

and '60s, as well as Americans such as CLAIRE MCCARDELL, HALSTON, and MAINBOCHER. After Parsons, Meyer worked as assistant designer at Anne Klein Studio, and from 1978 to 1989 for GEOFFREY BEENE, where he designed everything from evening gowns to shoes. He has taught shoe design at Parsons; he is a member of the Council of Fashion Designers of America.

When Meyer opened his own business in late 1989, he chose to join the small handful of designers specializing in made-to-order, which not only required less money up front than ready-to-wear but also gave him, he felt, greater control over quality. In 1991 he turned away from making clothes and began designing scarves. This led to necktie designs and eventually to other men's furnishings such as pocket squares and boxer shorts, and to men's ready-to-wear and accessories. Although the designs are made by cutting out colored paper, his print patterns have a freehand quality. Familiar motifs — stripes, circles, plaids — are given new proportions; colors are offbeat, bright and cheerful. His designs are also licensed for dinnerware and floor and wall tiles.

Miller, Nicole

Born ca. 1952

Nicole Miller was raised in Lenox, Massachusetts, the child of an American father and French mother. She attended the Rhode Island School of Design, and as a sophomore took a year off to study dress cutting in Paris. She was designing coats at Rain Cheetahs in 1975 when she was hired as head dress designer at P.J. Walsh; in 1982 the company was renamed Nicole Miller.

She first gained attention for prints she designed for scarves, which when transferred to men's ties became an immediate hit. Boxer shorts followed and men's wear with the inimitable prints used as linings. The prints — representing everything from comic book characters to magazine covers to wine labels to brand logos — are in bold graphics and brilliant colors. In addition to her prints, Miller's design projects include clothes for women, men, boys, and girls; men's and women's swimwear, and men's underwear and

Above, Nicole Miller and (right) separates for fall 1994.

women's lingerie; also handbags, jewelry, fragrance for men and women, hosiery, eyewear, watches, shoes, and paper products. Her women's clothes are mid-priced, young and sexy, very much for party girls. The first boutique under her name opened in New York in 1986, others have followed internationally.

M

Missoni, Rosita & Ottavio

Born Ottavio (Tai); Yugoslavia, 1921
Rosita; Golasecca, Varese, Italy, November 20, 1931
Awards Neiman Marcus Award, 1973

The Missonis met in 1948 in London where Rosita was studying English and Tai was competing with the Italian Olympic track team. He was a manufacturer of track suits, a business he had begun in 1946 after his release from a prisoner-of-war camp, and his suits were part of the official Italian team uniform. She had worked for her parents in their small bedspread manufacturing company. They married in 1953, and the same year went into business together, starting with four knitting machines. Their first efforts appeared anonymously in department stores or under the names of other designers. Looking for more adventurous styling, they hired Paris designers, first EMMANUELLE KHANH and later Christiane Bailly. After a few seasons Rosita took over design of the clothes, while Ottavio created the knits.

At a time when knits were considered basics, Ottavio's startling geometric and abstract patterns created a furor, as did the first Missoni showing in Florence in 1967. For this show, Rosita had the models remove their bras so they would not show through the thin knits. The stage lighting caused the clothes to look transparent, resulting in a scandal in the Italian press. The Missonis were not invited back to Florence and decided to show in Milan, which was also nearer home.

The collections are a joint effort. Ottavio creates the distinctive patterns and stitches on graph paper and works out the colorings. He and Rosita then work together on the line. She does not sketch, but with an

Rosita and Ottavio Missoni (top left) wearing their creations and celebrating their 30 years in fashion. Bottom left, illustration from WOMEN'S WEAR DAILY, 1976.

assistant, drapes directly on the model. Shapes are kept simple to set off the knit designs — each collection is built around a few classics: pants, skirts, long cardigan jackets, sweaters, capes, dresses. Production is limited and the clothes are expensive. In addition to the women's styles, there are a limited number of designs for men and children. The patterns have been licensed for bed and bath linens and there is a line of interior decorating textiles.

In April 1978, the Missonis gave a party to celebrate the 25th anniversary of their business and their marriage. First at an art gallery in Milan and again at the Whitney Museum in New York, their designs were shown as works of art. Live mannequins in new styles posed next to dummies displaying designs from previous years, arranged without regard to chronological order. Except for miniskirts and hot pants it was nearly impossible to date the designs, effectively demonstrating their timeless character.

The three Missoni children have all been in the family business: Vittorio in charge of administration, Luca helping his father in the creation of new patterns, and Angela in public relations. In 1993, Angela went into business on her own, calling her firm Team Angela Missoni and aiming at a younger woman.

Miyake, Issey

Born Hiroshima, Japan, April 22, 1938
Awards Mainichi Newspaper Fashion Award: 1976, 1984 • Council of Fashion Designers of America (CFDA) *Special Award,* 1983 • Neiman Marcus Award, 1984

A 1964 graduate of Tama Art University in Tokyo, Miyake moved to Paris in 1965 to study at L'Ecole de la Chambre Syndicale. Starting in 1966 he spent two years as assistant designer at GUY LAROCHE, went to GIVENCHY in the same capacity, and in 1969 and 1970 was in New York with GEOFFREY BEENE. In 1970 he formed Miyake Design Studio and Issey Miyake International in Tokyo, showed his first collection in 1971 in Tokyo and New York. His first Paris showing was in 1973. Licenses range from home furnishings and hosiery to bicycles and luggage; a fragrance, *eau d'Issey*, appeared in 1994.

One of the earliest Japanese to make the move to Europe, Miyake shows regularly at the Paris *prêt-à-porter* collections. He designs a full range of sportswear, but sportswear at a far remove from the conventional. The 1968 Paris student revolution shook up his thinking, leading him to question traditional views of fashion as applied to the modern woman. At that time he began to use wrapping and layering, combining Japanese attitudes toward clothes with exotic fabrics of his own design. He has developed steadily, going his own way as a designer, and has exerted a considerable influence on younger iconoclasts. His design credo is, "the shape of the clothing should be determined by the shape of the body of the wearer, and clothing should enhance, not restrict, freedom of the body." He is known for beautiful fabrics, brilliant use of textures, and mastery of proportion.

Top left, Issey Miyake in his showroom, 1993; from 1984 (bottom left) and 1994 separates (above right).

M

Mizrahi, Isaac

Born New York City, October 14, 1961

Awards Council of Fashion Designers of America (CFDA) *Perry Ellis Award for New Fashion Talent*, 1988; *Designer of the Year:* 1989, 1991 • Dallas Fashion Award *Fashion Excellence Award*

When Isaac Mizrahi opened his own company he was twenty-six years old, having already worked on Seventh Avenue for six years. He grew up in Brooklyn, the son of a children's wear manufacturer and of a fashionable mother whose clothes came from BALENCIAGA and NORELL. He attended the Yeshiva of Flatbush, then went to the High School of Performing Arts and Parsons School of Design. At Parsons he received the Chester Weinberg Golden Thimble Award and a Claire McCardell schol-

---

Isaac Mizrahi (below) and an outfit from his 1994 collection (left).
Also see Color Plate 18.

arship. In 1981, his last year at Parsons, Mizrahi worked at Perry Ellis Sportswear, staying there until 1983, when he went to Jeffrey Banks. From there he moved to CALVIN KLEIN, leaving in June 1987 to form his own business.

Working in the luxury sportswear category, which covers everything from raincoats to evening clothes, Mizrahi is notable for a constant flow of new ideas and for his audacity —he doesn't play it safe. In the American idiom that stems from CLAIRE MCCARDELL, his clothes are young and inventive, in unexpected colors and fabrics. They are comfortable and easy with a pared-down glamour, appealing to a sophisticate with a sense of adventure in dressing and an appreciation of quality.

Mizrahi's projects now include men's wear (1990) and accessories (1992). He has designed costumes for Twyla Tharp's ballet *Brief Fling*, for Mikhail Baryshnikov, Mark Morris, Liza Minelli, and for Spike Lee's *Jungle Fever*.

He was the subject of a film, *Unzipped*, documenting the creation of his fall 1994 collection. Prepared for an AIDS benefit, it was released commercially in August 1995.

Model, Philippe

Born Sens, France, 1956

Best known in this country for his shoes, Philippe Model also designs knitwear, bags, gloves, scarves, and hats. He embarked on a fashion career in 1974 with a bachelor's degree in science and an award as "best French artisan in hatmaking." Following a three-year period styling for himself and for such designers as GAULTIER, MUGLER, and MONTANA, he established his own company in 1981. By 1993 his designs were distributed to over two hundred stores throughout the world, including three shops of his own in Paris. He also free-lances for other shoe companies. Model's designs are elegant and refined, not strident but meant to be noticed. They could be called accessory haute couture. Additional projects include men's knitwear, perfume, interior design, and costumes and shoes for opera, which is one of his passions.

Molyneux, Captain Edward

Born Hampstead, England, September 5, 1891
Died Monte Carlo, March 23, 1974

Molyneux is remembered for fluid, elegant clothes with a pure, uncluttered line, well-bred and timeless. These included printed silk suits with pleated skirts, softly tailored navy-blue suits, coats and capes with accents of bright Gauguin pink and *bois de rose*. He used zippers in 1937 to mold the figure, and was partial to handkerchief-point skirts and ostrich trims. His distinguished clientele included Princess Marina of Greece, whose wedding dress he made when she married the Duke of Kent, the Duchess of Windsor, and such stage and film personalities as Lynn Fontanne, Gertrude Lawrence, and Merle Oberon.

Sketch of Molyneux's evening gown from HARPER'S BAZAAR, June 1931.

Of French descent and Anglo-Irish birth, Molyneux got his start in fashion in 1911 when he won a competition sponsored by the London couturiere, LUCILE, and was engaged to sketch for her. When she opened branches in New York and Chicago, he went with her to the U.S., remaining until the outbreak of World War I. He joined the British army in 1914, earned the rank of captain and was wounded three times, resulting in the loss of one eye. He was twice awarded the Military Cross for bravery.

In 1919 he opened his own couture house in Paris, eventually adding branches in Monte Carlo, Cannes, and London. He enjoyed a flamboyant social life, assembled a fine collection of 18th century and Impressionist paintings, opened two successful nightclubs, and was a personal friend of many of his clients. At the outbreak of World War II he escaped from France by fishing boat from Bordeaux and during the war worked out of his London house, turning over profits to national defense. He established international canteens in London and was one of the original members of the Incorporated Society of London Fashion Designers.

In 1946 he returned to Paris and reopened his couture house, adding furs, lingerie, millinery, perfumes. Because of ill health and threatened blindness in his remaining eye, he closed his London house in 1949, and in 1950 turned over the Paris operation to Jacques Griffe. He retired to Montego Bay in Jamaica, devoting himself to painting and travel. Persuaded by the financial interests behind his perfumes to reopen in Paris as Studio Molyneux, he brought his first ready-to-wear collection to the U.S. in 1965. The project was not a success; Molyneux's elegant, lady-like designs were totally out of step with the youth-obsessed 1960s. He soon retired again, this time to Biot, near Antibes.

Art lover, war hero, bon vivant, sportsman, Molyneux gave generously of his personal resources — money, time, and energy. He worked with the British Government during World War II and later financed dressmaking schools for French workers.

Montana, Claude

Born Paris, France, 1949

Montana began designing in 1971 on a trip to London. To make money, he concocted papier-maché jewelry encrusted with rhinestones, which were featured in fashion magazines and earned him enough money to stay on for a year. On his return to Paris, he went to work for MacDouglas, a French leather firm. Montana has also designed knitwear for the Spanish firm, Ferrer y Sentis, collections for various Italian companies, including Complice, his reputation growing throughout the 1970s and 1980s. In 1989. he joined LANVIN to design their couture collection, while continuing his own ready-to-wear business. His couture designs were very well received by the press,

Montana suit, 1994 (left) and men's wear looks from 1983 (right).

praised for their elegance and modernity, but he and Lanvin parted company in 1992.

Beyond the biker's leathers that made his name, Montana has developed into one of the more interesting of the contemporary French designers, with an exacting eye for proportion, cut, and detail. He is a perfectionist, with the finesse of a true couturier and a leaning toward

Claude Montana with the bride from his 1994 collection.

operatic fantasy. His clothes feature strong, uncompromising silhouettes and a well-defined sense of drama. They are sold in fine stores in the U.S. as well as in Italy, Germany, and England. Under license, they are made and distributed in Japan.

Mori, Hanae

Born Tokyo, Japan, January 8, 1926
Awards Neiman Marcus Award, 1973

Illustration of a hand-screened print by Hanae Mori, 1975.

A graduate of Tokyo Christian Women's College with a degree in Japanese literature, Mori went back to school after her marriage to learn sewing, sketching, and designing. She opened a small boutique in the Shimjuku section of Tokyo where her clothes attracted the attention of the burgeoning Japanese movie industry. In 1955, after designing costumes for innumerable films, she opened a shop on the Ginza, Tokyo's famous shopping street, and has gone on to develop a multi-million dollar international business. Her husband Ken Mori, formerly in the Japanese

textile industry, helps manage the company.

Hanae Mori brought her couture collection to Paris in January 1977 and continues to show there each season. Her ready-to-wear is sold at fine stores throughout the world while her boutiques in many countries also sell her accessories, sportswear, and innerwear. Her fabric designs are licensed for bed and bath linens; she designed skiwear for the Sapporo Winter Olympic Games in 1972. In June 1978 she opened a building in Tokyo which houses boutiques, the couture operation, and her business offices.

While her design approach is the most international of her compatriots, Mori makes extensive use of her Japanese background in her fabrics, which are woven, printed, and dyed especially for her. She has utilized the vivid colors and bold linear patterns of Hiroshige prints, while butterflies and flowers, the Japanese symbols of femininity, show up frequently in her prints. She is best known for her cocktail and evening dresses, carefully executed in Eastern-flavored patterns, with Western styling and fit.

Morlotti, Dominique

Born Paris, France, January 8, 1950

After a classical education, Morlotti entered the fashion field professionally with Ted Lapidus, worked for another house before taking charge of men's wear at PIERRE BALMAIN in 1980. He moved on to CHRISTIAN DIOR in 1983, as designer for Christian Dior Monsieur and in 1990, while continuing with Dior, launched a collection of men's ready-to-wear under his own label.

In 1992 Morlotti moved to LANVIN as designer of both the men's department and the women's ready-to-wear. His women's clothes show the influence of his men's wear background — clean, controlled, and beautifully tailored, combining refinement and seduction. In 1995, he was replaced by Ocimar Versolato as designer for women, continuing to design the Lanvin men's wear. He planned to add women's ready-to-

Dominique Morlotti and (left) his 1994 coat for Lanvin.

wear to the men's collection he designs under his own Dominique Morlotti label, starting for fall-winter 1996.

Morris, Robert Lee

Born Nuremberg, Germany, 1947

Awards Coty American Fashion Critics' Award *Jewelry Design (for Calvin Klein)*, 1981 • Council of Fashion Designers of America (CFDA) *Special Award (for founding Artwear and for jewelry design)*, 1985; *Women's Accessory Award*, 1994 • International Gold Award, 1987

Air Force brat, jewelry designer, entrepreneur, Robert Lee Morris taught himself the basics of jewelry after graduation from Beloit College in 1969, in a commune he set up in a Wisconsin farmhouse. The house burned down while he was visiting in Vermont and he decided to stay there. His work was discovered and first exhibited by Sculpture to Wear, a gallery in the Plaza Hotel in New York City which showed the jewelry of recognized artists, including Picasso, Arp, and Miro. After Sculpture to Wear closed, he opened Artwear in 1977 in New York's Soho district, a gallery devoted solely to exhibiting and selling the work of jewelry artists, including his own. He closed the gallery in 1993.

Working in metals ranging from brass and bronze to silver and gold, Morris pioneered in the use of organic, sculptural shapes, alluding in his designs to ancient history, religion, myth, and legend. He translates timeless symbols such as crosses, daggers, keys, and fertility symbols into modern forms; there is a strong

----

Robert Lee Morris at work in his studio (below left); (below right) his flaming hair cross pendant and choker, 1994.

anthropological influence in his work. He has experimented with new patinas and iodized finishes, and has designed accessories for the runway shows of GEOFFREY BEENE, DONNA KARAN, CALVIN KLEIN, and KANSAI YAMAMOTO. Other design projects include handbags, belts, dinnerware, fragrance, pet accessories, and cosmetic containers for Elizabeth Arden.

M

Moschino, Franco

Born Abbiategrasse, Italy, ca. 1950
Died Lake Annone, Italy, September 18, 1994

Moschino's father, the owner of an iron foundry, died when his son was four. As a child, Franco amused himself by drawing; at eighteen he ran off to Milan to study art at the Accademia Belle Arte, supporting himself by work as a waiter and a model. In the early 1970s, the fashion drawings he was making for various magazines attracted the attention of GIANNI VERSACE, who used his work in a publicity campaign. He worked as a sketcher for GIORGIO ARMANI on collections for Beged'Or and Genny, and for 11 years designed for Cadette. In 1983 he launched his own company.

Moschino became known, if not universally admired, for his irreverent send-ups of conventional fashion thinking. He sent pairs of models out on the runway in the same outfit, one wearing it as it would appear in a serious fashion presentation, the other as it might be worn on the street. He distributed fresh tomatoes to the audience so they could let fly at any styles they disliked. He incorporated statements such as "Ready to Where?" and "Waist of Money" into jackets, shirts, and belts. These pieces and others of the same kind became best sellers, in part because of the gags but also because the clothes were carefully tailored and of fine quality.

He believed that fashion should be fun and that people should take clothes and wear them with their own particular style. His motto was *"De gustibus non est disputandum"* — "Who's to say what is good taste?" The paradox was, that as much as he made fun of the fashion establishment, he was in the end so successful that he became part of the very thing that he was ridiculing. At the time of Moschino's death there was, in addition to the signature collection, a secondary line called Cheap & Chic, men's wear, children's wear, jeans, accessories, perfumes, and two Milan shops. His last collection was shown after he died and was well received. With a design staff of about a dozen and licenses ranging from swimwear and lingerie to perfume and sunglasses, the firm was expected to continue in business without its founder.

Moses, Rebecca

Moses graduated from the Fashion Institute of Technology in 1977 in the same class as ANDREA JOVINE, receiving the ILGWU Designer of the Year award. For three years she designed coats and suits for Gallant International, decided the times called for sportswear and went into business for herself, starting with a huge, 200-piece collection. Her company closed in June 1982 and in August of the same year Moses went into business with Victor Coopersmith. Her first offering was a small, tightly edited group of mixable sports separates. At the time she said "You learn fast that fashion is not just pretty clothes. It's a business and if you don't understand it you go out of business, fast." She left Coopersmith in October 1986, reopened doing business as R. M. Pearlman, her married name. The Moses Collection appeared in March 1988 and included everything from sportswear to suits and blouses, from evening coats to accessories. In 1992 she broke with her Italian backers and has since been designing on a consultant basis for other firms, including the Italian firm Genny.

Mugler, Thierry

Born Strasbourg, France, 1946

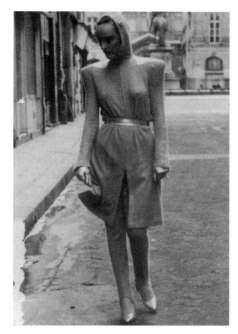

The son of a doctor, Mugler started making his own clothes while in his teens. He was part of a Strasbourg ballet company, dressed windows in a Paris boutique, moved to London in 1968. After two years he moved on to Amsterdam, then back to Paris. His first collection appeared in 1971 under the label Café de Paris; by 1973 he was making clothes under his own name.

Inventive and individual, Mugler came into prominence in the late 1970s with high-priced separates and dresses marked by broad-shouldered, defined-waistline silhouettes. While he claims to admire Madame GRÈS, his clothing appears to be descended more from the structured chic of JACQUES FATH. His tendency toward histrionic, often outrageous presentations tends to obscure what he is trying to say but he cuts a sexy, saucy

suit as well or better than anybody, and his collections are known for a sunny freshness and gaiety. As shown, the clothes are apt to appear aggressive and tough. Close up, they prove to be simple, well-cut, body-fitted, not overly detailed, the ready-to-wear more accessible than the couture. They have sold well in the U.S.

Thierry Mugler, 1987 (below); bold-shouldered designs from 1979 (top left) and 1982 (bottom left); 1994 coat (right).

Muir, Jean

Born London, England, ca. 1929
Died London, England, May 28, 1995
Awards Maison Blanche "Rex" Award, New Orleans: 1967, 1968, 1974, 1976 • Fellow of the Royal Society of Arts, 1973 • Neiman Marcus Award, 1973 • Commander of British Empire, 1983 • British Fashion Councils Hall of Fame, 1994

Of Scottish descent, Muir began her career in 1950 in the stockroom at Liberty; she sold lingerie, then became a sketcher in Liberty's made-to-measure department. In 1956 she joined Jaeger and soon became responsible for designing the major dress and knitwear collections. Starting in 1961, she designed under her own label for Jane and Jane, which she established in partnership with her husband, Harry Leuckert, a former actor, but which they did not own. In 1966 the two founded their own company, Jean Muir, Inc.

Muir was one of the breed of anti-couture, anti-establishment designers who came on the scene in the late 1950s and early 1960s. While others have disappeared, she not only survived but flourished, her clothes

Jean Muir in her studio (above) and a knit design, 1984 (right).

treasured by women looking for a low-profile way of dressing and quality of a very high order. She created a signature look of gentle, pretty clothes in the luxury investment category, flattering, and elegant, usually in the finest English and Scottish wools, cashmeres, and suedes. She was especially admired for her leathers, which she treated like jersey, and for her jerseys in tailored shapes that are completely soft and feminine, distinguished by the most refined details - the slight bell cut of a cuff, the subtle flare of a jacket.

Hard working and demanding, Muir believed in technical training as

the only serious foundation for a designer; she encouraged and worked with British art students, urging more emphasis on craft, less on art. Following her death, the company was to continue under Leukert's direction, with a design team that had worked with Muir.

N

Josie Natori
Charlotte Neuville
Norman Norell

Natori, Josie

Born Manila, Philippines, May 9, 1947

Josie Natori design from 1993.

Educated in the U.S. and the Philippines, with B.A.s in economics and music, Josie Natori was already a success in the investment banking world and a vice president at Merrill Lynch when she decided to establish her own business. Her main criterion was that whatever she did had to benefit the Philippines, her homeland. Her original plan was to make embroidered blouses to utilize the embroidery skills for which the Filipinos are famous, but at the suggestion of a Bloomingdale's buyer she switched to lingerie. The Natori Company was founded in 1977.

Sophisticated and sensuous, Natori designs rely on simple, sexy shapes in luxurious fabrics, most with the stylistic signatures of the Philippines: intricate embroidery, elaborate appliqués, lace, and feminine detailing. In addition to the gowns, there are bras and panties, robes, slippers and jewelry, with a fragrance collection in the works. She believes that "There is a whole new way of dressing with no categories and no boundaries...between dressing to entertain at home or clothes to wear out at night." The usual definitions of intimate apparel do not apply, as many women choose to wear her creations as evening gowns.

Mrs. Natori has received much recognition: the Galleon Award from her native country, the New York City Asian-American Award, the Philippine-American Foundation Friendship Award, among others. She has also served as a delegate to the Clinton Economic Summit and as Commissioner to the White House Conference on Small Business.

Neuville, Charlotte

Born Sausalito, California, June 22, 1951
Awards Mouton Cadet Young Designer Award, 1988 • *Metropolitan Home's* "Design 100" Award, 1990

After graduation from Williams College with a B.A. in art, Neuville attended Parsons School of Design, graduating in 1977. She worked as a design assistant to PERRY ELLIS and ADRIENNE VITTADINI, then as a designer for Jones New York Sport and Outlander. She set up a design studio in 1985, established her own label in 1986, closing her business in 1992. She then went as Creative Director and Vice President for Design to Cygne Designs, a large private label company supplying various firms including Ann Taylor, The Limited, and Express. Although her business venue changed from a small, tightly focused company to a large diverse firm, her fashion philosophy remains constant: it is important to have a constant flow of new, refreshing ideas at affordable prices.

Neuville is engaged in the Parsons Student/Critic Program and is a member of the Council of Fashion Designers of America (CFDA).

Norell, Norman

Born Noblesville, Indiana, 1900
Died New York City, October 25, 1972
Awards Coty American Fashion Critics' Award *First "Winnie,"* 1943; *First Return Award,* 1951; *First to be elected to Hall of Fame,* 1958 • Neiman Marcus Award, 1942 • Parsons Medal for Distinguished Achievement, 1956 • City of New York Bronze Medallion, 1972 • Pratt Institute, Brooklyn, Honorary Degree of Doctor of Fine Arts, 1962, conferred upon him in recognition of his influence on American design and taste, and for his valuable counseling and guidance to students of design, the first designer so honored.

Norell and HATTIE CARNEGIE could be said to be the parents of American high fashion, setting standards of taste, knowledge, and talent, and opening the way for the creators of today.

As a young child, Norell moved with his family to Indianapolis, where his father opened a haberdashery. From early boyhood his ambition was to be an artist and in 1919 he moved to New York to study painting at Parsons School of Design. He switched to costume design and in 1921 graduated from Pratt Institute. His first costume assignment was for *The Sainted Devil,* a Rudolph Valentino picture. He did Gloria Swanson's costumes for *Zaza,* then joined the staff of the Brooks Costume Company.

In 1924, in a move from costume to dress design, he went to work for dress manufacturer Charles Armour, remaining until 1928 when he joined Hattie Carnegie. He stayed with

Norman Norell at the Coty Fashion Critics' Award rehearsal. Dress uses hundreds of yards of silk net for the skirt, topped by a spangled white and satin halter bodice.

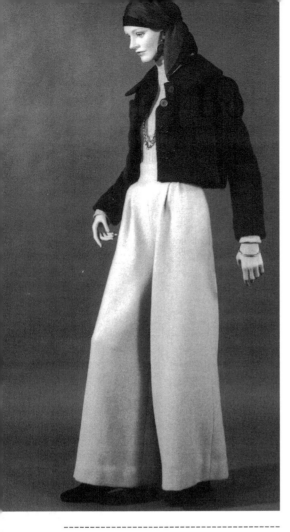

Above, Norell's brown jacket and tan pants from 1972; right, his black wool jersey dress and red wool jacket, ca. 1965. *Also see Color Plate 20.*

Carnegie until 1940, not only absorbing her knowledge and sense of fashion, but traveling with her to Europe where he was exposed to the best design of the day. In 1941 he teamed with manufacturer Anthony Traina to form Traina-Norell. The association lasted nineteen years, at which time Norell left to become president of his own firm, Norman Norell, Inc. The first collection was presented in June 1960.

From his very first collection under the Traina-Norell label, the designer established himself as a major talent, quickly becoming known for a lithe, cleanly proportioned silhouette, an audacious use of rich fabrics, for faultless workmanship, precise tailoring, and purity of line. Over the years he maintained his leadership, setting numerous trends that have become part of the fashion vocabulary and are taken for granted today. He was first to show long evening skirts topped with sweaters, initiated cloth coats lined with fur for day and evening, spangled them with sequins. He revived the chemise, introduced the smoking robe, perfected jumpers and pantsuits. His long, shimmering, sequined dresses were so simple they never went out of date, worn as long as their owners could fit into them and treasured even longer. *Norell* perfume, made in America, was a major success and is still popular.

He was a founder and president of the Council of Fashion Designers of America (CFDA). On October 15, 1972, the eve of his retrospective show at the Metropolitan Museum of Art, Norell suffered a stroke. He died ten days later. His company continued for a brief period with GUSTAVE TASSELL as designer.

O

Bruce Oldfield
Todd Oldham
Frank Olive
André Oliver
Rifat Ozbek

Oldfield, Bruce

Born London, England, 1950

Oldfield was educated as a teacher and taught English and art before turning to fashion. He attended Ravensbourne College of Art from 1968 to 1971 and St. Martin's School of Art from 1972 to 1973. He freelanced in London, designed a line for Henri Bendel, New York, and sold sketches to other designers. His first collection under his own name appeared in 1975.

Oldfield opened his own London retail shop in 1984 as the only outlet for his ready-to-wear, previously sold in the U.S. to such stores as Saks Fifth Avenue, Bergdorf Goodman, Henri Bendel. He has a considerable custom business and is especially recognized for his eveningwear, worn by British royalty and aristocracy as well as by entertainment personalities.

Oldham, Todd

Born Corpus Christi, Texas, November 22, 1961
Awards Council of Fashion Designers of America (CFDA) *Perry Ellis Award for New Fashion Talent,* 1991 • Dallas Fashion Award *Rising Star,* 1992; *Fashion Excellence Award,* 1993

Todd Oldham is the designer as showman. His desire to be a film director finds an outlet in the bravura of his showings, attended by celebrity friends and characterized by such features as rap music and drag performers on the runway. Oldham bypassed the usual routes to design prominence — by his own account he barely made it through high school, never went to design school, and taught himself pattern making. His first fashion experience was in the alterations department of a Polo/Ralph Lauren boutique.

He started in business in Dallas in 1985, two years later moved to New York. There he started Times 7, making women's shirts in basic styles with the uninhibited buttons that have become a trademark: some are

Above, Todd Oldham in 1994; right, separates from the same collection. *Also see Color Plate 11.*

antique, many are designed by his brother, Brad. In 1989 he signed with a Japanese company for a designer collection; his first formal presentation was for fall 1990, attracting considerable attention from the press and orders from stores. Branching out, Oldham signed as a design consultant with the German firm Escada in 1994 and in 1995 a license for designer jeans; he has also worked successfully with MTV. A fragrance appeared in April 1995.

Taking simple shapes, Oldham adds unconventional prints or beading and embroidery done in India, sometimes quirky and whimsical, sometimes lavish. A mixture of the commercial with the offbeat, the clothes are very well made and are sold in such bastions of the establishment as Bergdorf Goodman and Saks Fifth Avenue.

Olive, Frank

Born Milwaukee, Wisconsin, 1929

Olive studied art and fashion in Milwaukee and Chicago before going to California to try costume design. He worked in San Francisco for a dance company, came to New York in the early 1950s hoping to design for the stage. His sketches were seen by NORELL, who persuaded Olive to try his hand at hats. He apprenticed with Chanda, sold fabrics, worked in the Tatiana custom hat department at Saks Fifth Avenue, and then for Emme.

His first boutique was in Greenwich Village on MacDougal Street, where he designed hats and clothes. Even through the 1960s when hat makers "had everything going against them," Olive worked with Seventh Avenue designers on hats for their collections and also had fashionable private customers who considered a hat a necessary part of their total appearance. With the revival of interest in hats, he works with designers for their showings and continues to produce his sophisticated, original creations for fine stores and a wide-ranging list of celebrities and other fashionable women. Hats bearing the Frank Olive designer label and those marked Private Collection by Frank Olive are not only seductive and beautiful, but also notable for the quality of the materials and the meticulous craftsmanship.

Oliver, André

Born Toulouse, France, 1932
Died Paris, France, April 22, 1993

Oliver studied at L'Ecole des Beaux-Arts in Paris. After serving in the French Army he went to work for PIERRE CARDIN in 1952. He worked on the first Cardin men's wear collection, which was successful in both Europe and the U.S., and also on the couture collection. Eventually he took over design duties for both the men's and women's ready-to-wear collections, showing special affinity for soft, fluid clothes and women's evening wear.

In July 1987 Oliver was named artistic director of the Cardin couture house with total artistic control, sharing design responsibilities for the collection with Cardin. In their long association, Cardin acknowledged Oliver's design contribution with a generosity rare in the fashion world. On Oliver's death, Cardin resumed direction of both couture and ready-to-wear.

Ozbek, Rifat

Born Turkey, 1954

Ozbek arrived in England in 1970. He studied architecture for two years at the University of Liverpool then switched to fashion, studying at St. Martin's School of Art. After graduation in 1977 he worked in Italy for Walter Albini and an Italian manufacturer before returning to London and a stint designing for Monsoon, a made-in-India line. He presented his first collection under his own label in October 1984, showing out of his apartment; by his third collection he had a stylish new studio off Bond Street. In 1991 he moved his business to Milan, where he showed his collections until 1994, when he began showing in Paris.

The influence of London street fashion was evident in Ozbek's early work but translated with refinement and understatement. He has also been inspired by the way African

natives mix traditional and Western elements in their dress and by the Italian and French movies he saw when growing up. He admires the fashion greats: BALENCIAGA for cut, SCHIAPARELLI for her sense of humor, CHANEL for timelessness, YVES SAINT LAURENT for classicism. From his first collections and whatever the inspiration, his clothes have been sophisticated and controlled, without the rough-edged wackiness associated with much of London fashion.

Ozbek (near right) and (far right) coat, sweater and pants, 1994.

P-Q

Paquin
Mollie Parnis
Emeric Partos
Jean Patou
Sylvia Pedlar
Elsa Peretti
Barbara Perlin
Paloma Picasso
Robert Piguet
Gérard Pipart
Walter Plunkett
Paul Poiret
Miuccia Prada
Emilio Pucci
Mary Quant

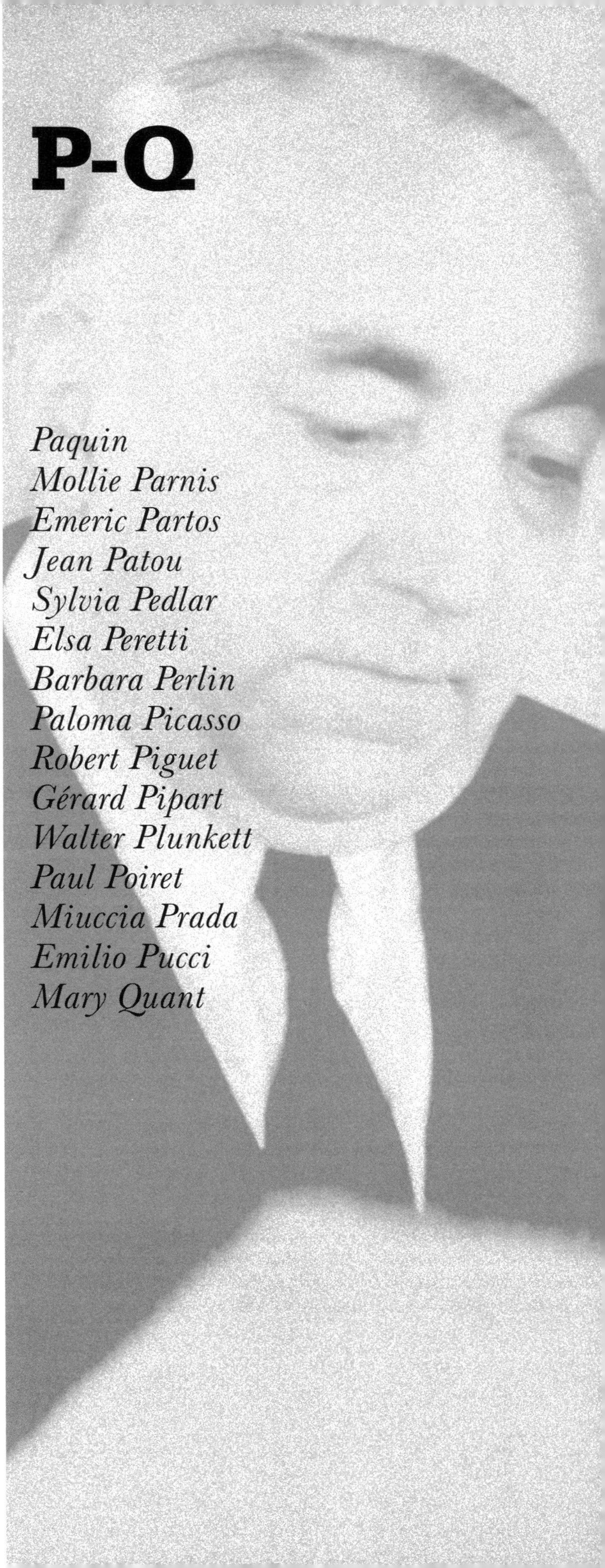

Paquin

Founded Paris, France, 1891
Closed 1956

One of the couture's great artists, Mme. Paquin trained at Maison Rouff; she opened her house with initial backing from her husband Isidore, a banker and businessman. The house of Paquin developed into a major couture force, becoming synonymous with elegance during the first decade of the 20th century.

The Paquin reputation for beautiful designs was enhanced by the decor of the establishment and the lavishness of its showings, as well as by the Paquins' extensive social life. Management of the house and its relations with its employees were

----

Two Paquin suits from 1941.

excellent, some workers remaining for more than forty years; department heads were women. The Paquin standards were so high that there was always a demand from other couture houses for any employees deciding to leave.

Mme. Paquin was the first woman to achieve importance in haute couture. She was chairman of the fashion section of the 1900 Paris Exposition and President of the Chambre Syndicale from 1917 to 1919. Hers was the first couture house to open foreign branches — in London, Madrid, Buenos Aires. She was the first to take mannequins to the opera and the races, as many as ten in the same costume. The house was credited with being the first to make fur garments that were soft and supple.

She was a gifted colorist, a talent especially evident in her glamorous and romantic evening dresses. Other specialties were fur-trimmed tailored suits and coats, furs, lingerie, blue serge suits with gold braid and buttons; accessories were made in-house. She claimed not to make any two dresses exactly alike, individualizing each model to the woman for whom it was made. Customers included queens of Belgium, Portugal, and Spain, as well as the actresses and courtesans of the era. The first perfume was produced in 1939, after Mme. Paquin had retired and sold her house to an English firm, an event that occurred in 1920. She died in 1936.

Parnis, Mollie

Born New York City, March 18, 1905
Died New York City, July 18, 1992

Mollie Parnis produced flattering, feminine dresses and ensembles for the well-to-do woman over thirty, emphasizing becomingness in beautiful fabrics, a conservative interpretation of current trends. She felt that good design did not mean dresses that had to be thrown away each year or that went out of date. The boutique collection followed the same principles but with a moderate price tag and the Studio collection, started in 1979, aimed at a younger woman.

The eldest of five children of Austrian immigrants, Parnis always knew she'd have to work for whatever she got. After leaving high school, she went to work in a blouse showroom as an assistant saleswoman and was soon designing. In 1933 she and her husband Leon Livingston, a textile designer, opened a ready-to-wear firm, Parnis-Livingston. From there she went on to become one of the most successful businesswomen on Seventh Avenue, heading a firm which grew into a multimillion dollar enterprise, Mollie Parnis Inc. She closed her business briefly in 1962 when her husband died, but reopened it again three months later. She shut down again in 1984 but quickly became bored and went back to work full time at Chevette Lingerie, owned by her nephew, Neal Hochman. Her first loungewear collection was for fall 1985.

A formidable organizer, Parnis routinely managed to administer her business, plan and edit collections with her design staff, supervise selling, advertising and promotion, and follow through on her civic interests, all in a day that began at 10 a.m. and seldom went beyond 5 p.m. She collected art and was also a noted hostess with a special affinity for journalists and politicians.

Parnis was well known as a philanthropist. She contributed scholarships to fashion schools and gave vest-pocket parks to both New York City and Jerusalem, which have honored her for her outstanding contributions to the two cities. She was a founder of the Council of Fashion Designers of America and served on the Board of Directors.

Partos, Emeric

Born Imré; Budapest, Hungary, March 18, 1905
Died New York City, December 2, 1975
Awards Coty American Fashion Critics' Award *Special Award (furs)*, 1957

Partos studied art in Budapest and Paris, jewelry design in Switzerland. He served in the French Army during World War II and in the underground movement, where he met Alex Maguy, a couturier who also designed for the theater. After the war, Partos joined Maguy, designing coats and also ballet costumes.

In 1947 he went to work for his friend CHRISTIAN DIOR, whom he considered the greatest living designer. He stayed with Dior for three years creating coats and suits, was wooed away in 1950 to be design consultant for Maximilian Furs. He designed furs for Maximilian for five years before moving to Bergdorf

P

Goodman to head their fur department, remaining there until his death twenty years later.

At Bergdorf's Partos was given a free hand with the most expensive pelts available. He showed a sense of fantasy and fun with intarsia furs such as a white mink jacket inlaid with colored mink flowers, and mink worked in two-tone stripes or box shapes. He designed coats that could be shortened or lengthened by zipping sections off or on, further innovated with silk or cotton raincoats used as slipcovers for mink coats. In addition, he was noted for subtle, beautifully cut classics in fine minks, sables, broadtail. One of the first to treat furs as ready-to-wear, Partos was a prolific source of ideas, noted for his theatrics but also as a master of construction and detail. He was a favorite with conservative customers as well as with personalities such as Barbra Streisand.

Coat by Partos of Foulke-processed Matara Alaska fur seal, 1975.

Patou, Jean

Born Normandy, France, 1887
Died Paris, France, March 1936

Patou's first couture venture was a small house called Parry, which opened just in time for World War I to cancel his first major showing scheduled for August 1914. After four years in the army as a captain of Zouaves, he reopened under his own name in 1919. The house was an immediate success with private clients; the clothes had simplicity and elegance and looked as if they were intended to be worn by real women, not just by mannequins.

An admirer of American business methods, Patou introduced daily staff meetings, a profit-sharing plan for executives, and a bonus system for mannequins. He was also an excellent showman: he brought six American models to Paris in 1925, using them alongside his French mannequins; instituted gala champagne evening openings; had a cocktail bar in his shop; chose exquisite bottles for his perfumes. These included *Moment Suprême* and *Joy*, promoted as the world's most expensive perfume. He was among the first couturiers to have colors and fabrics produced especially for him, is given credit for being the first in 1929 to return the waistline to its normal position and to lengthen skirts, which he dropped dramatically to the ankle.

One of many on Chanel's hate list, he returned her dislike with interest, on occasion complaining to fashion magazines of what he considered their favoritism toward her in covering collections. After Patou's death, the house remained open under the direction of his brother-in-law, Raymond Barbas, with a series of resident designers including: MARC BOHAN (1953-1957), KARL LAGERFELD (1958-1963), Michel Goma (1963-1974), ANGELO TARLAZZI (1973-1976), Roy Gonzalez (1976-1981), and CHRISTIAN LACROIX (1981-1987).

Patou's printed chiffon evening gowns (near right) and day dress with longer skirt (far right), both with waistlines at their normal locations, 1929.

P

Pedlar, Sylvia

Born New York City, 1901
Died New York City, February 26, 1972
Awards Coty American Fashion Critics' Award *Special Award (lingerie),* 1951; *Return Special Award (lingerie),* 1964 • Neiman Marcus Award, 1960

Intending to become a fashion illustrator, Pedlar studied at Cooper Union and the Art Students League. Instead, she took a design job and discovered her true direction; in 1929 she founded her own firm, Iris Lingerie.

Pedlar was a gifted designer working in a field where the temptation for vulgarity is strong. She specialized in soft, pure shapes that a woman of any age could wear, and to her, comfort was the most important consideration. Among her more famous creations were sleep togas, the bed-and-breakfast look, and the bedside nightdress for the woman who sleeps in the nude but wants a little something decorative to wake up to. Iris Lingerie was known for exquisite fabrics and laces, also perfectionist workmanship, as well as for the originality and beauty of the designs. Its uniqueness was recognized internationally and European designers such as DIOR, GIVENCHY, and PUCCI would visit Iris to buy Pedlar models. Pedlar closed her firm after forty-one years because "the fun has gone out of our work now." She was married to William A. Pedlar, whom she survived by one year.

Peretti, Elsa

Born Florence, Italy, May 1, 1940
Awards Coty American Fashion Critics' Award *Special Award (jewelry),* 1971 • Award for Outstanding Contribution to the Cultured Pearl Industry of America and Japan, 1978 • The Fashion Group "Night of the Stars" Award, 1986

The daughter of a well-to-do Roman family, Peretti earned a diploma in interior design and worked briefly for a Milanese architect. In 1961 she went to Switzerland, then moved on to London and started modeling. She was seen by models' agent Wilhelmina, who suggested that Peretti come to New York. In New York she worked for a handful of top houses, including HALSTON and OSCAR DE LA RENTA.

In 1969 Peretti designed a few pieces of silver jewelry, which Halston and GIORGIO SANT'ANGELO showed with their collections. These witty objects — a heart-shaped buckle, pendants in the form of small vases, a silver urn pendant that holds a fresh flower — were soon joined by a horseshoe-shaped silver buckle on a long leather belt and other designs in horn, ebony, and ivory. She also designed the containers for Halston's fragrance and cosmetics lines. In 1974 she began working with Tiffany

Elsa Peretti in 1992.

& Co., the first time in twenty-five years the company had carried silver jewelry. Among her much-copied designs are a small, open, slightly lopsided heart pendant that slides on a chain, and Diamonds-by-the-Yard, diamonds spaced at intervals on a fine gold chain. Her perfume, a costly scent in a refillable rock crystal bottle, is carried by Tiffany and she has also designed desk and table accessories for the firm.

Peretti is influenced in her work by a love of nature and inspired by Japanese designs. She works in Spain and New York, has travelled to the Orient to study semiprecious stones. Prototypes for the silver and ivory designs are made by artisans in Barcelona, the crystal pieces are produced in Germany. As a celebration of her fiftieth birthday and fifteen-year association with Tiffany,

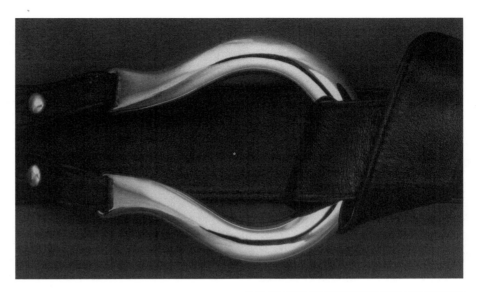

Peretti horseshoe buckle, sterling silver with leather belt, c. 1970.

Peretti was honored by the Fashion Institute of Technology in April 1990 with a retrospective exhibit of her work. It was called "Fifteen of My Fifty with Tiffany."

Perlin, Barbara

Born Los Angeles, California, March 4, 1961

Credited with revolutionizing boys' clothing, Barbara Perlin studied design at the University of California at Los Angeles, graduating in 1983. After a year in her own company, she established Monkey Wear in 1985, of which she is owner and designer. She produces boys' dress clothes and sportswear in the better price range, sold at fine department stores and specialty boutiques. She lists her design philosophy as "mini adultwear." Perlin has been honored by her industry for her designs for boys and toddler boys, and in 1993 was named as one of the top one hundred women-owned businesses in Los Angeles.

Picasso, Paloma

Born Paris, France, April 19, 1949

Not only is she the daughter of two artists, one of them a monumental figure in 20th-century art, Paloma Picasso is also a successful designer in her own right. She is at the center of a burgeoning business, involved in everything from jewelry to perfume and cosmetics to home design. Her first jewelry collection was in 1971 for the Greek firm, Zolotas. In 1972 she met Rafael Lopez-Cambil, an Argentine-born playwright, for whose plays she designed sets and costumes. After their marriage in

Paloma Picasso (left) with a hand-bag design, 1991 and (below) 18-karat gold jewelry for Tiffany & Co.

1978, Picasso's husband devised a strategy aimed at establishing her name and work in the world of design. In 1980, Paloma Picasso joined Tiffany & Co. with a collection of gold jewelry set with precious and semi-precious stones. Her style is marked by bold, sensuous shapes, sometimes inspired by urban graffiti, sometimes of a Renaissance opulence. In addition to cosmetics and perfume, her other U.S. design projects include top-of-the-line accessories and a less-expensive, more casual accessories collection, eyewear, tablewear, fabrics and wall coverings. There are boutiques in Paris, Japan, and Hong Kong.

Piguet, Robert

Born Yverdon, Switzerland, 1901
Died Lausanne, Switzerland, February 22, 1953

Piguet was the son of a Swiss banker and was expected to follow his father's profession. Instead, he went to Paris in 1918 to study design. He trained with the conservative Redfern and the brilliant POIRET, then opened his own house on the rue du Cirque. In 1933 he moved his salon to the Rond Point where he designed little himself, relying largely on the work of free-lance designers. A number of designers, including DIOR and GIVENCHY, worked for him at the outset of their careers; JAMES GALANOS spent three months there working without salary. Dior said, "Robert Piguet taught me the virtues of simplicity...how to suppress!" Piguet's clothes appealed to a younger customer: perfectly cut, tailored suits with vests, black-and-white dresses of refined simplicity, afternoon dresses, fur-trimmed coats especially styled for petite women. He had a flair for dramatic effects, which he used to advantage in his extensive work for the theater. In the U.S. his influence was greater on manufacturers than on custom design.

An aristocratic, solitary man, Piguet was super-sensitive and changeable, with a love of intrigue. Elegant and charming, he was a connoisseur of painting, literature, and music. He suffered from ill health throughout his life, retiring to seclusion after each showing to recuperate from the strain of his profession. He closed his house in 1951.

Pipart, Gérard

Born Rueil-Malmaison, near Paris, France, November 25, 1933
Awards Chambre Syndicale de la Couture Parisienne *Golden Thimble,* 1987

Pipart started in fashion at the age of sixteen, selling sketches to PIERRE BALMAIN and JACQUES FATH, and working for both for brief periods. He sketched for GIVENCHY, was assistant to BOHAN when at PATOU and during the short time he had his own house. After completing his two-year army service, he free-lanced in ready-to-wear, produced an unsuccessful couture collection in 1963, and returned to ready-to-wear with great success. In 1963 he succeeded JULES-

----

Gérard Pipart's bolero and trousers for Nina Ricci, 1994.

FRANCOIS CRAHAY as chief designer at NINA RICCI, where he has remained ever since.

Pipart has never learned to cut or sew. He works from detailed sketches and makes corrections directly on the *toiles.* Preferring simplicity, he detests gimmicks, and is known for young, spirited, elegant clothes, a very Parisian sophistication. He has been compared to Jacques Fath, whom he considers "the most wonderful personality I ever knew or saw." Among other designers, he greatly admires Givenchy and Balenciaga.

P

Plunkett, Walter

Born Oakland, California, 1902
Died March 8, 1982

Walter Plunkett was best known for period costumes, and particularly for *Gone With the Wind*. In the mid 1920s, after law studies and an attempt at an acting career, he took a job in the wardrobe department at FBO Studios (later RKO), then specializing in Westerns. Within a few months, the studio changed its name and Plunkett, without formal training, became its costume designer. He was soon put in charge of setting up a design department. In 1931, after a series of potboilers, he got his first important assignment, *Cimarron*, starring Irene Dunne. In 1933, he did *Flying Down to Rio*, the first film in which Fred Astaire danced with Ginger Rogers, and the same year costumed Katharine Hepburn in *Little Women*, the beginning of a long collaboration with the actress.

In addition to his design duties, Plunkett was manager of the RKO wardrobe department, and was in charge of payroll, budget, hiring and firing. Underpaid and overworked, he quit RKO in 1935, returning the next year at Katharine Hepburn's request to do her costumes for *Mary of Scotland*. From then until his retirement in 1966, he worked on his own terms as a free-lance designer, dressing some of the greatest stars in some of Hollywood's most ambitious productions, sometimes sharing design duties with other designers such as TRAVIS BANTON and IRENE SHARAFF.

Poiret, Paul

Born Paris, France, April 20, 1879
Died Paris, France, April 28, 1944

Fascinated by the theater and the arts, Poiret was himself a flamboyant and theatrical figure, shrewd and egotistical, spending fortunes on fetes, pageants, and costume balls, and on decorating his homes. He designed costumes for actresses such as Rejane and Sarah Bernhardt; his friends included Diaghilev, Leon Bakst, Raoul Dufy, ERTÉ, and Iribe.

As a youth, while apprenticed to an umbrella maker, Poiret taught himself costume sketching. He sold his first sketches to Mme. Cheruit at Raudnitz Soeurs, joined Jacques Doucet in 1896, and spent four years working for WORTH before opening his own house in 1904.

Considered by many to be one of the greatest originators of feminine fashion, Poiret was extravagantly talented, with a penchant for the bizarre and dramatic. While his forte was costume, the modern silhouette was to a great extent his invention. He freed women from corsets and petticoats and introduced the first, modern, straight-line dress. Yet he also invented the harem and hobble skirts, so narrow at the hem that walking was almost impossible. His minaret skirt, inspired by and named after a play he costumed, spread worldwide. Influenced by Diaghilev's Ballets Russes, he designed a Russian tunic coat, straight in line and belted, made from sumptuous materials. His taste for orientalism showed up in little turbans and tall aigrettes with which he adorned his models, and he scandalized society in 1911 by taking mannequins to the

Auteuil races dressed in *jupes culottes*, also called Turkish trousers.

He established a crafts school where Dufy for a while designed textiles, and was the first couturier to present a perfume. In 1912 he was the first to travel to other countries to present his collection, taking along twelve mannequins. In 1914, along with WORTH, PAQUIN, Cheruit, CALLOT SOEURS, he founded the Protective Association of French Dressmakers and became its first president.

Unable to adjust his style to changes brought about by World War I, Poiret went out of business in 1924. Bankrupt and penniless, he was divorced by his wife in 1929. Four years later he was offered a job designing ready-to-wear but his attitude toward money was so irresponsible that the venture failed. He took bit parts in movies, wrote his autobiography, moved to the south of France. He spent his last years in poverty and died of Parkinson's disease in a charity hospital. Poiret's extraordinary imagination and achievements flowered in the brilliant epoch of Diaghilev and Bakst. It influenced the taste of two decades.

Top left, Poiret consults with Joan Crawford at the MGM studios on his designs for her film OUR MODERN MAIDENS, 1929. Above, "Sorbet," a lampshade tunic, illustrated in LA GAZETTE DU BON TON, September 1913. *Also see Color Plate 15.*

Prada, Miuccia

Born — Italy, ca. 1950

Awards Council of Fashion Designers of America (CFDA) *International Award,* 1993

Miuccia Prada came into design through her connection with her family's firm, Fratelli Prada, since 1913 a maker of leather goods of the highest quality. A committed member of the Communist Party during and immediately after her university years, she resisted joining the family business until 1978 when she took over direction from her mother. Her first success was a black nylon backpack; later ones were handheld bags of the same fabric, washable, flexible, tough, and soft. Her first ready-to-wear collection was for fall 1989 and in 1994, Prada took part in the New York showings. Her clothes, much coveted by the more advanced fashion press, are described as supremely comfortable — nothing on the hanger but coming to life on the body — designed for nonconformists. There is a younger, less expensive Miu-Miu collection and a small line of men's clothes and accessories.

Coat from 1994 Prada collection.

Pucci, Emilio

Born Marchese di Barsento, Naples, Italy, 1914
Died Florence, Italy, November 29, 1992
Awards Neiman Marcus Award, 1954 • Council of Fashion Designers of America (CFDA) *Special Award,* 1990

Descendant of Russian nobility and member of the Italian aristocracy, Pucci was educated in Italy and the U.S. He was a member of his country's Olympic Ski Team in 1933-1934, and officer of the Italian Air Force during World War II, remaining in the service after the war. Even after he became involved with fashion, he retained his interest in politics and in the 1950s served two terms in the Italian Chamber of Deputies.

Pucci got into fashion by accident when ski clothes he was wearing in Switzerland caught the attention of photographer TONI FRISSEL. Snug and close-fitting, they were among the first made of stretch fabrics; when the Frissel photographs appeared and attracted attention, he decided to market the clothes. However, it was his simple chemises of thin silk jersey that made him a favorite of the international jet set in the 1960s. These dresses, wrinkle-resistant and packable in no space at all, were beloved by fashion professionals everywhere, and the brilliant signature prints in designs inspired by heraldic banners were copied in every price range. In 1990 there was a worldwide revival of interest in the prints. Design projects have included accessories, sportswear, underwear, fragrances for women and men, porcelain, sheets, bath linens, rugs, airline uniforms. After his death, his family planned to carry on the business.

Pucci beachwear, 1965. *Also see Color Plate 3.*

Quant, Mary

Born Blackheath, Kent, England, February 11, 1934
Awards O.B.E. (Order of the British Empire)

Quant was a leading figure in the youth revolution of the 1950s and 1960s — her awareness of social changes and understanding of the young customer made her a celebrity and helped put London on the fashion map. She studied at Goldsmith's College of Art in London

Quant (right in photo) with one of her "Jolly Sailor's" from her spring 1972 collection. Hardly typical of her early work it is white gabardine with navy-framed neckline.

where she met Alexander Plunket Greene, whom she later married. In 1955, with a partner, she and her husband opened a small boutique called Bazaar, the first on King's Road in London's Chelsea district. At the start they sold clothes from outside designers, but soon became frustrated by the difficulty of getting the kind of clothes they wanted from manufacturers. Mary Quant then began to make her own designs, spirited, unconventional, and instant hits with the young, probably because they were totally unlike anything their mothers had worn, or ever would wear.

She began on a small scale, running up her designs in her own flat, but her fame grew along with that of "swinging London." By 1963 she had opened a second Bazaar, had moved into mass production with her less expensive Ginger Group, and was exporting to the U.S. With her husband as business partner she had become a full-scale designer and manufacturer. She designed for J.C.Penney in the U.S. and for Puritan's Youthquake promotion; a highly successful cosmetics line was established in 1966 and sold worldwide. Her autobiography, *Quant by Quant*, was published the same year. In the 1970s, while no longer a fashion innovator, she added to her business with licenses for jewelry, carpets, household linens, men's ties, and eyeglasses. In 1973-1974, an

exhibition, "Mary Quant's London," was presented at the London Museum.

In approximately 1964 she became interested in makeup, and in 1966 launched a cosmetics line with the colors presented in a paint box and crayon kit. With Japanese partners she has since developed a complete body and skin-care collection as well as makeup, sold in freestanding shops in Japan that also sell clothes, swimsuits, and lingerie. There is a showcase shop in London and shops are scheduled for other parts of the Far East, Australia, and New Zealand.

Quant is given credit for starting the Chelsea or Mod Look of the mid 1950s and the miniskirts of the late 1960s. Whether or not she actually originated the mini, she certainly popularized it in England and the U.S. She initiated ideas that are now commonplace, using denim, colored flannel, and vinyl in clothes that only the young could wear and showing them with colored tights. For her innovative showings she used photographic mannequins rather than regular runway models and had them dance down the runway. Whatever her final stature as a designer, she was a pivotal figure in a fashion upheaval that reflected major social changes taking place around the world. Forty years later, a number of designers in Europe and the U.S. showed a Mod Look in their fall 1995 collections.

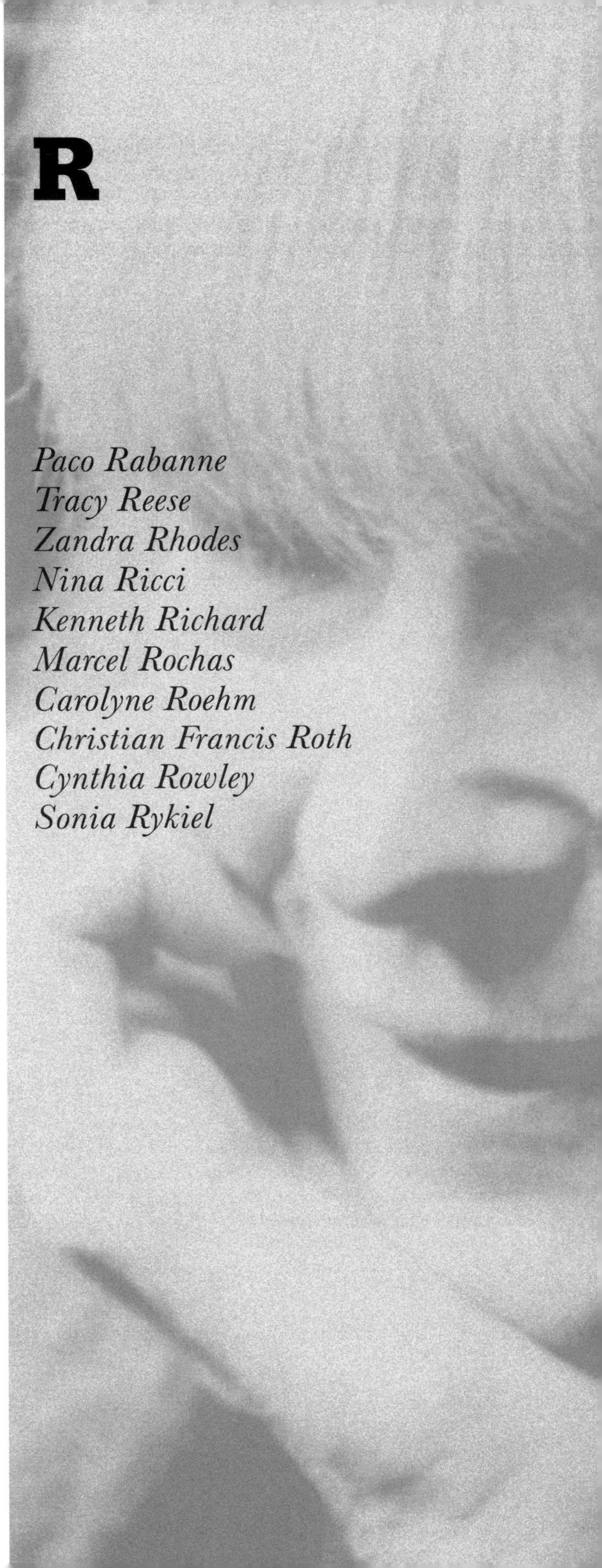

R

Paco Rabanne
Tracy Reese
Zandra Rhodes
Nina Ricci
Kenneth Richard
Marcel Rochas
Carolyne Roehm
Christian Francis Roth
Cynthia Rowley
Sonia Rykiel

Rabanne, Paco

Born San Sebastian, Spain, 1934

Rabanne's family fled to France in 1939 to escape the Spanish Civil War — at the time, his mother was head seamstress at BALENCIAGA in San Sebastian. In Paris, Rabanne studied architecture at the Ecole Supérieure des Beaux-Arts, began designing on a free-lance basis —handbags, shoes, plastic accessories, and embroideries.

In 1966 he attracted attention with dresses made of plastic discs linked with metal chains, accessorizing them with plastic jewelry and sun goggles in primary colors. He continued the linked-disc theme in coats of fur patches and dresses of leather patches, and also used buttons and strips of aluminum laced with wire. In 1970 he was one of the first to use fake suede for dresses. He likes to combine unlikely materials, and has designed coats of knit and fur, dresses made of ribbons, feathers, or tassels, linked for suppleness. While hardly wearable in the conventional sense, his experiments have had considerable influence on other designers. He has two successful fragrances, *Calandre* for women, *Paco* for men.

Left, Paco Rabanne in 1965 with long and short versions of his signature dresses made of linked plastic discs. Below, an African-inspired gown from Rabanne's 1994 couture collection.

204

Reese, Tracy

Born Detroit, Michigan, February 12, 1964

Tracy Reese specializes in young designer sportswear — separates, knits, and dresses for women with careers and busy, varied lives. Her influences range from historical costume to modern technology, with further inspiration from dance, theater, and music. The clothes combine a playful spirit with shape and structure.

After childhood weekends spent in art classes, Reese took a fashion design class at Cass Technical High School in Detroit. She attended Parsons School of Design on scholarship, graduating in 1984, and in the same year went to work as design assistant to Martine Sitbon. In 1987, she opened her own company, which two years later fell victim to the recession, then worked at PERRY ELLIS as designer for the Portfolio division. When the division closed the following year she free-lanced briefly with GORDON HENDERSON; from 1990 to 1995 she was design director at Magaschoni under the label Tracy Reese for Magaschoni. After leaving Magaschoni in January 1995, Reese designed an exclusive line for The Limited and in the same year started her own company, Tracy Reese Meridian.

Tracy Reese (below) and one of her designs from 1993 collection.

R

Rhodes, Zandra

Born Chatham, England, 1942
Awards British Clothing Institute Designer of the Year, 1972

Zandra Rhodes came into view in the late 1960s when she established her own dress firm. She had planned to be a textile designer and had set up her own print works and a shop to sell dresses made of her fabrics, then decided she was better able to interpret them than anyone else. She was undoubtedly right — her designs are of a piece with the fabrics they are made of — unmistakably hers, as eccentric and original as she is.

Rhodes's father was a truck driver; her mother was head fitter at WORTH in Paris before her marriage and afterward a senior lecturer in fashion at Medway College of Art. Zandra studied textile design and lithography at Medway, then went to the Royal College of Art, graduating in 1966. By 1969 she was producing imaginative clothing, for the most part working in very soft fabrics that float and drift — chiffon, tulle, silk — handscreened in her own prints. These have included Art Deco motifs, lipsticks, squiggles, teddy bears, stars, teardrops, big splashy patterns.

She has always made news, alternately criticized and applauded. She has finished edges with pinking shears, made glamorized Punk designs with torn holes or edges fastened with jeweled safety pins, sleeves held on by pins or chains. Her champagne bubble dresses drawn in at the knee with elastic were acclaimed, and flounced hems finished with uneven scallops and adorned with pearls or pompoms or braid have become a signature. The clothes are beautiful and romantic, a fantasy of dressing that's entirely distinctive and personal.

Rhodes's own appearance is as imaginative as her clothing: hair dyed in a rainbow of colors — magenta and bright green, for

Zandra Rhodes (top left): champagne bubble dress, 1978 (bottom left); loose top and flowing pants, 1994 (right).

example — and such makeup effects as eyebrows drawn in one continuous arc. Unlike many of her contemporaries from 1960s "swinging London" who have faded from the scene, she has continued to thrive and take risks. Other design projects have included sportswear, sleepwear, textiles, sheets, rugs. She pays frequent visits to the U.S. where her clothes are sold in fine department and specialty stores.

Ricci, Nina

Born Turin, Italy, 1883
Died Paris, France, November 29, 1970

Ricci moved to Paris with her family when she was twelve. As a child she made hats and dresses for her dolls, and at the age of thirteen was apprenticed to a couturier. At eighteen she was the head of an atelier, and at twenty-one a premier stylist. In 1932, encouraged by her jeweler husband, Louis, she opened her own house.

Ricci was a skilled technician who usually designed by draping the cloth onto the mannequin, but she was not an originator of fashion ideas. The house specialized in graceful clothes for elegant women who preferred to be in fashion rather than in advance of it; trousseaux were a specialty. Typical of her attention to elegance and detail is the Ricci perfume, *L'Air du Temps*, presented in a Lalique flacon with a frosted glass bird on the stopper. She was one of the first in the couture to show lower-priced models in a boutique. Since 1945 the house has been managed by her son Robert. In 1951 JULES-FRANCOIS CRAHAY became Mme. Ricci's collaborator on the collections; he took over complete design responsibility in 1959. He was succeeded in 1963 by GÉRARD PIPART.

Richard, Kenneth

Born Anchorage, Alaska, June 8, 1965

Combining a talent for tailoring with a romantic vision and unswerving conviction, Kenneth Richard tries to make each collection evolve naturally from the previous one and each piece work with everything else; he does not believe that fashion should change direction drastically each season. A dedicated reader, he takes his inspiration from literature, often

Kenneth Richard's separates, 1994.

giving a collection a theme borrowed from a favorite book.

After graduation from Miami University in Ohio, Richard worked as a buyer at Macy's then went on to the Fashion Institute of Technology, graduating in 1990. He spent a year with Dianne B. as associate designer, opened his own business in 1991. His clothes fall into the sportswear category and are in the better price range.

Rochas, Marcel

Born Paris, France, 1902
Died Paris, France, March 14, 1955

Rochas, who was known for young, daring designs, opened his couture house in 1924 in the Faubourg Saint-Honoré, moved to the avenue Matignon in 1931. According to legend, his reputation was made by the scandal that ensued when eight women wore the identical dress from his house to the same party, each having thought she had the exclusive.

Rochas had an abundance of fantastic, original ideas. He used as many as ten colors in combination, was lavish in his use of lace, ribbon, and tulle. He showed a broad-shouldered military look before SCHIAPARELLI, long skirts and an hourglass silhouette several years before the New Look, and invented a waist-cincher. His perfume, *Femme*, was packaged in black lace and became a classic. He maintained a boutique for separates and accessories, also designed for films. In 1951 he published *Twenty-five Years of Parisian Elegance, 1925-50*.

In March 1990, Parfums Rochas announced a new luxury ready-to-wear line with Peter O'Brien as designer. The firm had not been in the apparel business in France since the death of Rochas in 1955 although they had licensed a Japanese line.

Roehm, Carolyne

Born Kirksville, Missouri, ca. 1952

After nine years as assistant to OSCAR DE LA RENTA, Roehm went into business in 1985 with the backing of her financier husband, Henry Kravis. She brought a young, feminine look to "benefit dressing" with sleek suits and glamorous evening clothes; her customer was the woman in her thirties with a heavy social schedule. She closed her business in 1991, relaunching her career as an upscale catalogue business. After her divorce, Roehm produced a 1993 holiday catalogue exclusively for Saks Fifth Avenue; a holiday boutique at Saks the same year that included shoes and accessories was highly successful. Despite these successes, she again closed her business at the end of February 1994.

Roth, Christian Francis

Born New York City, February 12, 1969

Roth combines an antic wit with iron determination. A fashion prodigy, he knew when he was eleven years old that he wanted to make clothes and at sixteen, while attending the Fashion Institute of Technology at night, served a summer apprenticeship with KOOS VAN DEN AKKER. At Van den Akker, first as apprentice then as a full-time employee, he learned pattern making, sewing, draping, and other design skills, working by day and going to school at night. Through a special program at F.I.T., he finished high school in 1987, then studied at Parsons at night for a year; in 1988 he produced his own small first collection in the Koos Van den Akker design studio. Van den Akker eventually helped him start his own business. His first full showing was for fall 1990.

Roth aims to make clothes "without attitude — with wit, fun and quality," for "a woman with a sense of humor and an American Express card." Young and buoyant, his designs could be described as a cross between cartoon and couture,

----

Left, Roth outfits from fall 1994; above right, the designer with the bride at this showing.

with high-spirited appliqués on basic shapes and quality of a very high order. Because such quality is never cheap, the clothes are also expensive.

Twice nominated for the Mouton Cadet Young Designer Award, Roth was disqualified both times because he was not yet twenty-one. In 1989, along with RALPH LAUREN, MICHAEL KORS, and ISAAC MIZRAHI, he was honored by Cotton Inc. at their annual "Celebration of American Style" fashion show.

R

Rowley, Cynthia

Born Highland Park, Illinois, July 29, 1958

Awards Council of Fashion Designers of America (CFDA) *Perry Ellis Award for New Fashion Talent,* 1994

Cynthia Rowley was just seven when she made her first dress. She was also precocious in business, selling her first eight-piece collection, a senior design project, while still at the Art Institute of Chicago. After a few seasons in Chicago, she moved to New York in 1983; five years later she incorporated her business with herself as sole owner. While truly interested in the money side of the business, she still retains a creative wackiness that shows in fresh and fanciful clothes, witty takeoffs on high-priced fashion that are still functional and affordable. In addition to ready-to-wear, where her greatest strength lies in dresses, she also designs footwear. Other projects include clothes for films and costumes for choreographer Hilary Easton. Rowley has also served as critic at the Fashion Institute of Technology.

Above, Cynthia Rowley, 1994; right, white-collared and cuffed jacket with lace-trimmed skirt.

Rykiel, Sonia

Born Paris, France, 1930
Awards The Fashion Group "Night of the Stars" Award, 1986

Rykiel began in fashion by making her own maternity dresses, continued to design for friends after her child was born, and then for her husband's firm, Laura. The first Sonia Rykiel boutique opened in 1968 in the Paris department store Galeries Lafayette, followed by her own boutique on the Left Bank.

She has made her name with sweaters and sweater looks in apparently endless variations, usually cut seductively close to the body, softened with detail near the face. Her mannequins are, of necessity, the thinnest in Paris. When her daughter became pregnant, Rykiel put pregnant-looking mannequins in over-sized sweaters, and added a new line of children's wear when her granddaughter reached an age to appreciate them.

Rykiel presents a dramatic appearance, with a pale complexion and a mane of red hair, almost invariably dressed in black. Her Paris apartment is also in black, brightened by colored neon lights and a menagerie of friendly stuffed animals.

Top right, Rykiel in 1985; knit separates from 1984 (bottom right): designs for fall 1994 (far right).

R

S

Yves Saint Laurent
Fernando Sanchez
Jil Sander
Giorgio Sant'Angelo
Tanya Sarne
Arnold Scaasi
Jean-Louis Scherrer
Elsa Schiaparelli
Jean Schlumberger
Mila Schön
Ronaldus Shamask
Irene Sharaff
Simonetta
Adele Simpson
Willi Smith
Luciano Soprani
Mark Spirito
Per Spook
Stephen Sprouse
Cynthia Steffe
Walter Steiger
Anna Sui
Sybilla
Viola Sylbert

Saint Laurent, Yves

Born Oran, Algeria, August 1, 1936
Awards Neiman Marcus Award, 1958 • Council of Fashion Designers of America (CFDA)
Special Award, 1981

Son of a well-off family of Alsatian descent, Saint Laurent left Oran for Paris to study art. When he was seventeen his sketch won first prize in a fashion contest sponsored by the International Wool Secretariat; at nineteen he was introduced to CHRISTIAN DIOR, who hired him immediately. On Dior's death in 1957, Saint Laurent was chosen to succeed him as head designer of the house, a post he held until called up for military service in 1960. In the Army, he became ill and was discharged after three months. Saint Laurent opened his own couture house in January 1962. He began his Rive Gauche *prêt-à-porter* in 1966, established his men's wear in 1974. Since then his name and YSL initials have been licensed for everything from sweaters to bed and bath linens, eyeglasses to scarves to children's clothes. His fragrances include *Y*,

**Right, Yves Saint Lauren, 1994;
above, design from 1987 collection.**

Rive Gauche, *Opium*, *Paris*, and *Champagne*.

Within twenty years Saint Laurent reached the peak of his profession and established himself as the king of fashion, alternately taking inspiration from the street and exerting influence on it. Above all, he understood the life of the modern woman, designing simple, wearable day clothes with a slightly masculine quality in beautiful fabrics, and for evening, clothes of unabashed luxury and sensuousness, enriched with fantasy and drama.

In 1983 the Costume Institute of the Metropolitan Museum of Art mounted a twenty-five year retrospective of his work, the first time a living designer had been so honored. In it could be seen many of the highlights of his career, from the 1958 Trapeze of his first Dior collection, to such classics as the pea coat and the Smoking, and the fantasy of the rich peasants. It was possible to track his increasing mastery and polish, and the blending of vision and rigorous dedication that led to his preeminence.

Saint Laurent leaves the business side of his ventures to his partner, Pierre Bergé, who has described him as "born with a nervous breakdown." He remains devoted to the ideal of haute couture and the art of dressing women sensibly yet with a sense of poetry.

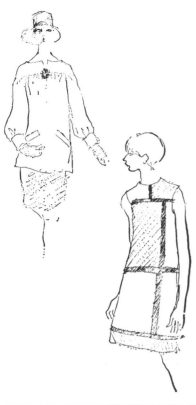

Some Saint Laurent career highlights. From the left, Fisherman's
shirt, 1962; Trapeze, 1965;
Mondrian dress, 1987; See-through
blouse, 1968; Longuette, 1970.
Below from left to right: evening
tuxedo, 1978; bow-tied evening
gown, 1979; evening jacket and
ankle-length skirt, 1994. *Also see
Color Plate 4.*

Sanchez, Fernando

Born Spain, 1930s

Awards Coty American Fashion Critics' Award *Special Award (lingerie):* 1974, 1977, 1981; *Special Award (fur design for Revillon),* 1975 • Council of Fashion Designers of America (CFDA) *Special Award (homewear and lingerie),* 1981

His mother was Belgian, his father Spanish, and Sanchez received his design education in France, making him a complete international. He studied at L'Ecole Chambre Syndicale de la Couture Parisienne in Paris and was a prize winner in the same International Wool Secretariat competition in which SAINT LAURENT won an award. He interned at NINA RICCI before joining Saint Laurent at CHRISTIAN DIOR, where Sanchez designed lingerie, accessories, and sweaters for the Dior European boutiques.

He first came to New York to do the Dior American lingerie line and for several years commuted between Paris and New York. At the same time he began designing furs for Revillon, working for them for twelve years and becoming known for such unconventional treatments as his hide-out mink coats with the fur on the inside. He opened his own lingerie company in 1973, re-signed with Revillon in 1984 to produce a collection for the U.S.

Sanchez's first successes for his own firm were glamorous lace-trimmed silk gowns, followed by camisole tops, boxer shorts, bikini pants. He went on to develop lingerie on the separates principle, mixing colors, lengths and fabrics to make a modern look. In 1983 he extended the same ideas into the men's market, and in 1987 introduced eveningwear for women, possibly in response to the fact that much of his lingerie was already migrating to public venues. He calls his designs "homewear," although many styles can also be worn on the beach or for dancing. Seductive, luxurious, trend-

Fernando Sanchez (top left) and designs for men and women, 1994.

setting, and expensive, his lingerie has been given credit for reviving interest in extravagant underthings.

Sander, Jil

Born Wesselburen, Germany, November 27, 1943

The preeminent designer working in Germany today, Jil Sander has in recent years also become a major international fashion force. Raised in Hamburg, she studied textile design, spent two years in the U.S., and worked as a fashion journalist before deciding to create fashion herself. She opened a boutique in Hamburg-Poseldorf in 1968 when such shops did not exist in Germany, and worked as a fashion designer for a major fabric manufacturer.

When she began, the only German with an international design reputation was KARL LAGERFELD, and he was working in Paris. From the start her objective has been clear design without decoration, proportions refined to perfection, lines and cuts that are out of the ordinary. Sander brings a subtle fluidity to the most severe tailoring, her suits are extraordinary for their combination of authority and sensuality, her dresses have a purity and sexy austerity. Her demands for the highest quality in materials and craftsmanship are matched by her prices.

As astute in business as she is creative in design, Sander has built her company by logical steps from 1969, when she founded a sales organization for future fashion and accessories collections that did not yet exist, to 1973 when she produced her first collection, to a public stock offering in 1989. Cosmetics were added in 1979, leathers and eyewear in 1984. There are boutiques in Europe, Japan, Hong Kong, and the U.S.; the flagship store opened in Paris in 1993. Sander has been much

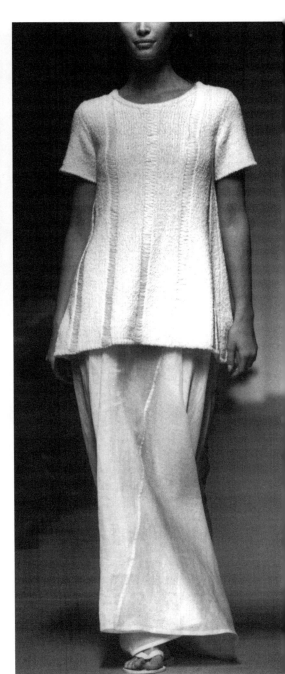

Top left, fur-trimmed coat; bottom left, Jil Sander; right, tunic and skirt, 1993.

honored in Europe for her accomplishments, both in design and in business.

S

Sant'Angelo, Giorgio

Born Florence, Italy, May 5, 1936

Died New York City, August 29, 1989

Awards Coty American Fashion Critics'Award *Special Award (fantasy accessories and ethnic fashions),* 1968; *"Winnie,"* 1970 • Council of Fashion Designers of America (CFDA) *Special Award (contribution to evolution of stretch clothing),* 1987

Sant'Angelo spent much of his childhood in Argentina and Brazil where his family owned property. He trained as an architect and industrial designer before going to France to study art, came to the U.S. in 1962. His art background runs the gamut from high to pop, including studies with Picasso and work with Walt Disney. Moving to New York in 1963, he free-lanced as a textile designer and stylist and served as design consultant on various environmental projects. This brought him into contact with the DuPont Company, resulting in commissions for experiments with Lucite® as a material for the home and for fashion accessories. The accessories were a sensation and received extensive press coverage.

While Sant'Angelo's initial success was with accessories, his first clothing collection of gypsy dresses and modern patchwork clothes was extremely influential. He went on to break more ground with clothes of ethnic inspiration, particularly a collection dedicated to the American Indian. Always very much an individualist, he was interested in new uses for materials such as stretch fabrics incorporating spandex. His designs were for those who like their clothes a bit out of the ordinary and he maintained a couture operation for a roster of celebrity customers. He also did film costumes.

His many businesses included Sant'Angelo Ready-to-Wear (1966), di Sant'Angelo, Inc. (1968), women's ready-to-wear and separates under the Giorgio Sant'Angelo label, as well as extensive licenses. These covered swimwear and active sportswear, furs, tailored suits, outerwear, men's outerwear, neckties and men's wear, environmental fragrances, sheets and domestics, furniture, rugs and carpets. After his death the business went on for several years with Martin Price as designer; the licensing operation continues.

Designs by Sant'Angelo from 1977 (right) and 1984 (below).

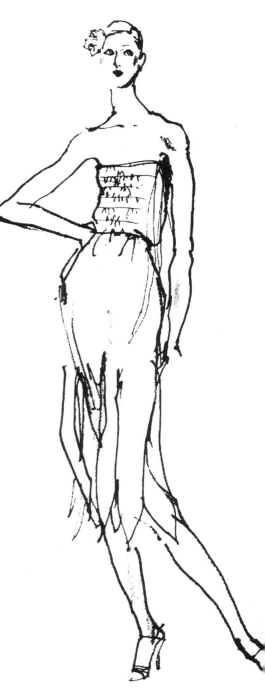

Sarne, Tanya

Born Tanya Gordon; England, ca. 1948
Awards British Export Award, Women's Wear, 1993

Tanya Sarne and her collaborators design for their label Ghost in the subversive spirit of English fashion of the sixties and seventies — not surprising, since Sarne was a fashion model in the late sixties. Her uncontroversial aim is to make unstructured, comfortable, feminine clothes that each woman can wear and adapt to please herself — her means are another matter. Using an unconventional manufacturing technique, Ghost's designs are made from "grey" unfinished cloth specially developed so that when washed and dyed, the pieces shrink up to 50 percent. This achieves exceptional density and texture. Multi-functional and easy the result is fashion in a moderate price range for independent, free-spirited women who don't want to look like everyone else.

Sarne attended the University of Sussex, where she took her B.A. with honors in History and Social

Tanya Sarne (above) and a design for Ghost, 1994 (right).

Psychology. After her marriage broke up she was sales manager for Entrepais, an ethnic fashion company (1976-1978), then chairman and designer for Miz (1979-1984). From 1984 to the present, she has held the same posts at Ghost Ltd. Future plans for the company include a fragrance.

S

Scaasi, Arnold

Born Montreal, Canada, May 8, 1931
Awards Coty American Fashion Critics' Award *"Winnie,"* 1958 • Neiman Marcus Award, 1959 • Council of Fashion Designers (CFDA) *Special Award (extravagant evening dress),* 1987 • Dallas Fashion Award *Fashion Excellence Award*

The son of a furrier, Scaasi finished high school then left Canada for Melbourne, Australia to live with an aunt who dressed at CHANEL and SCHIAPARELLI. With her disciplined approach to dress and living she was an important influence. He began art studies in Australia then returned to Montreal to study couture. There he designed clothes for private clients and saved enough money to go

to Paris to continue his fashion studies at the L'Ecole de la Chambre Syndicale de la Couture Parisienne. On their completion, he traveled in Europe for a year then returned to Paris and went to PAQUIN as an apprentice.

Arriving in New York in 1955, Scaasi worked as a sketcher for CHARLES JAMES, designed coats and suits for a Seventh Avenue manufacturer, and in 1957, on a shoestring, opened his own wholesale business. In 1960 he bought and renovated a Manhattan town house for his ready-to-wear presentations, then switched to couture in 1963. Another twenty years elapsed before he returned to ready-to-wear with Arnold Scaasi Boutique, for cocktail and evening dresses.

One of the last of the true custom designers in the U.S., Scaasi is known for spectacular eveningwear in luxurious fabrics. He has designed costume jewelry, furs, sweaters, men's ties. Licenses have also included a bridge dress line, loungewear, bras and panties, furs, bridalwear, and a better-priced line of sportswear and knits.

Left, evening gown, 1993 and right, Scaasi with the bride from the same collection.

Scherrer, Jean-Louis

Born Paris, France, 1936

Scherrer trained as a dancer at the Paris Conservatory but turned to fashion when he injured his back at the age of twenty. The sketches he made during his recuperation were shown to DIOR and he became Dior's assistant at the same time as SAINT LAURENT. It was at Dior that he learned the intricacies of cutting and draping that are the basis of his craft. After Dior's death and the choice of Saint Laurent as his successor, Scherrer left the house, found a backer, and in 1962 opened his own business. Since then he has had considerable success in both couture and ready-to-wear, with

Scherrer evening pyjamas, 1994.

elegant clothes in the more elaborate couture tradition.

In April 1990, majority control of the company was acquired by a holding company, which in December 1992, citing heavy losses, dismissed Scherrer and replaced him with Eric Mortensen as couturier and artistic director. The shock waves caused by the firing of a founding designer while still alive and well, one who owns a 10 percent share of the company, were considerable. Scherrer sued and negotiated a cash settlement and permission to resume designing, but did not recover the use of his name. He intended to find a design post with another company.

Schiaparelli, Elsa

Born Rome, Italy, September 10, 1890
Died Paris, France, November 13, 1973
Awards Neiman Marcus Award, 1940

The daughter of a professor of Oriental languages, Schiaparelli studied philosophy, also wrote poetry and articles on music. She married and moved to the U.S., where she lived until the end of World War I. When her husband left her in 1920, she returned to Paris with no money and her daughter Marisa to support.

Her involvement in fashion came about in the 1920s, when a sweater she designed for herself and had knitted by a member of the Paris Armenian colony was seen and ordered by a store buyer. By 1929 Schiaparelli had established Pour le Sport on the rue de la Paix; by 1930 she was doing an estimated yearly

business of 120 million francs from twenty-six workrooms employing two thousand people. In 1935 she opened a boutique on the Place Vendôme for sport clothes, later added dresses and evening clothes.

Like her great rival, CHANEL, Schiaparelli was not simply a dressmaker but also a part of the brilliant

S

artistic life of Paris in the 1920s and 1930s. She had close friendships with artists, among them JEAN SCHLUMBERGER, who also designed jewelry for her, Salvador Dalí, with whom she worked on designs for prints and embroideries, Jean Cocteau, Kees van Dongen, and MAN RAY. Highly creative and unconventional she shocked the couture establishment by using rough "working class" materials for evening, colored plastic zippers as decorative features, huge ceramic buttons in the shape of hands or butterflies or whatever caught her fancy, and wildly imaginative accessories.

She showed little "doll hats" shaped like a lamb chop or a pink-heeled shoe, gloves that extended to the shoulders and turned into puffed sleeves. She fastened clothing with colored zippers, jeweler-designed buttons, padlocks, clips, dog leashes. She showed witty lapel ornaments in the shape of hands, teaspoons, hearts, or angels, and amusing novelties such as glowing phosphorescent brooches and handbags that lit up or played tunes when opened. She was spectacularly successful with avant-garde sweaters worked with tattoo or skeleton motifs.

Schiaparelli changed the shape of the figure with broad, padded shoulders inspired by the London guardsman's uniform, a silhouette that lasted until the advent of the New Look. Both a genius at publicity and a trailblazer, she commissioned a fabric patterned with her press clippings then used the material in scarves, blouses, and beachwear, and she pioneered the use of synthetic fabrics. Her signature color was the brilliant pink she called "shocking," the name she also gave to her famous fragrance in its dressmaker dummy bottle.

Following the fall of France, she came to the U.S., where she sat out the war. She returned to Paris after Liberation and reopened her house in 1945. While she continued in business until 1954, she never regained her prewar position. She continued as a consultant to companies licensed to produce hosiery, perfume, and scarves in her name, living out her retirement in Tunisia and Paris.

Schiaparelli's irreverence and energy could result in vulgarity but she also produced clothes of great elegance and extreme chic. Perhaps her major contribution was her vitality and sense of mischief, a reminder not to take it all too seriously.

Schlumberger, Jean

Born Mulhouse, Alsace-Lorraine, June 24, 1907
Died Paris, France, August 29, 1987
Awards Coty American Fashion Critics' Award *Special Award (the first given for jewelry)*, 1958
• Chevalier of the National Order of Merit of France, 1977

Schlumberger was the son of an Alsatian textile magnate, who sent him to America while still in his teens to work in a New Jersey silk factory. On his return to France he abandoned textiles and took a job with an art publishing firm, becoming part of the inventive Paris world of fashion, art, and society. His first jewelry designs were clips made from china flowers found in the Paris flea market. These pieces attracted the attention of ELSA SCHIAPARELLI, who admired their originality and commissioned him to design costume jewelry. He progressed to gold and precious stones and developed an influential international clientele, which included the Duchess of Windsor and Millicent Rogers.

Schlumberger went into the Army at the advent of World War II, was evacuated from Dunkirk, and eventually came to the U.S. He designed clothes for Chez Ninon, opened an office on Fifth Avenue,

then joined the Free French and served in the Middle East. After the war, he returned to New York in 1946 and opened a salon on East 63rd Street. In 1956 he joined Tiffany & Co. where he had his own salon on the mezzanine, reached by a private elevator.

Schlumberger fantasy jewel for Tiffany. Bird of platinum, 18-karat gold and pavé diamonds, perched on a citrine rock.

Schlumberger has been equated with Fabergé and Cellini. His virtuosity, imagination, and skill brought forth exuberant fantasies: a sunflower of gold, emeralds, and diamonds with a 100-carat sapphire heart planted in a clay pot set in a gold cachepot; snowpea clips of malachite and gold; moss-covered shells dripping with diamond dew. He revived the Renaissance technique of enamelwork, adopted the custom of mixing semiprecious stones with diamonds, used enamel and stones as if they were paint. His work was the subject of a lecture at the Metropolitan Museum of Art and a loan exhibition of jewelry and objects at the Wildenstein Gallery, New York.

Schön, Mila

Born Trau, Dalmatia, Yugoslavia

Schön's parents left Yugoslavia for Trieste, Italy, to escape the Communists; she moved on to Milan where she led a privileged life until a change in financial circumstances forced her to earn a living. In 1958 she opened a small workroom to copy Paris models, in 1965 showed her own designs in Florence.

Although based in Milan, Schön for many years showed her couture and deluxe ready-to-wear in Rome. She became well known for beautifully cut suits and coats in double-faced fabrics and for exquisitely beaded evening dresses. She moved with the times toward a softer, more fluid look but always upheld the highest standards of design and workmanship. Men's wear, swimsuits, and sunglasses were later additions.

In August 1991, Schön showed her couture collection in Paris. As of 1994, she was honorary president of the firm and a new design team consisting of Marisa Modiana, Romy Godwin, and Christophe Lemaire, was hired to give the house a fresh, younger attitude. Each of the three has worked for a major Paris or Milan firm.

Shamask, Ronaldus

Born Amsterdam, Holland, 1946
Awards Coty American Fashion Critics' Award *"Winnie,"* 1981 • Council of Fashion Designers of America (CFDA) *Men's Wear Designer of the Year,* 1988

One of a small group of designers with a strong architectural bent, Shamask arrived in New York City in 1971 by a circuitous route — Australia, London, and Buffalo, New York. Essentially self-taught, he moved with his family to Australia when he was fourteen, worked in the display department of a large Melbourne department store, and in 1967 moved to London where he worked as a fashion illustrator and began to paint. Then came Buffalo and three years designing sets and costumes for ballet, theater, and opera, then New York City and design commissions from private clients for interiors and clothing.

Shamask next undertook a twenty-piece collection in muslin, cut from patterns that were actually life-sized blueprints. In 1978 he and a friend, Murray Moss, formed a partnership called Moss and opened a pristine, all-white shop and "laboratory" on Madison Avenue. The first presentation in 1979 consisted of the original muslin collection executed in three weights of linen. The clothes, which combined strong architectural shapes with beautiful fabrics, were cut with the utmost precision and exquisitely made. They were praised for their purity of design and exceptional workmanship.

In 1986, starting with two coats, he branched out into men's fashion and by spring 1988 was turning out a full line of men's wear. These, made in Italy of European fabrics, were individual pieces intended to be chosen separately and put together in matched or unmatched outfits. The women's business closed in the early 1990s but Shamask continues in men's wear. In 1994 he designed costumes for the modern dancer Lucinda Childs.

Sharaff, Irene

Born Boston, Massachusetts, ca. 1910

Died New York City, August 16, 1993

Awards Motion Picture Academy Awards: *An American in Paris* (color; for scenery and costume for ballet sequence), 1951; *The King and I*, 1956 (color); *West Side Story*, 1961 (color); *Cleopatra* (color; with Nino Novarese and Renie), 1963; *Who's Afraid of Virginia Woolf*, 1966 (black and white)

Sharaff adjusts costume for Elizabeth Taylor for CLEOPATRA, 1963.

In a remarkable career that spanned more than sixty years, Irene Sharaff designed costumes for sixty stage productions and forty films, in addition to work for ballet and television, and even fashion illustration. Her first work, in 1928 while she was still in art school, was for Eva Le Gallienne's Civic Repertory Theatre in New York; her last film costumes were for *Mommie Dearest* in 1981; the last for the stage were for *Jerome Robbins' Broadway* in 1989. Sometimes she designed sets as well as costumes. In the process, she earned two Donaldson awards and a Tony for her stage work, and for film received five Oscars and fifteen Academy Award nominations.

Sharaff studied at the New York School of Fine and Applied Arts and the Art Students League, working part time; by 1931 she had enough money saved to spend a year in Paris where she attended the Grande Chaumière. Even more important than school was her exposure to the theatrical designs of painters Christian Bérard, Pavel Tchelitchew, and André Derain, and her discovery of the French couture with its emphasis on perfection in both design and execution. All had a great influence on her subsequent work. For ten years after her return she worked with great success on the New York stage, moving to Hollywood in 1942 to work on musicals at MGM. Ultimately, her designs ranged from *Meet Me in St. Louis* to *Who's Afraid of Virginia Wolf*, from *Madame Curie* to *Hello Dolly* and *The Taming of the Shrew*. Most of her work was at MGM although she did a number of movies for other studios.

With rare versatility, Sharaff understood theater, dance, and film, and was at home in both modern and period settings, realism and fantasy. Her meticulous research translated into a combination of authenticity and function; the costumes were never overpowering and were exquisitely made.

S

Simonetta

Born Duchess Simonetta di Cesaro; Italy, before World War I

One of the Italian couturiers who gained international notice after the Second World War, Simonetta began designing clothes in the 1930s and became a leading dressmaker in Rome. After her marriage in 1952 to ALBERTO FABIANI, also a designer, they continued in their separate establishments before moving to Paris in 1962 and opening a joint business called Simonetta et Fabiani. Their clothes were well received critically but the business was not a success and Fabiani moved back to Rome in 1966, Simonetta remaining in Paris. She had her own boutique, worked for a while at Chloé at the same time as KARL LAGERFELD. Her designs were in the couture tradition, graceful, elegant, and feminine.

After her divorce, she left Paris and the fashion business, later traveled to India on a religious pilgrimage, and set up a leper colony there before returning to Rome.

Simpson, Adele

Born Adele Smithline; New York City, December 8, 1903
Died Greenwich, Connecticut, August 25, 1995
Awards Neiman Marcus Award, 1946 • Coty American Fashion Critics' Award *"Winnie,"* 1947 • National Cotton Fashion Award, 1953

The youngest of five daughters of an immigrant tailor, Simpson started designing at seventeen while attending Pratt Institute at night. When she was just twenty-one she replaced her older sister, Anna, as head designer for an important Seventh Avenue manufacturer and was soon earning the then staggering sum of $30,000 annually and traveling regularly to Paris for her firm. She married Wesley Simpson, a textile executive, in 1927; worked for another firm Mary Lee until 1949, when she took over the company and named it for herself.

Simpson always saw her purpose as dressing women, not just selling dresses — her clothes were pretty, feminine, and wearable and could be coordinated into complete wardrobes. They were known for excellent design and impeccable quality, intended for women of discerning taste, conservative but not old fashioned. When Donald Hopson took over the designing of the collection, a younger, more fluid look developed. An exhibition, "1001 Treasures of Design," items collected by Adele and Wesley Simpson, was presented by the Fashion Institute of Technology in 1978. The family sold the firm in 1991.

Smith, Willi

Born Philadelphia, Pennsylvania, February 19, 1948
Died New York City, April 17, 1987
Awards Coty American Fashion Critics' Award *Special Award,* 1983

One of a number of black designers who came to the fore in the late 1960s, Smith was the son of an iron-worker and a housewife. He originally intended to be a painter, studied fashion illustration at the Philadelphia Museum College of Art, and in 1965, at the age of seventeen, arrived in New York with two scholarships to Parsons School of Design. He got a summer job with ARNOLD SCAASI, spent two years at Parsons, during which he free-lanced as a sketcher. He then worked for several manufacturers, including Bobbie Brooks, Talbott, and Digits.

After several failed start-up attempts, WilliWear Ltd. was established in 1976 with Laurie Mallet as president, Smith as designer and vice president. His innovative, spirited clothes — described as classics with a sense of humor — were fun to wear as well as functional, brought fashion verve to the moderate price range. Collections were consistent in feeling from one year to another so that new pieces mixed comfortably with those from previous years. Preferring natural fibers for their comfort and utility, he designed his own textiles

and went to India several times a year to supervise production of the collections. Men's wear was introduced in 1978 "to bridge the gap between jeans and suits." Smith also designed for Butterick Patterns, did lingerie and loungewear, textiles for Bedford Stuyvesant Design Works, furniture for Knoll International. He was a sponsor of the Brooklyn Academy of Music's "Next Wave" festival and designed one of the 1984 dance presentations. His name continues to be licensed — WilliWear for sportswear (essentially weekend wear) and Willismith Loungewear.

Right, designer Willi Smith and (left) separates from 1978.

S

Soprani, Luciano

Born Reggiolo, Italy, 1946

Soprani was born into a farming family, studied agriculture, and farmed for a year and a half before breaking away in 1967 to become a designer. His first job was with MaxMara, the Italian ready-to-wear firm, where he stayed for eight years, plus another two years free-lance. He free-lanced for a number of firms until 1981, when he signed his first contract with Basile to design their women's line. After a year he was given the added responsibility for the men's wear. He has also designed for Gucci. His first collection under his own name appeared in 1981. Essentially, Soprani works with strong shapes, enlivened by interesting details. His clothes are original and lively and appeal to sophisticated women worldwide.

Spirito, Mark

Born Elizabeth, New Jersey, November 24, 1954

Mark Spirito began making jewelry in 1977, the year after his graduation from Cooper Union where he studied painting, photography, and sculpture. He opened his own business in 1979. In addition to jewelry design, he has accessorized collections for DONNA KARAN and LOUIS DELL'OLIO at Anne Klein, designed sportswear for Benetton (1985-1986).

Spirito's jewelry is modern and graphic, somewhat talismanic, combining richness with minimalism. He combines precious metals with semi-precious stones for their color and because he feels they bring a healing quality to the piece. His wide-ranging design influences include fashion designers of the past and present, for example, CHANEL, CHARLES JAMES, and REI KAWAKUBO, as well as Gothic and Renaissance architecture and Chinese culture. Byzantine, Celtic, and tribal motifs are recurring themes but he strives to evoke a feeling of the ancient without mimicking a particular style. His fine jewelry is sold at top specialty stores around the U.S.

Spook, Per

Born Oslo, Norway, 1939
Awards Chambre Syndicale de la Couture Parisienne, *Golden Needle*, 1978; *Golden Thimble*, 1979

One of the Paris designers who brings a distinctive personal twist and a more casual look to fashion, Per Spook arrived in Paris at eighteen to study art at L'Ecole des Beaux-Arts, then switched to L'Ecole de la Chambre Syndicale de la Couture Parisienne to learn fashion design. His first job was at DIOR; he freelanced at SAINT LAURENT and Féraud and in 1977 opened his own house. His first collections were enthusiastically praised for a fresh, lively view of shape and color. Both his couture and his ready-to-wear are designed with a relaxed sportswear sensibility.

Like many small couture houses, Spook operates on a thin financial edge and has had to close his business more than once.

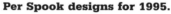

Per Spook designs for 1995.

Sprouse, Stephen

Born Ohio, 1954

Sprouse burst triumphantly on the New York design scene in 1983, and at the time was considered the archetypal "downtown" designer (as opposed to Seventh Avenue). He disappeared from view just as dramatically only five seasons later. His first collection of chemises and separates was reminiscent of the 1960s, except that the pieces were printed or painted in graffiti-like designs or sequined and colored in a Day-Glo spectrum. He was particularly admired for the perfection of his coats. Since June 1987, when he resurfaced with a new backer, Sprouse has been in and out of business, sometimes working on a custom basis. Despite the brevity of his appearances, his fashion influence has been extensive, particularly the hot, wild colors of the early collections.

At the center of the rock music scene of the 1980s, Sprouse saw his designs worn by a number of rock stars, including Debbie Harry, Iggy Pop, and Mick Jagger. In 1995, in his role as costume curator, he recreated the era for the opening of the Rock-and-Roll Hall of Fame and Museum in Cleveland, Ohio.

S

Steffe, Cynthia

Born Molville, Iowa, June 30, 1957

Steffe grew up in Molville, came to New York and studied at Parsons School of Design (1978-1982). She won many awards during her four-year stay: the Claire McCardell Scholarship her sophomore year, an award for the most original children's wear design, the Willi Smith Silver Thimble award during her junior year, and both the Donna Karan Gold Thimble and 1982 Designer of the Year awards in her senior year. In 1982, while still in school, she started working as a design assistant at Anne Klein & Co., leaving there in October 1983 to design for Spitalnick under the label Cynthia Steffe for Spitalnick & Co. She left in 1988 to form her own company with her husband, Richard Roberts.

Essentially Steffe's clothes are luxury sportswear, combining ease, comfort, and sophistication, with an emphasis on unusual and original fabrics. Her goal is timeless clothes with a distinctly American viewpoint; she sees her customer as a knowledgeable professional woman who needs clothes of elegance and style for both her public and private lives.

Steiger, Walter

Born Geneva, Switzerland, February 7, 1942

Walter Steiger's elegant shoes for women and men are sold in fine stores internationally. Apprenticed as a shoemaker at St. Gall, Switzerland (1958-1961), he moved on to design shoes in Paris (1962) and London (1962-1967). He established his own label in 1968 and opened his first Paris shop in 1974. He has since added accessories to his design projects.

Sui, Anna

Born Dearborn Heights, Michigan, ca. 1955
Awards Council of Fashion Designers of America (CFDA) *Perry Ellis Award for New Fashion Talent*, 1992

Anna Sui's restless curiosity and eclectic, unconventional approach to dress made their appearance early: while still in junior high she sewed many of her own clothes, even appliquéing some of the dress fabrics onto her shoes. In her teens she began to save clippings from fashion magazines in what she calls her "Genius Files" (she still refers to them). After high school she enrolled at Parsons School of Design in New York where she became close friends with Steven Meisel, soon to be a top fashion photographer. Sui left Parsons in her second year to work for a junior sportswear company, designing everything from swimsuits to knits and moonlighting as a stylist for Meisel's fashion shoots. Torn between styling and designing, she continued to design and in 1980, after selling six of her pieces to Macy's, opened her own business. Her first runway show was in April 1991. By September 1993 Sui had moved her business out of her apartment into quarters on Seventh Avenue and opened two boutiques, one in New York's SoHo, the second in Los Angeles.

Described as a mixture of hip and haute, romance and raunch, the clothes are a tribute to their designer's imagination and are popular with a younger crowd, although Sui maintains that anyone with an adventurous spirit can wear them. A great deal of their effect is based on the free-wheeling way she puts them together, "It's like playing dress-up; you keep adding things and taking bits away." She works hard to maintain a moderate price structure so that her young customers will continue to be able to afford her designs and says that the most important thing she's learned is to ship the clothes on time with good quality.

Anna Sui (bottom right) and two of her designs for 1994.

S

Sybilla

Born Sybilla Sorondo; New York City, 1964

The daughter of a Polish-born mother (a painter and couturiere) and an Argentine-diplomat father, Sybilla was seven when her father moved the family to Madrid. At seventeen, she went to Paris to study drawing, and while there spent a year at SAINT LAURENT, where she learned to sew and discovered her desire to design. Returning to Spain, she showed her first collection in October 1983, to an audience consisting largely of her own friends and a few small shops. In 1985 she signed her first agreement with a manufacturer and designed her first shoe collection; in 1987 she opened a boutique in Madrid. Although based in Madrid,

From Sybilla's 1992 collection.

she has shown at Milan, one of a group of enthusiastic and creative young designers. She has also had her own shop in Paris for bed and bath designs.

Devoid of frills and elaborate ornamentation, Sybilla's style is discreet yet sexy. The clothes are adventurous in cut, marked by intricate, gracefully spiraling seaming and a strong sculptural sense, both original and spirited. The best known of the current crop of Spanish designers, she has been compared to the great BALENCIAGA.

Sylbert, Viola

Born New York City
Awards Coty American Fashion Critics' Award *Special Award (fur design)*, 1975

Now best known for her furs, Sylbert's first successes were in leathers, sportswear, and sweaters. The daughter of a dress manufacturer, she earned her B.A. and M.Sc. in retailing at New York University. Her first love was writing, her second theatrical costume design, but to earn a living she became a fashion coordinator at Ohrbach's and gradually worked into designing.

Recognizing early that "I'm not a 9-to-5 person," she began to free-lance, enjoying the stimulation of working with different people on different kinds of projects. She established a routine of sketching and research at home, travels to Europe and Hong Kong.

In 1970, at the suggestion of Geraldine Stutz of Henri Bendel, she began designing furs, easy and casual

in feeling with a unique fit and unusual colorings. She is fascinated with textures and the visual variations of different materials. In addition to furs she is identified with outerwear and knitwear, has designed "trend collections" of jersey dresses and men's sweaters for the Wool Bureau. She has also ventured into loungewear, children's clothes, and accessories.

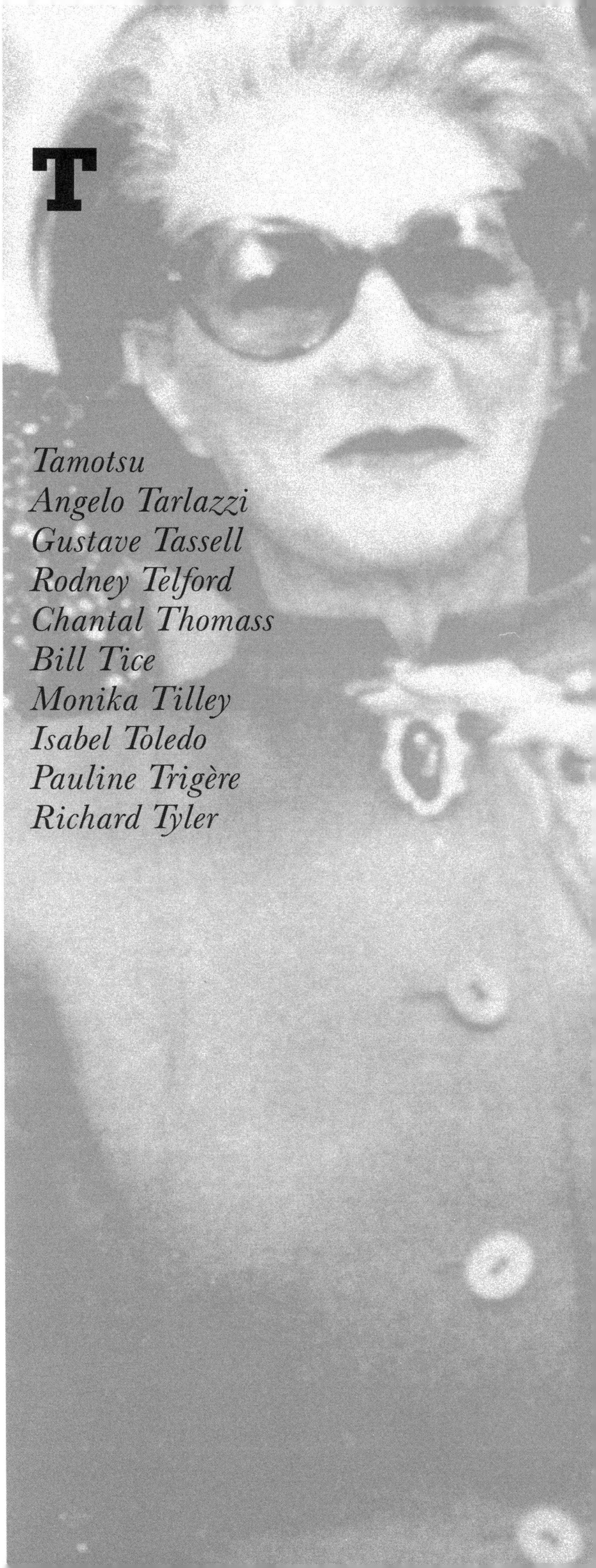

T

Tamotsu
Angelo Tarlazzi
Gustave Tassell
Rodney Telford
Chantal Thomass
Bill Tice
Monika Tilley
Isabel Toledo
Pauline Trigère
Richard Tyler

Tamotsu

Born Tokyo, Japan, July 29, 1945

Tamotsu studied textiles, fashion, and costume design at the Kuwazawa Design School. Following school, a job with one of Japan's largest textile producers exposed him to color, texture, and fashion, and further stimulated his interest in clothing design. On a visit to the U.S. in the early 1970s, he decided to stay. He studied pattern making and apparel at the Fashion Institute of Technology in New York, supporting himself with odd jobs in the workrooms of designers and costume makers. In his spare time he made clothes for friends. His career took off when jumpsuits and dresses he designed for a New York boutique became hot items.

In Tamotsu's early clothes, sophisticated color and fabric choices and away-from-the-body cuts revealed his Japanese heritage and training in textiles. He has since developed a more Western look, while retaining his interest in fabrics. Design projects have included sportswear, dresses, outerwear, and Vogue Patterns, and he has developed a thriving business in larger sizes. His chosen customer is "the woman who goes to work."

Tarlazzi, Angelo

Born Ascoli Piceno, Italy, 1942

While he now works and presents his ready-to-wear in Paris, Tarlazzi received his fashion initiation and education in Italy. At nineteen he went to work at Carosa in Rome, stayed five years and became chief designer. In 1966 he left for Paris and a job with PATOU. After three years at Patou he went to New York but could not find work and returned to Europe. He then free-lanced for Carosa, went back to Patou (1972-1977), then established his own business. He has also free-lanced for Basile and BIAGIOTTI.

Tarlazzi's clothes have been described as a blend of Italian fantasy and French chic. His knits, termed "suave and sexy," are produced in Italy, the remainder of his collection is French-made.

Tassell, Gustave

Born Philadelphia, Pennsylvania, February 4, 1926
Awards International Silk Association Award, 1959 • Coty American Fashion Critics' Award *"Winnie,"* 1961

Tassell studied painting at the Pennsylvania Academy of Fine Arts. After Army service he did window displays for HATTIE CARNEGIE, where he was exposed to the designs of NORELL and was inspired to become a dress designer. He had his own small couture business in Philadelphia then returned to Carnegie as a designer, leaving in 1952 to spend two years in Paris. While there he supported himself by selling sketches to visiting Americans, including GALANOS. He returned to the U.S. and in 1956, aided by Galanos, opened his own ready-to-wear business in Los Angeles. After Norell's death in 1972, Tassell took over as designer, remaining until the firm closed four years later. He then reopened his own business.

Tassell was a friend of Norell, sharing with him a sure sense of proportion, an insistence on simplicity of line and refined detail. He was known for clothes of near-couture sophistication and perfect finish.

Telford, Rodney Vaughn

Born Durban, South Africa, 1967

Rodney Telford is one of the young designers interested less in the trendiest last word than in construction detail, believing that true design is found not in styling alone but in styling wedded to intriguing engineering. He displays a talent for fine tailoring developed at Parsons School of Design, where he graduated in 1988. He honed his skills during one-year stints at KOOS VAN DEN AKKER and CHRISTIAN FRANCES ROTH, opened his own firm in 1990. He is a member of the Council of Fashion Designers of America (CFDA).

Telford (near right) and characteristically refined pantsuit (far right), both 1994.

Thomass, Chantal

Born Paris, France, 1947

Thomass began designing without formal training. In her teens she invented clothes for herself, which were made up by her mother, later she made dresses from silk scarves painted by an art student boyfriend. In 1967 she sold these to DOROTHÉE BIS and to a shop in Saint Tropez where they were bought by Brigitte Bardot. The same year she married Bruce Thomass and together they started a firm called Ter et Bantine, making "very junior," rather eccentric clothes. The firm, Chantal Thomass, was established in 1976 for a more expensive line, pretty and feminine, with a young, up-to-the-minute spirit.

Tice, Bill

Born Tipton, Indiana, 1942
Died Glendale, Arizona, March 9, 1995
Awards Coty American Fashion Critics' Award *Special Award (loungewear),* 1974 • American Printed Fabrics Council "Tommy" Award: 1971, 1988

Tice designs from 1976.

Tice majored in fashion design at the University of Cincinnati, graduating in 1964. After arriving in New York he spent several years working in ready-to-wear, found his niche in 1968 when he became designer for Royal Robes. In 1972 he took another detour into designer ready-to-wear, moved back into the intimate apparel field in 1975 as vice president of design at Swirl. From 1986 to 1991, he was involved in various businesses, running the gamut from his own firm, Entice Ltd. for ready-to-wear and intimate apparel, to a licensing agreement for robes, loungewear, and lingerie under the Bill Tice name, to upscale private label for Victoria's Secret and others. In 1991 he retired and moved to Arizona to spend more time with family and friends, but continued to work on special projects.

Bill Tice originated many key at-home ideas, the jersey float and the quilted gypsy look among them. In his eleven years at Swirl he produced widely imitated fleece robes, as well as innovative and salable loungewear, ranging from sundresses to printed sarongs to quilted silk coats and narrow pants. Known as a perfectionist who truly loved loungewear, he designed his own prints and accessories for his collections, as well as slippers and evening shoes. Other design projects included patterns and domestic linens.

Innovative and energetic, Tice extended his role far beyond that of designer, initiating off-shore manufacturing, supervising workrooms and production, as well as all aspects of sales promotion, including public relations and national advertising. He produced videos for store use at point of sale before anyone else, traveled tirelessly to promote his products, and was the first intimate apparel designer to have his own boutiques in major fashion stores. His book, *Enticements, How to Look Fabulous in Lingerie*, was published by Macmillan in 1985.

Tilley, Monika

Born Vienna, Austria, July 25, 1934

Awards Coty American Fashion Critics' Award *Special Award (swimsuits),* 1975 • American Printed Fabrics Council "Tommy" Award, 1976 (twice in one year: once for beach clothes and sportswear, once for loungewear and lingerie "for her original designs and use of prints")

Monika Tilley made her name with swimwear. She has always been involved in sports so that her sportswear designs, while fashionable and often seductive, are thoroughly functional. She has used bias cuts, cotton madras shirred with elastic, a technique of angling the weave of a fabric so it shapes the body. While she explains her reputation as a top swimwear designer as a matter of longevity — "I've stuck to swimwear longer than anyone else has" — it is based on fit. She is very product oriented and insists on strict production control; she also works hard at promoting new lines with trunk shows and personal appearances.

Born into a family of conservative government officials and diplomats, Tilley grew up in Austria and England. After graduation in 1956 from the Academy of Applied Arts in

Swimwear by Tilley from 1973.

her native Vienna, she studied in Stockholm and Paris before leaving Europe for the U.S. She worked briefly as an assistant to JOHN WEITZ, then as a free-lance designer of skiwear and children's clothes. Her career began in earnest at White Stag and Cole of California. She has also held design positions at the Anne Klein Studio, Mallory Leathers, and in 1968, Elon of California. In 1970 she incorporated as Monika Tilley Ltd., a full-service studio covering color and fiber consulting, textile and print design, and designing/marketing, specializing in men's and women's sportswear, women's lingerie and loungewear. Her list of past and present clients includes the Color Association of America, Monsanto, Malden Mills, Levi Straus, Munsingwear, Vassarette, Miss Elaine, and Elon.

Toledo, Isabel

Born Cuba, April 9, 1961

Toledo is one of the designers working in a very personal way somewhat out of the main stream. She learned to sew as a child in Cuba and started making her own clothes because everything ready made was too big for her. Arriving in the U.S. with her family, she attended the Fashion Institute of Technology and Parsons School of Design, studied painting and ceramics before switching to design. She worked with DIANA VREELAND at the Costume Department of the Metropolitan Museum, restoring clothes from the Museum's collection. Her fashion career began in December 1985. At the urging of her artist husband Ruben Toledo, she made up a few pieces, which he then took around to the stores. Patricia Field and Henri Bendel were her first customers, followed by Bergdorf Goodman, which gave her the 57th Street windows for clothes from her first full collection.

Line and shape are paramount with Toledo, who starts with a shape such as the circle and experiments to see how far she can take it. She believes in simplicity arrived at through innovation, insists that the design must not be contrived but must evolve naturally. Her clothes, which she calls classic, range from sportswear to evening, from simple to flamboyant; they derive their uniqueness from the strength of their shapes and from her eye for details. The designs transcend age categories and appeal to women with a liking for the different.

Below, 1994: Isabel Toledo (left); dress and floating jacket (center); back detail of jacket (right).

Trigère, Pauline

Born Paris, France, November 4, 1912
Awards Neiman Marcus Award, 1950 • Coty American Fashion Critics' Award *"Winnie,"* 1949; *Return Award,* 1951; *Hall of Fame,* 1959 • Medaille de Vermeil of the City of Paris: 1972, 1982

The daughter of a dressmaker and a tailor who came to Paris from Russia in 1905, Trigère learned to cut and fit in her father's shop, where she made her first muslins. She worked with her father until his death in 1932. In 1937, en route to Chile with her family, she arrived in New York and decided to stay. She found work with Ben Gershel & Co. and as assistant to Travis Banton at Hattie Carnegie. In 1942, with a collection of eleven styles, she opened her own business.

Trigère cut and draped directly from the bolt — coats, capes, suits, and dresses of near-couture quality in luxurious fabrics, unusual tweeds and prints. The deceptive simplicity of the clothes was based on artistic, intricate cut, especially flattering to the mature figure. She took care of the designing for her firm while her elder son, Jean-Pierre Radley, as president of Trigère Inc., was in charge of the business end. The Trigère name has appeared on scarves, jewelry, furs, men's ties, sunglasses, bedroom fashions, paperworks, servingware, and a fragrance.

Trigère closed her business in August of 1993 but a year later was

once again involved in design, this time a small line of jewelry intended to complement clothes of hers that her customers were still wearing.

Left, evening gowns from 1962. Top right, Trigère in her signature tinted glasses in 1985; bottom right, tweed coat from 1985.

Tyler, Richard

Born Sunshine, Australia, 1948

Awards Council of Fashion Designers of America (CFDA) *Perry Ellis Award for New Fashion Talent,* 1993; *Best Designer,* 1994 • Dallas Fashion Award *Fashion Excellence Award (for Anne Klein)*

When Richard Tyler succeeded LOUIS DELL'OLIO as designer for ANNE KLEIN, he was already a highly regarded fashion name in Los Angeles, producing beautiful clothes of near-custom quality for women and men and selling them from his own boutique. His jackets are particularly admired, not only for their inventive, graceful cut, but also for their perfectionist tailoring and finish, so flawless they could be worn inside out. Their high quality places the clothes firmly in the deluxe category.

When he was eight years old, Tyler was taught to sew by his

Tyler (right) and (above) suit from his own resort collection, 1995.

mother, who designed costumes for the ballet. Her credo, "Don't send it out unless it's perfect," has guided him ever since. In his teen years, Tyler apprenticed with the tailor who made suits for the Australian Prime Minister; at eighteen he opened his first boutique, Zippity-doo-dah, attracting a clientele from the music industry. After touring with a music group, he landed in Los Angeles in 1977, from there spent time designing in Europe, then returned to L.A. In 1987, Tyler/Trafficante, a partnership with his second wife, Lisa Trafficante, and her sister Michelle, was established in Los Angeles, to design, manufacture, and wholesale the clothes. The first New York showing of the women's collection was in April 1993.

In May 1993 Tyler was named as designer for Anne Klein. While the collections were well received by his peers and the press, the traditional Anne Klein customer evidently found them too advanced and in December 1994 the company announced the end of the arrangement. Tyler continues to produce his signature lines in Los Angeles.

U-V

Patricia Underwood
Emanuel Ungaro
Valentino
Maggie Vall
Joan Vass
Phillipe Venet
Gianni Versace
Madeleine Vionnet
Adrienne Vittadini
Roger Vivier
Diane Von Furstenberg

Underwood, Patricia

Born Maidenhead, England, 1948

Convent educated, Underwood worked in Paris as an *au pair* and at Buckingham Palace as a secretary before moving to New York in 1968. She studied at the Fashion Institute of Technology and then, with a friend, went into business making hats. Her strength is in elegantly updating classic, simple shapes from the past, such as boaters, milkmaids' hats, and nuns' coifs. Her designs have been bought by leading stores, featured in fashion magazines, and have frequently been chosen by ready-to-wear designers to complement their collections.

Above, boldly-brimmed hats from Underwood's 1987 fall collection and (right) the designer.

Ungaro, Emanuel

Born Aix-en-Provence, France, February 13, 1933
Awards Neiman Marcus Award, 1969

Ungaro's parents were Italian immigrants. He gained his initial training working with his father, a tailor, from whom he learned to cut, sew, and fit men's clothes. In 1955, at twenty-two, he left Provence for Paris and a job in a small tailoring firm. Three years later he went to work for BALENCIAGA, where he stayed until 1963, then spent two seasons with COURRÈGES. He opened his own business in 1965. His first collections were reminiscent of Courrèges — tailored coats and suits with diagonal seaming, little girl A-line dresses, blazers with shorts. The clothes were widely copied in the youth market. Many of his special fabrics and prints were designed by Sonja Knapp, a Swiss graphic artist who still designs most of his fabrics.

In the 1970s he turned to softer fabrics and more flowing lines, mingling several different prints in a single outfit and piling on layers. His designs became increasingly seductive, evolving into a body-conscious, sensuous look, strategically draped and shirred. As it was immediately and extensively copied Ungaro himself moved on, retaining his penchant for mixing patterns and prints. His excellent tailoring has always remained in evidence in creations as diverse as a men's wear striped jacket tossed over a slinky flowered evening dress, or daytime suits with soft trousers cut on the bias. He has added ready-to-wear, a perfume, *Diva*, also Ungaro boutiques in Europe and the U.S. Other projects have included furs and men's wear, sheets, wallcoverings, curtains, knitwear.

Clockwise from top left: Ungaro, 1993; accesory extravaganza, 1993; soft tailoring, 1994; evening pouf, 1988.

Valentino

Born Valentino Garavani; Voghera, Italy, ca. 1932
Awards Neiman Marcus Award, 1967

Valentino left Italy for Paris at age seventeen to study at L'Ecole de la Chambre Syndicale de la Couture Parisienne, having prepared himself by studying both fashion and the French language in Milan. In 1950 he went to work for JEAN DESSÈS, stayed five years, then worked as design assistant at GUY LAROCHE until 1958.

In 1959, he opened his own couture house with a tiny atelier in Rome's Via Condotti, within a few years was successful enough to move to his present headquarters. His first major recognition came in 1962 when he showed for the first time in Florence. In 1975 he began showing his ready-to-wear collections in Paris and has continued to do so. His couture showings are still held in Rome. His first boutique for ready-to-wear opened in Milan in 1969, followed by one in Rome and then others around the world, including Japan. Other interests include men's wear, Valentino Piu for gifts and interiors, bed linens, and drapery fabrics.

Valentino's clothes are noted for refined simplicity and elegance — well-cut coats and suits, sophisticated sportswear, entrance-making evening dresses — always feminine and flattering. They are notable for beautiful fabrics and exquisite workmanship and are worn by a diverse international clientele ranging from the late Jacqueline Onassis to Elizabeth Taylor. With Giancarlo Giammetti, his partner and business manager, Valentino understands the grand gesture. In 1978 he introduced his signature fragrance in France, spon-

Valentino (bottom right). Above and top right from the 1995 couture collection. *Also see Color Plate 17.*

soring a ballet performance in Paris, with after-theater parties at Maxim's and the Palace. In 1984, he celebrated his 25th year in business and 50th couture collection with an enormous outdoor fashion show in Rome's Piazza d'Espagna. His 30th anniversary celebration was a week of lavish lunches, dinners, a ball, and two exhibitions, attended by an international assemblage of friends and clients. A Valentino retrospective was part of an Italian promotion at the Park Avenue Armory in 1992.

Vall, Maggie

Born Germany

Maggie Vall began designing hats and headgear in 1974 at a time when hats were a nearly extinct fashion species. She studied at the Pennsylvania Academy of Fine Arts in Philadelphia and the Art Students League in New York; her first job, during summer vacation, was in the millinery department at Wanamaker's in Philadelphia. Her first hat was the result of a challenge from her husband to do something with her talent that would make more money than painting. The hat was made of blue-and-white Dutch wax batik and Henri Bendel bought it. As her education and background were in the fine arts, she says she learned her craft on the job.

Vall believes in soft, unconstructed forms, emphasizing shape, color, line, and fabric, often using two or more fabrics in one hat. She has added soft shoulder bags and hair accessories to her line.

Vass, Joan

Born New York City, May 19, 1925
Awards Smithsonian Institution, Washington, D.C., "Extraordinary Women in Fashion", 1978
• Coty American Fashion Critics' Award *Special Award (crafted knit fashions),* 1979

Joan Vass (above) and knits from 1987.

Vass has built her reputation on crochets and handmade or hand-loomed knits, and imaginative, functional clothes in simplified shapes and subtle colorings, usually in her preferred natural fibers. She is recognized by retailers and the press as a highly creative, original designer.

A graduate of the University of Wisconsin, she majored in philosophy, did graduate work in aesthetics, was a curator at the Museum of Modern Art, an editor at art book publisher Harry N. Abrams. With no formal fashion training, she got into designing in the early 1970s when two of her concerns intersected. First, she was bothered by the plight of women with salable skills but no

outlet for them — specifically, women who either could not work away from home or did not want to be shut up in an office or factory; second, she was convinced there was a market for handmade articles of good quality.

Vass, who had always knitted and crocheted, found a number of women with superior craft skills and in 1973 began designing things for them to knit and crochet, selling the articles privately. This new enterprise took so much time that she wanted to give it up but was dissuaded by her workers. Then came her first large order from

Henri Bendel; other stores followed and she was in business. Her firm was incorporated in 1977. In addition to Joan Vass New York — better-priced clothes for men and women — there are Joan Vass boutiques and the moderately priced Joan Vass USA collection.

Vass's 1994 knit separates.

Venet, Philippe

Born Lyons, France, May 22, 1929

Venet started in fashion at fourteen when he was apprenticed to the best couturier in Lyons. He stayed six years then moved on to Paris and at twenty-two was working at SCHIAPARELLI, where he met GIVENCHY. In 1953 he went to Givenchy as master tailor, leaving in 1962 to open his own house. In addition to couture, he has designed costumes for the Rio de Janeiro Carnival, done sumptuous furs for Maximilian, produced a ready-to-wear line and men's wear, and operated a boutique. A superb tailor, Venet is especially admired for his coats and suits. His clothes are beautifully cut and have great elegance and ease.

Above, Venet in his studio, 1991; right, coat from 1992.

Versace, Gianni

Born Calabria, Italy, 1946

As Versace's mother was a dress-maker his exposure to fashion began early. He studied architecture but became more and more involved in his mother's couture business until in the late 1960s he was acting as buyer for their atelier. He finished his architectural studies and moved to Milan where he became even more interested in fashion and textile design and began designing for several *prêt-à-porter* firms, including Genny and Callaghan. In 1979 he showed for the first time under his own name, a collection of men's wear.

Since then Versace has become one of Europe's most popular designers, with a vivid and far-ranging imagination. He offers women many options, always sensuous and sexy. Like SCHIAPARELLI, he can go over the top into vulgarity, but also produces clothes of great sophistication and elegance. In the early 1980s he introduced a fabric of metal mesh, so soft and pliable it is sewn by machine, and used it in beautiful, slithery evening dresses worn from California to the Riviera.

There are Gianni Versace boutiques around the world for men's and women's clothing, Versace accessories, knits, leathers, furs, and fragrances for men and women. He has also designed for the theater, including ballet costumes for La Scala and for Béjart's Ballet of the 20th Century. "Signatures," a retrospective exhibit celebrating fifteen years of his work was mounted at the Fashion Institute of Technology in November 1992.

The many facets of Versace: sultry, 1988 (top left); from 1994, suave tailoring (bottom left), and sex kitten (top right). Above, Versace and bride, 1994. *Also see Color Plate 2.*

Vionnet, Madeleine

Born Aubervilliers, France, 1876
Died Paris, France, March 2, 1975
Awards Légion d'Honneur, 1929

Gerber, for whom she made *toiles* and whom she considered even greater than POIRET. In 1907 she moved to Doucet and in 1912 opened her own house, which closed during World War I. She reopened in 1918 on the avenue Montaigne, closed for good in 1940.

Even while working for others, Vionnet had advanced ideas not always acceptable to conservative clients. She eliminated high, boned collars from dresses and blouses, and claimed to have eliminated corsets before Poiret. One of the couture's greatest technicians, she invented the modern use of the bias cut, producing dresses so supple they eliminated the need for fastenings of any kind. Without the aid of placket openings, they could be slipped on over the head to fall back into shape on the body. For even more suppleness, seams were often stitched with fagotting.

She did not sketch, but instead draped, cut, and pinned directly on the figure. For this purpose she used a small-scaled wooden mannequin with articulated joints. Designs were later translated into full-size *toiles*, then into the final material. Most probably she chose this method for convenience. It is doubtful she could have achieved her effects as economically or with as little physical effort

One of the towering figures of 20th century couture, Vionnet still influences us. Her bias technique, her cowl and halter necklines, her use of pleating, are part of the designer's vocabulary. The daughter of a gendarme, she began her apprenticeship when she was twelve and at sixteen was working with a successful

dressmaker called Vincent. By the age of nineteen she had married, had a child who died, and was divorced. At twenty she went to London, where she stayed five years working first in a tailor's workroom and then for CALLOT SOEURS. She returned to Callot Soeurs in Paris, working closely with one of the sisters, Mme.

by any other means. Vionnet introduced crêpe de Chine, previously confined to linings, as a fabric suitable for fashion; she transformed Greek and medieval inspirations into completely modern clothes, graceful and sensuous. She did not allow herself to become set in her fashion ways and it is said that in 1934 she scrapped her nearly finished collection when she realized it was out of step with the new romantic mood, completing an entirely new one in two weeks to show on the scheduled date.

Many designers trained with her. Her assistant for years was Marcelle Chaumont, who later opened her own house. Others included Mad Maltezos of the house of Mad Carpentier, and Jacques Griffe. Herself a person of complete integrity, Vionnet was the implacable enemy of copyists and style pirates. Her motto was, "To copy is to steal."

Additional sketches made for WWD in 1969 with Vionnet's input.

1912   1913   1918-19   1920

1931   1931   1936   1939

Vittadini, Adrienne

Born Hungary

Awards Coty American Fashion Critics' Award *Special Award,* 1984

Vittadini left Hungary with her family in 1956, grew up in Philadelphia where she studied at the Moore College of Art. She always wanted to be a fashion designer and in 1965 won a fellowship to study in Paris with Louis Féraud. Back in the U.S., she went to work as a designer for Sport Tempo, then for the Rosanna division of Warnaco. In the early 1970s, she met and married Gianluigi Vittadini, a Milanese businessman, and retired. She soon went back to work part time for Warnaco, then for Kimberly Knits, and in January 1979 established her own business.

Vittadini reflects current trends in wearable clothes with a sophisticated viewpoint. Although her sportswear now includes woven fabrics, she finds knits more challenging than wovens because the designer must begin by creating the fabric itself. She also likes the practicality of

Vittadini (above) and a knit design from her 1994 collection.

knitted clothes, the way they travel, their ease of care, and the seductive way they cling to the body. Other projects have included swimsuits for Cole of California.

Vivier, Roger

Born Paris, France, 1913
Awards Neiman Marcus Award, 1961

Creator of some of this century's most beautiful shoes, Roger Vivier studied drawing and sculpture at L'Ecole des Beaux-Arts before going to work for a shoemaker. Light-hearted and with a spirited sense of fantasy, his shoes have a strong structural foundation traceable to his training in sculpture.

Vivier started his own business in the 1930s and soon developed a fashionable international clientele. Delman brought him to New York to design an upscale line, and in 1953 he went to work for CHRISTIAN DIOR. During his time at Dior he produced a myriad exquisite evening shoes — refined, streamlined silhouettes exuberantly jeweled and embroidered. He again opened his own firm in 1963, moved to the rue Royale in 1974, and has since created shoes for some of the top Paris couture houses.

Von Furstenberg, Diane

Born Brussels, Belgium, December 31, 1946

Von Furstenberg has had at least three separate fashion careers. She started in 1971 with moderately priced dresses of lightweight jersey, had her own custom shop for a few years on Fifth Avenue, and continues with the Diane Von Furstenberg Studio and direct TV selling on QVC.

Educated in Spain, England, and Switzerland, Von Furstenberg took a degree in economics from the University of Geneva, moved to the U.S. in 1969. When she saw a need for dresses that were affordable, comfortable, and fashionable, she decided to try designing. Her first patterns were cut on her dining table, shipped to a friend in Italy to be made up. In 1971, she packed her first samples in a suitcase and started showing them to store buyers. The jersey wrapdress with surplice top and long sleeves was an immediate

success and made her name. This is the dress Von Furstenberg says taught her three essential F's in designing for women. "It's flattering, feminine and, above all, functional." A perfume followed, a cosmetics line and shop, home furnishings, and the usual licenses, from eyewear to luggage.

She left the moderate-price dress market in 1977, re-entered it briefly in 1985 with a collection based on her signature wrapdress. This was followed by her retailing venture and her current design-and-marketing studio and involvement with televised home shopping. In 1994 she was appointed Creative Planning Director for Q2, QVC's weekend channel.

Men's and women's wear by Von Furstenberg, 1974.

W

Ilie Wacs
Chester Weinberg
John Weitz
Vivienne Westwood
Wittall & Shon
Workers for Freedom
Charles Frederick Worth

Wacs, Ilie

Born Vienna, Austria, December 11, 1927

Wacs comes by his fashion expertise naturally. His father was one of Vienna's leading men's custom tailors until 1938 when the Germans invaded Austria, and the family escaped to Shanghai. In 1941, when the Japanese occupied the city and forced all refugees into a ghetto, the elder Wacs supported the family by stripping old suits and reversing them to make new garments. He was helped by his son, who thus learned the art of tailoring quite literally from the inside out.

After the 1945 liberation, Wacs went to Paris with a scholarship to study art at L'Ecole des Beaux-Arts but turned to fashion and worked in the Paris couture. Brought to New York by Philip Mangone, a leading American tailor, he worked for Mangone and others, and had his own couture business. In 1964 he joined Originala, a top-ranking coat and suit maker, where he was head

designer until 1972. He then designed under his own label for a conglomerate, acquiring ownership of Ilie Wacs Inc. in 1975.

Working in the better price range, Wacs has a well-deserved reputation for superior tailoring in fine fabrics, definitely for women who are most comfortable in the mainstream of fashion and who appreciate excellent quality. He believes that contemporary clothes should be uncomplicated and free of gimmicks, and that good fit is synonymous with good fashion.

Coat design by Wacs, 1963.

Weinberg, Chester

Born New York City, September 23, 1930
Died New York City, April 24, 1985
Awards Coty American Fashion Critics' Award *"Winnie,"* 1970 • Maison Blanche "Rex" Award, New Orleans, 1972

Weinberg built his reputation on simple, elegant designs, sophisticated and classic, never exaggerated or overpowering. They were always marked by beautiful fabrics, which were his passion. "Fabrics set the whole mood of my collection. I cannot design a dress until I know what the fabric will be."

A 1951 graduate of Parsons School of Design, Weinberg went on to earn a B.S. degree in art education from New York University, studying at night while working as a sketcher during the day. After graduation, he worked for a number of better dress houses before opening his own business in 1966. From 1977 till 1981 his

company was a division of Jones Apparel Group, and when it closed he went to work for Calvin Klein Jeans as design director. He began teaching at Parsons in 1954 and continued to do so until the year before his death.

Weitz, John

Born Berlin, Germany, May 25, 1923
Awards Coty American Fashion Critics' Award *Special Award for Men's Wear,* 1974

Weitz is considered a pioneer of practical, modern clothes for sports and informal living. He introduced women's sports clothes with a men's wear look in the 1950s, showed pants for town wear, and in the 1960s presented "ready-to-wear couture," where the design could be chosen from sketches and swatches and made up to order. For men, he produced Contour Clothes inspired by jeans, cowboy jackets, fatigue coveralls. He was one of the first U.S. designers to show both men's and women's wear, one of the first to license his work worldwide.

Educated in England, Weitz

By John Weitz, 1994.

apprenticed in Paris at MOLYNEUX. He arrived in the U.S. shortly before Pearl Harbor, and served in U.S. Army Intelligence. After the war he showed his designs — women's sportswear based on men's clothes — to Dorothy Shaver, President of Lord & Taylor, who helped him get started in business. He began licensing in 1954, began his men's wear business in 1964. He has also designed accessories, among them watches, scarves, and jewelry.

A man of many interests, Weitz was a licensed racing driver and designed a two-seater aluminum sports car, the X600. His portrait photographs have been shown at the Museum of the City of New York.

Westwood, Vivienne

Born Tintwhistle, England, 1941

Westwood became involved in fashion around 1970 through her association with Malcolm McLaren of The Sex Pistols. At the time she was earning her living as a teacher, having left Harrow Art School after only one term. She went into business with McLaren and together, they have owned a London shop in King's Road and another in London's West End.

Westwood belongs to the anti-fashion branch of design exemplified by Comme des Garçons, although her approach is totally different. Sometimes beautiful, sometimes ridiculous, never dull, her clothes show a fierce rejection of polite standards of dress. They are often inspired by London street life, with wild swings in influences — from the leather and rubber fetishism, Punk Rock, and S & M of the 1970s, to the "new romanticism" and "pirate" looks of the early 1980s. For fall 1994, she showed bustles, placing fanny pillows under just about everything and proclaiming the rear to be the new erogenous zone. Despite poor finances, she has regularly shown in Paris, and her anarchic view of dressing has had a considerable influence on other designers, both in England and around the world.

Left, Westwood bustle dress, 1994; Dandy-inspired pantsuit, 1994 (top right); the designer (bottom right).

Whittall & Shon

Born Eliot Whittall; Greenwich, Connecticut, October 23, 1955
Richard Shon; Okinawa, Japan, January 6, 1958
Awards Dallas Fashion Award, 1989

Witty hats, caps, accessories, and casual separates are the stock in trade of this firm, the designs often extravagantly adorned and embellished with feathers and flowers, buttons, laces, and studs. Both partners came to design with thorough schooling: Whittall attended the Rhode Island School of Design (1975- 1979) and spent a year in Paris with PIERRE CARDIN; Shon, who graduated from Stamford University, studied at L'Ecole de la Chambre Syndicale de la Couture Parisienne (1981-1983), and went to work for Whittall & Javits in 1984. In 1986, Shon bought out ERIC JAVITS and the firm assumed its present name. Their work has appeared on the covers and in the editorial pages of major magazines, including *Vogue*, *Harper's Bazaar*, *Town & Country,* and *Seventeen*. Men's ready-to-wear and a retail store in Miami's South Beach district are other business interests.

Workers for Freedom

Born Graham Fraser & Richard Nott; both in 1948
Awards British Fashion Council Designer of the Year, 1989

The partners opened their business in a tiny shop in London in 1986 with a small stake and the intention of producing modern, wearable clothes. Fraser was a merchandise manager at Liberty of London; Nott, a former assistant to VALENTINO, was a lecturer at Kingston Polytechnic, where he received his training.

They had no plans to wholesale but were immediately besieged by retailers, including Henri Bendel and Saks Fifth Avenue. From the beginning they've been somewhat out of the mainstream. They were in the vanguard in the use of embroidery and with ethnic looks and continue to lead the way, evolving from the wildness of 1980s London into a more refined view of easy, softly tailored

Above, Graham Fraser (left in photo) and Richard Nott, 1989; far left, sexy lady look, 1990.

clothes that are both delicate and feminine, sexy and sophisticated.

Worth, Charles Frederick

Born Bourne, Lincolnshire, England, October 13, 1825
Died Paris, France, March 10, 1895

The founder of the house that became the world's longest-running fashion dynasty got his first job when he was just eleven and worked for a number of London drapers (a dealer in cloth or clothing) before leaving for Paris in 1845. He took a job with a shop selling fabrics, shawls, and mantles, and persuaded the firm to open a department of made-up dress models, which he designed. He was the first to present clothes on live mannequins, using his young French wife as a model. In 1858 he opened his own couture house on the rue de la Paix, which closed during the Franco-Prussian War. Re-established in 1874, Maison Worth maintained

Left, unable to draw, Worth sketched his designs on pre-drawn stock figures. Right, Worth, ca. 1864.

its fashion leadership for another eighty years.

Worth was court dressmaker to Empress Eugénie of France and to Empress Elizabeth of Austria. He dressed the ladies of European courts and society women of Europe and America. A virtual fashion dictator, he required his customers, except for Eugénie and her court, to come to him instead of attending them in their homes as had been the custom. He was an excellent businessman, was the first couturier to sell models to be copied in England and America, and was also widely copied by others without his permission. He enjoyed his success and lived in the grand manner.

Worth designs were known for their opulence and lavish use of fabrics, elaborate ornamentation of frills, ribbons, lace, braid, and tassels, which can strike the modern eye as suffocating excess. He is held responsible for the collapsible steel frame for crinolines and then for abolishing crinolines in 1867. Whether he actually invented it or not, he certainly exploited the crinoline to the utmost, as it reached its most extravagant dimensions during the Second Empire and disappeared when the Empire collapsed. Worth promoted the use of French-made textiles, and is said to have invented the princess-style dress, court mantles hung from

the shoulders, and the ancestor of the tailor-made suit for women. He was influenced by the paintings of Van Dyck, Gainsborough, and Velasquez.

After his death, the House of Worth continued under the leadership of his sons, Jean-Philippe and Gaston, then of his grandson, Jean-Charles, and finally of his great-grandsons, Roger and Maurice. When Roger retired in 1952, Maurice took over and in 1954 sold the house to PAQUIN. A London wholesale house continued under the Worth name until the 1970s. Parfums Worth was established in 1900, continues today with *Je Reviens* the best-known fragrance.

Y-Z

Yohji Yamamoto
Yeohlee
Yuki
Zang Toi
Zoran

Yamamoto, Yohji

Born Yokohama, Japan, ca. 1943

Yamamoto is a member of the Japanese avant-garde that includes REI KAWAKUBO and ISSEY MIYAKE. Oversize clothes and a playful diversity of textures are his signature, along with asymmetrical hems and collars, holes and torn edges. He likes surprise details: an unexpected pocket, a lapel that turns into a long, flowing shawl, a new placement of buttons.

A graduate of Keio University, he studied fashion at Tokyo's Bunka College of Fashion under Chie Kolke, who had attended L'Ecole de la Chambre Syndicale de la Couture Parisienne in Paris with SAINT LAURENT. From 1966 to 1968 he followed the standard course, studying all aspects of the clothing industry; by 1972 he had his own company. He showed his first collection in Tokyo in

Yamamoto (above) and a kimono-design from 1994.

1976. In 1981 he established himself in France with a boutique in Paris, and since then has shown at the Paris *prêt-à-porter* collections.

Yeohlee

Born Yeohlee Teng; Penang, Malaysia, ca. 1955

At the ripe old age of nine, Yeohlee talked her mother into letting her enroll in a pattern-making class. There was no ready-to-wear in Malaysia, clothes were made at home or by seamstresses and tailors, and she was dissatisfied with what her mother produced from English

patterns. At eighteen, she came to New York to study at Parsons School of Design and two years later sold her first five-piece collection to Henri Bendel. She founded her own company in 1981.

Her work is spare, often dramatic in impact, characterized by

clear lines and geometric forms. The clothes are also comfortable and flattering, cut to allow the wearer to move with easy elegance. Yeohlee designs a complete collection but is most admired for her coats, both long and short. Working in the better price range, she feels that the timeless quality of the design, combined with superior fabrics and workmanship, make her clothes long-term investments.

With their purity of form and distinct vision, Yeohlee's designs have been chosen for numerous exhibits, including shows at the Museum of the City of New York and the Massachusetts Institute of Technology, where they were featured with such designers as ARMANI, FERRÉ, MONTANA, and MIYAKE. They are also included in the permanent costume collection of the Metropolitan Museum of Art.

Yuki

Born Gnyuki Torimaru; Miyazaki-ken, Japan, ca. 1940

London-based Yuki worked in both couture and ready-to-wear, making refined, elegant clothes with the flowing, sculptural quality of Madame GRÈS, somewhat out of the main stream. His primary training was as a textile engineer but he also worked in Tokyo as an animator, studied the history of architecture at the Chicago Art Institute and fashion at the London College of Fashion (1964-1966).

After a two-year stint as design assistant to a London dressmaker, he worked for HARTNELL and for two years in Paris with CARDIN. He presented his first collection under his own name in 1972. He has designed for theater and television, and has supported his more visionary design efforts with a successful

Yuki (right) and a beautifully-draped silk jersey design from 1994.

licensing program. Best known for dramatic, bias-cut evening clothes, frequently in silk jersey, Yuki based all designs on the body, working to remove all unnecessary detail. In 1992, his work was honored by a twenty-year retrospective showing at the Victoria and Albert Museum.

Zang Toi

Born Malaysia, June 11, 1961

Zang Toi, the seventh child of a grocer, left Malaysia for Canada in 1980, moved on to New York City a year later intending to study painting or interior design. Instead, he switched to fashion, and while at Parsons School of Design went to work for MARY JANE MARCASIANO. He graduated from Parsons in 1983 and stayed on with Marcasiano for five years, concentrating on production. Following free-lance work at SHAMASK, he opened his own business in 1989.

Designing with a light touch, Zang Toi combines an Oriental sense of color and a taste for exotic details with the forthright flair of American sportswear. The result is a fresh twist for classic looks. The clothes are young and spirited, with a sophisticated attitude.

Right, Zang Toi and exuberant evening looks, 1994.

262

Zoran

Born Belgrade, Yugoslavia, 1947

Zoran belongs to the fashion mini- malists, confining himself to a few pure shapes, always in the most expensive, most luxurious fabrics. He studied architecture in Belgrade, moved to New York in 1971. His first fashion recognition came in 1977 when his designs were bought by Henri Bendel.

The early collections were based on squares and rectangles in silk crêpe de Chine, cashmere, and other luxurious fabrics. The designs have evolved from there, retaining their purity and luxury. Zoran works in a limited color range, usually black, gray, white, ivory, and red. It is a relaxed look, sophisticated and utterly simple, a perfection of under- statement by a master of proportion and balance. He prefers not to use buttons and zippers and as far as possible avoids any extraneous detail. Because his customers lead a highly mobile life, he has produced a jet-pack collection of ten pieces that fit into a small bag so that a woman can look casual and glamorous wherever her travels take her. At a less costly level, Zoran has produced daytime clothes in cotton knit, although evenings are still devoted to satin, velvet, and cashmere. Inevitably, his creations are for women of sophisticated tastes and well-filled bank accounts.

Below, Zoran and a typically spare design from 1991.

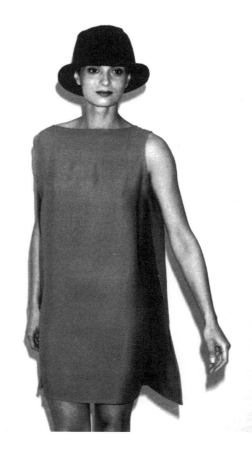

The Stylemakers

Antonio
Richard Avedon
Cecil Beaton
Edna Woolman Chase
Bill Cunningham
Louise Dahl-Wolfe
Jessica Daves
Baron Adolf de Meyer
Erté
Toni Frissell
Horst P. Horst
George Hoyningen-Huene
Man Ray
Martin Munkacsi
Irving Penn
Virginia Pope
Carmel Snow
Edward Steichen
Diana Vreeland

Antonio

Born Antonio Lopez; Puerto Rico, 1943
Died Los Angeles, California, March 17, 1987

Antonio was an illustrator of protean talent, sensitive to every social shift and art movement, changing styles innumerable times during his twenty-four-year career. At the start, his work was elegant and relatively conventional fashion illustration but by 1965 Pop Art had become the essence of his drawings, followed by Surrealism and by monumental figures clearly inspired by French artist, Fernand Léger. He later moved to a more fluid style, but each period was never less than flamboyant, dramatic in its use of black and white or color. In addition to women's and men's fashion, he also brought his unique point of view to bear on children's clothes.

When his family moved to New York, Antonio was nine years old but already committed to art — even as a very small child he would sketch little dresses to please his mother, a dressmaker. He attended the High School of Industrial Art (now the High School of Art and Design) and the Fashion Institute of Technology, from which he dropped out at nineteen to join *Women's Wear Daily*. He left *WWD* after only four months when he was refused permission to free-lance and began working for *The New York Times*. During the 1960s he traveled back and forth to Europe working for *Elle* and *British Vogue* among others, eventually spending so much time in Europe that at the end of the decade he decided to move to Paris. Seven years later he moved back to New York. Other publications he worked for were *Harper's Bazaar, Vogue,* and *Interview.*

In 1964, Antonio undertook what became a five-year project, recording the life work of CHARLES JAMES under the direct supervision of the designer. He also was a molder and maker of fashion models, advising them on makeup and hair styles to fit his ideas of their best look. He became interested in education and gave lectures and workshops to students of fashion illustration in the U.S. and the Dominican Republic. A retrospective of his work, 1963 to 1987, was mounted at F.I.T. in 1988.

Avedon, Richard

Born New York City, May 15, 1923
Awards (partial list) Art Directors Show highest achievement medal, 1950 • Pratt Institute citation of dedication to fashion photography, 1976 • Art Directors Club Hall of Fame, 1982 • Council of Fashion Designers of America (CFDA) *Lifetime Achievement Award,* 1989

The son of a retail store owner, Avedon received his first photographic training in the merchant marine. He took a class in experimental photography at the New School for Social Research, taught by Alexey Brodovitch, art director of *Harper's Bazaar,* and in 1945 joined the staff of the magazine. Thus began his long and distinguished career in fashion and commercial photography and an association with *Harper's Bazaar* that endured for twenty years. During that time he had non-fashion assignments from other publications, including *Theatre Arts.* In 1966 he moved to *Vogue,* remaining there until 1990.

His fashion photography, notable for its sense of style, freedom, and drama, captured the tone of the 1960s and recorded the sexual revolution. He took the action photography of MARTIN MUNKACSI to a more sophisticated level, working in the studio, and, for his simulated photo-journalism, on location. He also did photo-collages using the illustrations of Katerina Danzinger, was a visual consultant on the Fred Astaire film, *Funny Face,* and has been a TV consultant. Since leaving *Vogue,* he has been staff photographer at *The New Yorker,* their first, providing them with aggressively anti-glamour portraits. One-man shows of his work have been held at, among other venues, the Museum of Modern Art in 1975, the Metropolitan Museum of Art in 1978, and in 1994 at the Whitney Museum. This last was a retrospective placing emphasis on his non-fashion work, which presumably, he considered more serious than the fashion.

Beaton, Cecil

Born London, England, January 14, 1904
Died Broad Chalke, Wiltshire, England, January 18, 1980
Awards Antionette Perry (Tony) Award: *Quadrille,* 1955; *My Fair Lady,* 1957; *Coco,*1970 • Neiman Marcus Award, 1956 • Commander of the British Empire (C.B.E.), 1957 • Motion Picture Academy Award: *Gigi,* 1958; *My Fair Lady* (sets and costumes), 1965 • Légion d'Honneur, 1960

Photographer, artist, costume and set designer, writer, Beaton was educated at Harrow and at Cambridge University. In 1928 he began a long affiliation with *Vogue* magazine, where his first contributions were spidery sketches, caricatures of well-known London actresses, and drawings of clothes worn at society parties; photographs appeared later. In her memoirs, Edna Woolman Chase of *Vogue* describes him at their first meeting as "...tall, slender, swaying like a reed, blond, and very young..." He gave an impression that was "an odd combination of airiness and assurance". And later, "What I like best is his debunking attitude toward life and his ability for hard work." In photography he did both fashion and portraiture, and became the favored photographer of the British royal family. During World War II, he photographed for the Ministry of Information, traveling to North Africa, Burma, and China.

Beginning in 1935, Beaton designed scenery and costumes for ballet, opera, and theatrical productions in both London and New York. Among his credits: *Lady Windermere's Fan, Quadrille, The Grass Harp, The School for Scandal* (Comédie Française). He did the costumes for the New York, London, and film productions of *My Fair Lady,* costumes for the films *Gigi* and *The Doctor's Dilemma.* He also designed hotel lobbies and club interiors.

A prolific writer and diarist, Beaton published many books, illustrating them and those of others with drawings and photographs. He was knighted by Queen Elizabeth II in 1972. In 1975 he suffered a stroke, which left him partially paralyzed, but he learned to paint and take photographs with his left hand. From 1977 until his death, he lived in semi-retirement at his house in Wiltshire.

Chase, Edna Woolman

Born Asbury Park, New Jersey, March 14, 1877
Died Locust Valley, New York, March 20, 1957
Awards Légion d'Honneur, 1935 • Neiman Marcus Award, 1940

The child of divorced parents, Edna was raised by her Quaker grandparents, whose principles and plain style of dress were to prove a lasting influence. In 1895, when she was eighteen, she went to work in the Circulation Department of *Vogue,* then just two years old, with a salary of $10 a week. She was to spend fifty-six years at *Vogue,* thirty-seven of them as editor.

She fell in love with the magazine immediately. As she was enthusiastic, hard-working, and willing to take on any and all chores, she acquired more and more responsibility. By 1911 she was the equivalent of managing editor. Her name first appeared on the masthead as editor in February 1914. British and French *Vogue* were born in 1916 and 1920 respectively; Mrs. Chase was editor-in-chief of all three editions. During World War I she began to feature American designers in *Vogue*'s pages, and is credited with originating the modern fashion show in 1914 when *Vogue* produced a benefit "Fashion Fête" sponsored by prominent society women.

During her tenure *Vogue* survived two world wars, a depression, and tremendous social changes. With Condé Nast, who bought it in 1909, she helped shape the magazine according to her own strong sense of propriety and high standards of professionalism. She suffered the second-rate badly, respected talent and industriousness; she herself wrote directly to the point. Taste, business ability, and a capacity for hard work brought her to the top of her profession and kept her there for an amazing time span. She retired as editor-in-chief in 1952 and became chairman of the editorial board. Her requirements for success are still worth considering by those thinking of a career in fashion. They were: taste, sound judgment, and experience — the training and knowledge gained from actually working in a business, which she valued above formal course-taking.

She was married to and divorced from Francis Dane Chase and had one child, the writer and actress Ilka Chase. A second marriage in 1921 to Richard Newton ended with his death in 1950.

Cunningham, Bill

Born Boston, Massachusetts, ca. 1929
Awards Council of Fashion Designers of America (CFDA) *Eugenia Sheppard Award for Fashion Journalism,* 1993

A familiar New York figure in his beret, corduroys, and parka, camera unobtrusively at the ready, Bill Cunningham observes and records fashion, not as it is worn on the runway but as it appears in the real world on real people. In fair weather or foul, from one of his favorite posts at 57th Street and Fifth Avenue, in SoHo, or at the 26th Street flea market, he catches the passing scene for his "On the Street" column in the Sunday *New York Times;* his second feature, "Evening Hours," chronicles benefits, art show openings, and other social events.

Bill Cunningham's early attraction to fashion was totally alien to his conservative New England background. In Boston he worked after school at Bonwit Teller, and when he moved to New York after graduation, went to work for Nona Park and Sophie Shonnard in their Chez Ninon boutique at the New York Bonwit's. It was there he first saw the fashionable women who later became his photographic subjects. On his own time he made masks and headdresses for ladies attending the then-popular masked balls, and later opened his own hat shop called William J., backed by Rebecca Harkness, the noted ballet patron. Drafted into the Army, he was stationed in the South of France and was able to join his former employers, Nona and Sophie, in Paris when they were there shopping for their clients.

Once out of the Army he was hired by *Women's Wear Daily*'s John Fairchild to write a twice-weekly column, leaving after nine months to write about fashion for the *Chicago Tribune.* A friend, the illustrator ANTONIO, suggested that he use a camera to make notes, a move that opened his world and was the beginning of a new career. In the mid-70s, he began free-lancing at *The New York Times* and in 1993 went on staff. To attract his photographic attention, a subject must have more than mere perfection, which he finds uninteresting. For him, a person with style must have "something extra. Something so personal — flawless but with a dash."

Dahl-Wolfe, Louise

Born San Francisco, California, 1895
Died Allendale, New Jersey, December 13, 1989

Accomplished in both fashion and portrait photography, Louise Dahl-Wolfe attended the California School of Design (now San Francisco Institute of Design). Before buying her first camera in 1923, she worked at everything from designing electric signs to decorating. After travels to Europe and Africa, during which she met her future husband, Mike Wolfe, she moved to San Francisco, then to the Great Smoky mountains of Tennessee. Her first published photographs were documentary shots of her Tennessee neighbors, which were bought by Frank Crowninshield and appeared in *Vanity Fair* in 1933.

Dahl-Wolfe's first black-and-white fashion photography appeared in *Harper's Bazaar* in 1936, her first color in 1937; her elegant photographs graced the magazine until 1958. With dramatic lighting and backgrounds ranging from intricate Chinese screens to seamless paper, she caught the essence of individual fashions as simple as a CLAIRE MCCARDELL linen sundress, as structured as a pair of satin ball gowns by CHARLES JAMES. She was the first to use color effectively in fashion photography, driving both the color separators and Art Director Alexey Brodovitch to distraction with her insistence on perfection. Unlike many of her peers, she never considered photography as art but rather as a commercial medium. She left *Harper's Bazaar* after Carmel Snow and Brodovitch resigned, worked for a few months at *Vogue,* then retired to Frenchtown, New Jersey with her artist husband, who died in 1985.

Daves, Jessica

Born Cartersville, Georgia, February 20, 1898
Died New York City, 1974

Jessica Daves arrived in New York in 1921. She worked in the advertising departments of various New York stores, including Saks Fifth Avenue, writing fashion copy and learning about fashion merchandising. In 1933 she went to *Vogue* magazine as fashion merchandising editor, where her ability was spotted by EDNA WOOLMAN CHASE, then editor-in-chief. In 1936 she was made managing editor, became editor in 1946. Upon Mrs. Chase's retirement in 1952, Daves became editor-in-chief of American *Vogue*. She was a director of Condé Nast Publications from 1946 until she retired in 1963, served as editorial consultant for a year then worked on specialized books until November 1966.

An accomplished writer and editor, Miss Daves could fix a piece of ailing copy in minutes. She was known for clearheadedness and sound judgment — of all the great fashion editors she was probably the most astute at business. The years of her editorship coincided with a phenomenal growth of the American ready-to-wear industry. She recognized its increasing importance and broadened the magazine's coverage of domestic ready-to-wear, including more moderately priced clothes. Under her direction *Vogue* assumed a more serious tone and ran more articles of intellectual interest than before.

Short and plump, Miss Daves dressed well but her figure precluded real style. Her manner was warm, her voice retained charming overtones of her southern origin. In her later years she became rather regal with something of a queen mother effect. She was married to Robert A. Parker, a writer, who died in 1970. They had no children.

de Meyer, Baron Adolf

Born 1868
Died Los Angeles, California, 1949

Baron de Meyer is considered the first true fashion photographer, the one who transformed fashion photography from a photographic sideline to a major artistic expression. Born Adolf Meyer-Watson, he was of German extraction, the possessor of a modest fortune sufficient to allow him to circulate in fashionable English circles. He dropped the Watson from his name, gained a Saxon title, and in 1899, married Olga Alberta Caracciolo, the godchild of Edward VII of England and, it was rumored, his illegitimate daughter. The marriage opened society to de Meyer and the couple devoted themselves to the pleasures and pursuits of the English upper crust until the King's death in 1910 made it necessary to earn some money. De Meyer soon established a reputation as a photographer in Paris and London; his early pictures of Diaghilev's Ballets Russes captured the dazzling splendor and drama that so captivated the European avant-garde. In 1913, the imminent onset of World War I persuaded de Meyer and his wife to leave for New York where he went to work for the Condé Nast publications, *Vogue* and *Vanity Fair*. In 1923 he was hired away by Hearst, lured by more money and the opportunity to live and work in Paris, a privilege denied him by Condé Nast; it was a move he later regretted.

De Meyer's primary interest was in creating an ideal of feminine beauty and softness, of luxury and romance. His photographs relied on glamorous backgrounds and elaborate settings, reflecting a life of opulent ease and aristocratic idleness. They embodied the painterly traditions of 19th-century art with their emphasis on glowing light and romantic atmosphere. He employed soft focus, using a lens that was sharp in the center, soft at the edges, and sometimes stretched silk gauze over the lens. He made much use of backlighting, his most famous and influential technique. Many other photographers imitated his approach but failed to achieve the same extravagantly flattering and glamorously snobbish results. His influence declined with the disappearance of the way of life he glorified so brilliantly and with the liberation of women. A new age had begun and he could not move with the times.

Erté

Born Romain de Tirtoff; St. Petersburg, Russia,
November 10, 1892
Died Paris, France, April 21, 1990

The son of an admiral in the Russian Imperial Navy, Erté studied painting in Russia, went to Paris in 1912 to study at Académie Julian. He took a new name for himself from the French pronunciation of his initials R.T. (air-tay), got a job sketching for PAUL POIRET, went on to design for opera and theater, creating costumes for such luminaries as singer Mary Garden.

From 1914 into the 1930s, he produced illustrations and covers for various magazines, including *Harper's Bazaar.* He designed for the Folies Bergère, came to the U.S. in the 1920s to work for Ziegfeld and other impresarios, and tried Hollywood briefly in 1925. There he created beautiful and esoteric costumes for several silent films, including *The Mystic, Ben Hur,* and King Vidor's *La Boheme,* but impatient with the financial restrictions placed on him, returned to Paris after eight months.

In 1967, to celebrate his eightieth birthday, Erté selected over a hundred of his designs for clothes, jewelry, and accessories, to be shown in London and at the Grosvenor Gallery in New York. The exhibition contained some of the most elegant and individual designs of the Art Deco period. The New York exhibition was bought in its entirety by the Metropolitan Museum of Art.

Frissell, Toni

Born New York City, March 10, 1907
Died Saint James, New York, May 17, 1988

Before taking up photography, Toni Frissell worked for a painter and trained as an actress; she also worked in the advertising department of Stern Brothers and in 1929 went to work for *Vogue* as a caption writer. She had dabbled in photography but did not take it seriously until after the death of her brother, a documentary film maker, in an accident on location. It was at *Vogue* that she took her first fashion photographs in the informal style described by the magazine as "sunlit, windblown records of action outdoors." Outdoor work was her specialty: she would tilt her camera to achieve dramatic diagonals, and would often shoot from below with a short-focus lens to elongate the model's body. After World War II, Frissell did some location work but soon abandoned fashion. She worked for *Sports Illustrated* during its first four years and undertook assignments for *Life* and *Look* as well as some documentary projects.

Horst, Horst P.

Born Weisenfels-an-der-Saale, Germany, August 14, 1906

Horst studied furniture design with Walter Gropius at the School for Applied Arts in Hamburg, went to Paris in 1930 to study architecture with Le Corbusier. In Paris he met and modeled for HOYNINGEN-HUENE, who became a life-long friend, and took up photography himself. He photographed for French *Vogue*, then was brought to New York to work for American *Vogue*. He joined the Army during World War II, working as a photographer. Because his name, Paul Albert Bohrmann, was too close to that of one of Hitler's close associates, he had it changed legally.

At the time Horst went to work for the magazine, *Vogue* publisher Condé Nast exerted rigid control over photography, demanding that all work be done on large-format studio cameras. Sets were elaborate and each detail was expected to be perfect, resulting in refined, but static images. Despite these limitations, Horst introduced energy into his photographs through dramatic lighting and camera angles, and managed to take risks, giving an edge to the required elegance. With the acceptance of smaller cameras he moved outdoors and brought action into his shots. His influences include both Hoyningen-Huene and EDWARD STEICHEN, although he considers Steichen better at portraits than at fashion. In addition to fashion, he has also photographed interiors for *Vogue*.

Hoyningen-Huene, George

Born St. Petersburg, Russia, 1900
Died Los Angeles, California, 1968

Baron George Hoyningen-Huene was the son of the chief equerry to the Tsar; his mother was the daughter of a former American ambassador to Russia. His family fled the Russian Revolution, ending up in London. During World War I he served with the British, after the war moved to Paris where he supported himself with odd jobs, including work as an extra in the infant movie industry. It was there that he was able to observe and learn lighting techniques that were the basis for his later photographic work. He worked as a sketch artist in his sister's dress-making firm, in 1925 was designing and preparing backgrounds in the photo studios of French *Vogue*, and by 1926 was taking photographs. He was discovered by MAINBOCHER, then the magazine's editor, became chief photographer, was brought to New York briefly, then returned to Paris. In 1935 he moved back to New York and went to work for *Harper's Bazaar*. He lost interest in fashion during the 1940s, moved to Los Angeles in 1946 and taught photography at Art Center School. He was also color consultant to George Cukor. He traveled widely, taking what he called "archeological photographs" in Greece, Egypt, and Mexico, and subsequently published them in books.

At the start of his career, Hoyningen-Huene was influenced by STEICHEN but rapidly developed his own style. His photographs have an aristocratic assurance and innate, unforced elegance, which seem to come from within rather than be imposed from without. He was quite at home with his sitters, usually society women or other celebrities as there was at that time no corps of professionals, and this rapport may have contributed to the atmosphere. The later, non-fashion photographs have this same quality of confident communication.

Man Ray

Born Philadelphia, Pennsylvania, August 27, 1890
Died Paris, France, November 18, 1976

More interested in art than in commercial photography, Man Ray was nevertheless one of the fashion world's most innovative photographers, introducing elements of surrealism into his fashion work. He first worked for PAUL POIRET around 1921 or 1922, using glass plates and operating out of Poiret's darkroom. He photographed the couture section of the 1925 Decorative Arts Exposition in Paris. After working in New York, he returned to Paris with American models, who brought an American accent to his work. He photographed the Paris collections from 1938 to 1940, sometimes during air raid warnings, before returning to the U.S. After World War II he abandoned fashion to devote himself to art, including experimental photography.

Munkacsi, Martin

Born Cluj, Romania, May 18, 1896
Died Randalls Island, New York, July 14, 1963

Munkacsi became a news photographer in 1923 after an abbreviated apprenticeship as a housepainter and work on a sporting paper in Budapest. Within a few years he had risen to the top of his profession and was Hungary's highest-paid photojournalist. He left Europe in 1934 because of the rise of Nazism, and came to the U.S. with a contract with Hearst Press. His first fashion work appeared in *Harper's Bazaar* in April 1934, revolutionary action shots that are the ancestors of all the spontaneous, outdoor-action, fashion photography since. His career peaked in the early 1940s, when he claimed to be the world's highest-paid photographer. Witty and charming, Munkacsi could also be arrogant, and his hot temper alienated many. He considered his work as business, not art, and is quoted as saying "A photograph is not worth a thousand words, it's worth a thousand dollars."

Penn, Irving

Born Plainfield, New Jersey, June 16, 1917

A major figure in the field of fashion photography, Irving Penn attended the Philadelphia Museum School of Industrial Art, studied design from 1934 to 1938 with *Harper's Bazaar*'s renowned artistic director and developer of talent, Alexey Brodovitch. Penn worked as art director in a New York store and, from 1937 to 1939, free-lanced as an artist for *Harper's Bazaar.* In 1942 he spent a year painting in Mexico. His first *Vogue* photographs appeared in 1943, the beginning of a long and fruitful relationship. After war service in the American Field Service in Italy and India, his career blossomed, resulting in a wide variety of photographs of fashion, personalities, and travel. In addition to Condé Nast publications, his client roster included international advertising agencies. In 1947, he married model Lisa Fonssagrives, with whom he first collaborated in 1950 for photographs of the Paris collections; these were unadorned but rich in feeling. Their later location trip to Morocco foreshadowed his future interests and so-called anthropological pictures.

At a time when fashion photography was marked by elaborately artificial lighting, Penn used his lights to simulate daylight, an important and influential move. Posing his models against the plainest backgrounds, he achieved a monumental simplicity and clarity, an elegant femininity. On his location trips, he employed the same economy of means for portraits of native people. In the manner of 19th-century photographers he used a portable studio he built to ensure the desired conditions in the Cameroons, Peru, and other areas where no studios existed. His work has been exhibited in one-man shows at the Museum of Modern Art in New York and is in the permanent collection there, as well as that of the Metropolitan Museum of Art. He is also the author of numerous photographic books, from 1960 with *Moments Preserved*, through 1991 with *Passage*.

Pope, Virginia

Born Chicago, Illinois, June 29, 1885
Died New York City, January 16, 1978

As fashion editor at *The New York Times* from 1933 to 1955, Virginia Pope is credited with practically inventing fashion reportage. One of the first to look for news in the wholesale market, she reported on the people who made clothes at a time when only Paris fashion was considered newsworthy. She encouraged the American fashion industry in its early years, originating the "Fashions of The Times" fashion show in 1942 as a showcase for American designers and staging the show each fall for the next nine years. In 1952 the show became a twice-yearly fashion supplement of the same name, still published by *The Times*.

Following her father's death, the five-year-old Virginia was taken to Europe by her mother; together they toured the continent for the next fifteen years. She became fluent in French, German, and Italian, and familiar with the best of European art and music. They returned to Chicago in 1905. Virginia served in the Red Cross during World War I, then tried various careers in Chicago and New York, including social work, the theater, book translations, and writing.

A late starter in journalism, Miss Pope had a long run. Her first published pieces, which ran in *The New York Times*, were interviews with a visiting German theater group and articles about an Italian neighborhood, results of her facility in languages. She joined *The Times* as a member of the Sunday staff in 1925 and eight years later became fashion editor, a position she held and developed for twenty-two years. Following her retirement, Miss Pope joined the staff of *Parade* magazine as fashion editor; her name remained on the masthead until her death.

In addition, she held the Edwin Goodman chair established by Bergdorf Goodman at the Fashion Institute of Technology, giving a course on "Fashion in Contemporary Living." She could often be seen on Seventh Avenue with her students, escorting them to fashion shows and behind the scenes to see how a business worked. And because she believed that exposure to culture was essential to a designer's development, she regularly took students to performances of the Metropolitan Opera. While her personal style was of the establishment, she understood innovation and could look at clothes objectively. Referring to her conservative appearance and "grande dame" reputation, a fellow editor once said, "she could play the Queen of England without a rehearsal."

Snow, Carmel

Born Dublin, Ireland, 1888
Died New York City, May 9, 1961

Carmel Snow was raised in the fashion business — her mother came to the U.S. to promote Irish industries at the 1893 Chicago World's Fair and stayed on to found a dressmaking business, Fox & Co. One of the exhibitors at *Vogue*'s first "Fashion Fête" in 1914, the firm made the dress worn on that occasion by *Vogue*'s editor, EDNA WOOLMAN CHASE. A friendship developed and in 1921 Mrs. Chase offered Carmel a job in the magazine's fashion department. In 1929 she became editor of American *Vogue*.

In 1932, in a move that sent shock waves through the fashion world, Mrs. Snow went as fashion editor to *Harper's Bazaar*, *Vogue*'s great rival. *Vogue*'s publisher, Condé Nast, never spoke to her again. She remained with *Bazaar*, first as fashion editor then as editor, until 1957, when she became chairman of the editorial board. Her successor was Nancy White, her niece and godchild.

Tiny in stature but a major fashion presence and forceful personality, Mrs. Snow was a woman of wit and intelligence, of strong views expressed frankly and with passion. She dressed in great style in clothes from the Paris couture and like a high priestess of fashion, championed each change as it appeared. She recognized BALENCIAGA'S genius and well before the majority of the fashion press promoted him indefatigably; CHRISTIAN DIOR spoke of her "marvelous feeling for what is fashion today and what will be fashion tomorrow." A loyal and powerful champion of the talented, she demanded their best and received their finest efforts. After World War II, she took a leading role in helping the French and Italian textile and fashion industries get back on their feet. She was the stuff of legends: it was said that even when she dozed off at showings, her eyes would snap open when a winner appeared and that she had total ocular recall. It is a fact that Christian Dior delayed openings until she arrived. Even after she no longer had official connections and despite precarious health, she continued to go to Paris twice yearly for the collections.

She married George Palen Snow in 1926 and had three children. Her Irish accent never completely disappeared nor her attachment to the country of her birth. She worked there and in New York on her memoirs, written in collaboration with Mary Louise Aswell published in 1962, who was fiction editor at *Bazaar* for eleven years.

Steichen, Edward

Born Luxembourg, March 27, 1879
Died West Redding, Connecticut, May 25, 1973

Brought to the U.S. as an infant, Steichen grew up in the middle west, studied art at the Milwaukee Art Students League (1894-1898), during which time he was a lithography apprentice and began to teach himself photography. He became a U.S. citizen in 1900, lived in Paris, painting and doing photography from 1900 till 1902, and again from 1906 to 1914. During World War I he served as Lt. Colonel in the U.S. Army Expeditionary Forces (1917-1919) as commander of a photo division. Around 1922, he abandoned painting and committed himself entirely to photography.

His first fashion photographs were made in 1911 for PAUL POIRET; it was not until after he was hired by Condé Nast in 1923 as photographic editor-in-chief that he developed his mature style, deeply influenced by his involvement with modern art. He replaced the pictorialism of his predecessor, BARON DE MEYER, with a modernism based on strong, clean lines, plain backgrounds, and an all-new model, the "flapper." His influence was strong on the early work of HOYNINGEN-HUENE. He also worked for the advertising agency, J. Walter Thompson.

Steichen essentially abandoned his own photography in 1947 when he became director of the Department of Photography at New York's Museum of Modern Art, a post he held until his retirement in 1962. His best-known show from that era was "The Family of Man," which traveled to a number of other museums around the country. During his long and distinguished career he accumulated a staggering list of honors and affiliations.

Vreeland, Diana

Born Paris, France, ca. 1906
Died New York City, August 22, 1989
Awards Chevalier of the National Order of Merit of France, 1970 • Légion d'Honneur, 1976 • Lord & Taylor Dorothy Shaver "Rose" Award, 1976 • Parsons School of Design Honorary Doctor of Fine Arts Degree, 1977

For nearly five decades, Diana Vreeland was a powerful influence on the American fashion consciousness, first as fashion editor and last as museum consultant. Born in Paris to an American mother and English father, raised in a milieu saturated with fashion and the arts, she was by both nature and nurture ideally fitted for her eventual vocation. As a child, she was exposed to extraordinary people and events: Diaghilev, Nijinsky, Ida Rubinstein, Vernon and Irene Castle were all guests in her parents' apartment and she remembered being sent to London in 1911 for the coronation of George V. Her family moved to America at the outbreak of World War I. Married in 1924 to Thomas Reed Vreeland, she accompanied her husband as his job took him to Albany, New York, on to London, then back to New York City in 1937. The same year, at the invitation of Carmel Snow, she went to work for *Harper's Bazaar.*

At *Bazaar,* she first wrote "Why Don't You," a column that quickly became a byword for such suggestions as "Why Don't You ... rinse your blonde child's hair in dead champagne to keep it gold as they do in France...?" After six months she became fashion editor, working closely with Mrs. Snow and art director Alexey Brodovitch to make *Bazaar* the exciting, influential publication it was. In 1962 she left the magazine to go to *Vogue* as associate editor, then editor-in-chief, a post she held until 1971. After 1971 she was a consulting editor at *Vogue* and began a new career as consultant to the Costume Institute of the Metropolitan Museum of Art. There she mounted a series of outstanding exhibitions on such subjects as "BALENCIAGA," "American Women of Style," The Glory of Russian Costume," "Vanity Fair," "Man and the Horse."

Mrs. Vreeland, who as a child felt like an ugly duckling, recreated herself as an elegant, completely individual woman with a strong personal style: jet black hair, heavily rouged cheeks, bright red lips. For day and small dinners she dressed in simple uniforms — sweaters and skirts or sweaters and pants — appearing for big evenings in dramatic gowns from favorite designers: SAINT LAURENT, GRÈS, GIVENCHY. Her conversation and writing styles were as original as her appearance, dramatic, exaggerated, and quite inimitable. In her time at *Vogue,* the Vreeland memos were cherished, copied, and passed around among the staffers.

As an editor she not only reported fashion but promoted it vigorously, showing something she believed in repeatedly until it took hold. Perhaps her greatest achievement was her ability to understand the era of the 1960s with all its upheavals. To whatever she did she brought her sense of drama, her immense energy, and above all, her unquenchable enthusiasm for the unique and the beautiful. She credited her success to conscientiousness, thoroughness, and an inability to take short cuts. A fund in her name has been established to benefit the Metropolitan Museum of Art's Costume Institute.

Appendix

Council of Fashion Designers of America (CFDA) Awards

Year	Designer	Type
1989	Abboud, Joseph	menswear designer of the year
1990	Abboud, Joseph	menswear designer of the year
1994	Alfaro, Victor	Perry Ellis award for new fashion talent
1989	Avedon, Richard	lifetime achievement award
1981	Barnes, Jhane	outstanding menswear designer
1994	Bartlett, John	Perry Ellis award for new talent
1985	Beene, Geoffrey	special award
1986	Beene, Geoffrey	special award designer of the year
1989	Beene, Geoffrey	special award for fashion as art
1987, 1989	Blahnik, Manolo	outstanding excellence in accessory design
1986	Blass, Bill	lifetime achievement award
1985	Claiborne, Liz	special award
1993	Cunningham, Bill	Eugenia Sheppard award for fashion journalism
1981	Ellis, Perry	outstanding designer in women's fashion
1982	Ellis, Perry	outstanding designer in men's fashion
1983	Ellis, Perry	outstanding designer in men's fashion
1985	Gernreich, Rudi	special tribute
1989	Henderson, Gordon	Perry Ellis award for new fashion talent
1987	Jacobs, Marc	Perry Ellis award for new fashion talent
1981	Julian, Alexander	designer of the year
1982	Kamali, Norma	outstanding women's fashion
1985	Kamali, Norma	innovative uses of video in presentation and promotion of fashion
1985	Karan, Donna	special award
1986	Karan, Donna	special award
1990	Karan, Donna	women's wear designer of the year
1992	Karan, Donna	menswear designer of the year
1981	Kieselstein-Cord, Barry	excellence in design
1981	Klein, Calvin	best American collection
1983	Klein, Calvin	best American collection and women's wear designer of the year
1987	Klein, Calvin	best American collection
1993	Klein, Calvin	menswear designer of the year
1982	Lagerfeld, Karl	special award
1981	Lauren, Ralph	special award
1986	Lauren, Ralph	retailer of the year
1994	Leiber, Judith	lifetime achievement award
1994	Meyer, Gene	men's accessory award
1983	Miyake, Issey	special award
1988	Mizrahi, Isaac	Perry Ellis award for new fashion talent
1989	Mizrahi, Isaac	designer of the year
1991	Mizrahi, Isaac	designer of the year
1985	Morris, Robert Lee	special award for founding Artwear and for jewelry design
1994	Morris, Robert Lee	women's accessory award
1991	Oldham, Todd	Perry Ellis award for new fashion talent

Year	Designer	Type
1993	Prada, Miuccia	international award
1990	Pucci, Emilio	special award
1994	Rowley, Cynthia	Perry Ellis award for new fashion talent
1981	Saint Laurent, Yves	special award
1981	Sanchez, Fernando	lingerie and at-home wear
1987	Saint'Angelo Giorgio	contribution to evolution of stretch clothing
1987	Scaasi, Arnold	extravagant evening dress
1988	Shamask, Ronaldus	menswear designer of the year
1992	Sui, Anna	Perry Ellis award for new fashion talent
1993	Tyler, Richard	Perry Ellis award for new fashion talent
1994	Tyler, Richard	best designer

Coty American Fashion Critics' Awards

Year	Designer	Type
1955, 1969	Adolfo	Special Award (millinery)
1982	Adri	"Winnie"
1972	Anthony, John	"Winnie"
1977	Anthony, John	Return Award
1980	Barnes, Jhane	Men's Wear
1981	Barnes, Jhane	Men's Apparel
1984	Barnes, Jhane	Men's Wear Return Award
1964	Beene, Geoffrey	"Winnie"
1966	Beene, Geoffrey	Return Award
1974	Beene, Geoffrey	Hall of Fame
1975	Beene, Geoffrey	Hall of Fame Citation
1977	Beene, Geoffrey	Special Award (jewelry)
1979	Beene, Geoffrey	Special Award
1981	Beene, Geoffrey	Special Award (women's fashion)
1982	Beene, Geoffrey	Hall of Fame Citation
1961	Blass, Bill	"Winnie"
1963	Blass, Bill	Return Award
1968	Blass, Bill	First Coty Award for men's wear
1970	Blass, Bill	Hall of Fame
1971	Blass, Bill	Hall of Fame Citation
1975	Blass, Bill	Special Award (furs for Revillon America)
1982	Blass, Bill	Hall of Fame Citation
1983	Blass, Bill	Hall of Fame Citation
1974	Burrows, Stephen	Special Award (lingerie)
1977	Burrows, Stephen	"Winnie"
1950	Cashin, Bonnie	"Winnie"
1961	Cashin, Bonnie	Special Award (leather and fabric design)
1968	Cashin, Bonnie	Return Award
1972	Cashin, Bonnie	Hall of Fame
1975	Cesarani, Sal	Special Award (men's wear)
1976	Cesarani, Sal	Special Award (men's wear-neckwear)
1982	Cesarani, Sal	Men's Wear Return Award
1974	Cipullo, Aldo	Men's Wear (jewelry)
1943	Daché, Lilly	Special Award (millinery)
1967	de la Renta, Oscar	"Winnie"
1968	de la Renta, Oscar	Return Award
1973	de la Renta, Oscar	Hall of Fame
1984	Dell'Olio, Louis	Special Award (women's wear with Donna Karan)
1977	Dell'Olio, Louis	"Winnie" (with Donna Karan)
1982	Dell'Olio, Louis	Hall of Fame (with Donna Karan)
1979	Ellis, Perry	"Winnie"
1980	Ellis, Perry	Return Award
1981	Ellis, Perry	Hall of Fame
1981	Ellis, Perry	Special Award (men's wear)
1983	Ellis, Perry	Hall of Fame Citation (women's wear)

Year	Designer	Type
1983	Ellis, Perry	Men's Wear Return Award
1984	Ellis, Perry	Hall of Fame (men's wear)
1984	Ellis, Perry	Hall of Fame Citation (women's wear)
1951	Fogarty, Anne	Special Award (dresses)
1954	Galanos, James	"Winnie"
1956	Galanos, James	Return Award
1959	Galanos, James	Hall of Fame
1960	Gernreich, Rudi	Special Award (innovative body clothes)
1963	Gernreich, Rudi	"Winnie"
1966	Gernreich, Rudi	Return Award
1967	Gernreich, Rudi	Hall of Fame
1962, 1969	Halston	Special Award (millinery)
1971	Halston	"Winnie"
1972	Halston	Return Award
1974	Halston	Hall of Fame
1978	Helpern, Joan	Special Award (footwear)
1975	Horn, Carol	"Winnie"
1950	James, Charles	"Winnie"
1954	James, Charles	Special Award (innovative cut)
1943	John, Mr.	Special Award
1971	Johnson, Betsy	"Winnie"
1979	Julian, Alexander	Men's Wear Return Award
1977	Julian, Alexander	Men's Wear Award
1981	Julian, Alexander	Men's Apparel
1983	Julian, Alexander	Special Award Citation
1984	Julian, Alexander	Special Award (men's wear)
1984	Kahn, Robin	Special Award (belt and buckle designs for men's wear)
1981	Kamali, Norma	"Winnie"
1982	Kamali, Norma	Return Award
1983	Kamali, Norma	Hall of Fame
1977	Karan, Donna	"Winnie" (with Louis Dell'Olio)
1982	Karan, Donna	Hall of Fame (with Louis, Dell'Olio)
1984	Karan, Donna	Special Award (women's wear with Louis Dell'Olio)
1955	Kasper, Herbert	"Winnie"
1970	Kasper, Herbert	Return Award
1976	Kasper, Herbert	Hall of Fame
1979	Kieselstein-Cord, Barry	Outstanding Jewelry Design
1984	Kieselstein-Cord, Barry	Excellence in Women' Wear Design
1955	Klein, Anne	"Winnie"
1969	Klein, Anne	Return Award
1971	Klein, Anne	Hall of Fame
1973	Klein, Calvin	"Winnie"
1974	Klein, Calvin	Return Award
1975	Klein, Calvin	Hall of Fame
1975	Klein, Calvin	Special Award (fur design for Alexandre)
1979	Klein, Calvin	Special Award (contribution to international status of American fashion)
1981	Klein, Calvin	Women's Apparel

Year	Designer	Type
1966	Lane, Kenneth Jay	Outstanding Contribution to Fashion
1970	Lauren, Ralph	Mens Wear
1973	Lauren, Ralph	Return Award
1974	Lauren, Ralph	"Winnie"
1984	Lauren, Ralph	Special Award (women's wear)
1976	Lauren, Ralph	Return Award
1976	Lauren, Ralph	Hall of Fame (men's wear)
1977	Lauren, Ralph	Hall of Fame (women's wear)
1981	Lauren, Ralph	Men's Apparel
1973	Leiber, Judith	Special Award (handbags)
1945	Leser, Tina	"Winnie"
1951	Maxwell, Vera	Special Award (coats and suits)
1944	McCardell, Claire	"Winnie"
1958	McCardell, Claire	Hall of Fame (posthumous)
1976	McFadden, Mary	"Winnie"
1978	McFadden, Mary	Return Award
1979	Mcfadden, Mary	Hall of Fame
1981	Morris, Robert Lee	Special Award (jewelry for Calvin Klein)
1943	Norell, Norman	First "Winnie"
1951	Norell, Norman	First Return Award
1958	Norell, Norman	First designer elected to Hall of Fame
1951	Partos, Emeric	Special Award (furs)
1961	Pedlar, Sylvia	Special Award (lingerie)
1964	Pedlar, Sylvia	Return Special Award (lingerie)
1971	Peretti, Elsa	Special Award (jewelry)
1974, 1977	Sanchez, Fernando	Special Award (lingerie)
1975	Sanchez, Fernando	Special Award (furs for Revillon)
1981	Sanchez, Fernando	Special Award (lingerie)
1968	Sant Angelo, Giorgio	Special Award (fantasy accessories and ethnic fashions)
1970	Sant Angelo, Giorgio	"Winnie"
1958	Scaasi, Arnold	"Winnie"
1958	Schlumberger, Jean	Special Award (the first given for jewelry)
1981	Shamask, Ronaldus	"Winnie"
1947	Simpson, Adele	"Winnie"
1983	Smith, Willi	Special Award
1975	Sylbert, Viola	Special Award (fur design)
1961	Tassell, Gustave	"Winnie"
1974	Tice, Bill	Special Award (loungewear)
1975	Tilley, Monika	Special Award (swimsuits)
1949	Trigère, Pauline	"Winnie"
1951	Trigère, Pauline	Return Award
1959	Trigère, Pauline	Hall of Fame
1979	Vass, Joan	Special Award (crafted knit fashions)
1984	Vittadini, Adrienne	Special Award
1970	Weinberg, Chester	"Winnie"
1974	Weitz, John	Special Men's Wear Award

Neiman Marcus Awards

Year	Designer	Year	Designer
1955	Balmain, Pierre	1968	Lane, Kenneth Jay
1956	Beaton, Cecil	1980	Leiber, Judith
1964, 1965	Beene, Geoffrey	1945	Leser, Tina
1969	Blass, Bill	1955	Maxwell, Vera
1950	Cashin, Bonnie	1945	McCardell, Claire
1957	Chanel, Gabrielle	1973	Missoni, Rosita & Ottavio
1940	Chase, Edna Woolman	1984	Miyake, Issey
1962	Crahay, Jules-Francois	1973	Mori, Hanae
1940	Daché, Lilly	1973	Muir, Jean
1968	de la Renta, Oscar	1942	Norell, Norman
1947	Dior, Christian	1960	Pedlar, Sylvia
1955	Eiseman, Florence	1990	Pucci, Emilio
1979	Ellis, Perry	1958	Saint Laurent, Yves
1947	Ferragamo, Salvatore	1987	Scaasi, Arnold
1952	Fogarty, Anne	1940	Schiaparelli, Elsa
1954	Galanos, James	1946	Simpson, Adele
1947	Hartnell, Norman	1950	Trigère, Pauline
1953	James, Charles	1969	Ungaro, Emanuel
1959, 1969	Klein, Anne	1967	Valentino
1980	Lagerfeld, Karl	1961	Vivier, Roger

Bibliography

This bibliography is compiled to help the reader in the study of fashion. Not all the listed books have contributed to this edition of Who's Who in Fashion.

The Age of Worth. New York: Brooklyn Museum of Arts & Sciences, 1982.

Amies, Hardy. *Just So Far*. St. James Place, London: Collins, 1984.

_____. *ABC of Men's Fashion.* London: Newnes, 1964.

_____. *Still Here.* London: Weidenfeld and Nicolson, 1984.

Anscombe, Isabelle. *A Woman's Touch: Women in Design from 1860 to the Present Day.* London: Virago, 1984.

Ash, Juliet and Elizabeth Wilson, editors. *Chic Thrills.* London: Pandora Press, 1992.

Bailey, M.J. *Those Glorious, Glamour Years: The Great Hollywood Costume Designs of the Thirties.* Secaucus, NJ: Citadel Press, 1982.

Baillen, *C. Chanel Solitaire.* Translated by Barbara Bray. New York: Quadrangle/The New York Times Book Co., 1974.

Ballard, Bettina. *In My Fashion.* New York: David McKay Co., Inc., 1960.

Balmain, Pierre. *My Years and Seasons* (autobiography). Translated by E. Lanchbery and G. Young. London: Cassell & Co. Ltd., 1964. New York: Doubleday & Company, Inc., 1965.

Beaton, Cecil. *The Glass of Fashion.* New York: Doubleday & Company, Inc., 1954.

_____. *Fair Lady.* New York: Holt, Rinehart & Winston, 1964.

_____. *Cecil Beaton: Memoirs of the 40s.* New York: McGraw-Hill Book Co., 1977.

_____. *The Book of Beauty.* London: Duckworth, 1930

_____. *Cecil Beaton's New York.* London: Batsford, 1938.

_____. *Persona Grata* (with Kenneth Tynan). London: Wingate, 1953.

_____. *The Glass of Fashion.* London: Weidenfeld & Nicolson, 1954.

_____. *Cecil Beaton's Diaries—1922-1929, The Wandering Years* (1961); *1939-1944, The Years Between* (1965); *1944-1948, The Happy Years* (1972); *1948-1955, The Strenuous Years* (1973). London: Weidenfeld & Nicolson.

_____. *The Gainsborough Girls,* a play. 1951.

Bender, Marilyn. *Beautiful People.* New York: Coward, McCann & Geoghegan, Inc., 1967.

Bernhard, Barbara. *Fashion in the 60s.* New York: St. Martin's Press, 1978.

Bertin, Celia. *Paris à la Mode.* London: Gollancz, 1956.

Bianchino, Gloria, Grazietta Butazzi, Alessandra Mottola Molfino, and Arturo Carlo Quintavalle. *Italian Fashion.* New York: Rizzoli International Publications, 1988.

Black, J. Anderson and Madge Garland. *A History of Fashion.* New York: Morrow, 1980.

Blum, Stella. *Designs by Erte. Fashion Drawings & Illustrations from Harper's Bazaar.* New York: Harry N. Abrams, 1987.

Bond, David. *The Guinness Guide to Twentieth Century Fashion.* Middlesex, England: Guinness Superlatives Ltd., 1981.

Boucher, François with Yvonne Deslandres. *20,000 Years of Fashion: The History of Costume and Personal Adornment,* Expanded Edition. New York: Harry N. Abrams, 1987.

Brady, James. *Super Chic.* Boston: Little, Brown & Co., 1974.

Brogden, J. *Fashion Design.* London: Studio Vista, 1971.

Burris-Meyer, Elizabeth. *This Is Fashion.* New York: Harper, 1943.

Byers, Margaretta. *Designing Women.* New York: Simon & Schuster, 1938.

Calasibetta, Charlotte Mankey. *Fairchild's Dictionary of Fashion,* 2nd Edition. New York: Fairchild Publications, 1988.

Carter, Ernestine. *Magic Names of Fashion.* New Jersey: Prentice-Hall, Inc., 1980.

_____. *Twentieth Century Fashion, a Scrapbook: 1900 to Today.* London: Eyre Methuen, 1975.

_____. *The Changing World of Fashion.* New York: G.P. Putnam's Sons, 1977.

Chapkis, Wendy and Cynthia Enloe. *Of Common Cloth: Women in the Global Textile Industry.* Amsterdam: Transnational Institute, 1983.

Charles-Roux, Edmonde. *Chanel: her life, her world, and the woman behind the legend she herself created.* France: Editions Grosset & Faquelle, 1974. Distributed by Random House, New York.

_____. *Chanel and Her World.* London: Weidenfeld & Nicolson, 1979.

Chase, Edna Woolman and Ilka Chase. *Always in Vogue.* New York: Doubleday & Company, Inc., 1954.

Coleman, Elizabeth Ann. *The Genius of Charles James.* Published for the exhibition at the Brooklyn Museum. New York: Holt, Rinehart and Winston, 1982.

_____. *Changing Fashions, 1800-1970*. New York: Brooklyn Museum, 1972.

_____. *The Opulent Era: Fashions of Worth, Doucet and Pingat.* London: Thames and Hudson, 1989.

Creed, Charles. *Made to Measure.* London: Jarrolds, 1961.

Daché, Lilly. *Talking through My Hats.* Edited by Dorothy Roe Lewis. New York: Coward-McCann, Inc., 1946.

_____. *Lilly Daché's Glamour Book.* 1957.

Dars, Christine. *A Fashion Parade: The Seeberger Collection.* London: Blond & Briggs, 1979.

Davenport, Millia. *The Book of Costume.* New York: Crown Publishers, Inc., 1948.

Daves, Jessica. *Ready-Made Miracle.* New York: G.P. Putnam's Sons, 1967.

Daves, Jessica, Alexander Liberman, Bryan Holmes and Katherine Tweed. *The World in Vogue.* Compiled by The Viking Press and Vogue Magazine, 1963.

DeGraw, Imelda G. *25 Years, 25 Couturiers.* Denver: Denver Museum, 1975.

De Marly, Diana. *Costume on the Stage.* New York: Barnes and Noble Imports, 1982.

_____. *The History of Haute Couture, 1850-1950.* London: B.T. Batsford, 1980.

_____. *Worth, Father of Haute Couture.* London: Elm Tree Books, 1980.

Demornex, Jaqueline. *Madeleine Vionnet.* Translated by Augusta Audubert. New York: Rizzoli International Publications, 1991.

De Osma, Guillermo. *Mariano Fortuny: His Life and Work.* New York: Rizzoli International Publications, Inc., 1980.

Deschodt, Anne-Marie. *Mariano Fortuny, un Magicien de Venise.* Tours, France: Editions du Regard, 1979.

Deslandres, Yves. *Poiret.* New York: Rizzoli International Publications, Inc., 1987.

Devlin, P. *Fashion Photography in Vogue.* London: Thames and Hudson, 1978.

Diamonstein, Barbaralee. *Fashion: The Inside Story.* New York: Rizzoli International Publications, Inc., 1985.

Dior, Christian. *Talking about Fashion.* Translated by Eugenia Sheppard. New York: G.P. Putnam's Sons, 1954.

_____. *Christian Dior and I.* Translated by Antonia Fraser. New York: E.P. Dutton & Company, Inc., 1957.

_____. *Dior by Dior.* Translated by Antonia Fraser. London: Weidenfeld & Nicolson, 1957. Harmondsworth, England: Penguin Books, 1968.

Dixon, H. Vernon. *The Rag Pickers.* New York: David McKay Co., Inc., 1966.

Dorner, Jane. *Fashion: The Changing Shape of Fashion through the Years.* London: Octopus Books, 1974.

_____. *Fashion in the 40s and 50s.* London: Ian Allen, 1975.

Duncan, N.H. *History of Fashion Photography.* New York: Alpine Press, 1979.

Elegance et Creation: Paris 1945-1975. Paris: Musee de la Mode et du Costume, 1977.

Emanuel, Elizabeth and David. *Style for All Seasons.* 1983.

Erte. *Erté Fashions.* New York: St. Martin's Press, 1972.

_____. *Erté—Things I Remember* (autobiography). London: Peter Owen Limited, 1975.

Etherington-Smith, Meredith. *Patou.* New York: St. Martin's/Marek, 1983.

Ewing, Elizabeth. *History of 20th Century Fashion.* New York: Charles Scribner's Sons, 1974.

Fairchild, John. *The Fashionable Savages.* New York: Doubleday & Company, Inc., 1965.

Farber, R. *The Fashion Photographers.* New York: Watson Guptill, 1981.

Fashion, 1900-1939. London: Scottish Arts Council; Victoria and Albert Museum, 1975.

Fashion Illustration. New York: Rizzoli International Publications, 1979.

Ferragamo, Salvatore. *Shoemaker of Dreams* (autobiography). England: George G. Harrap & Co. Ltd., 1972.

Fine Fashion. Philadelphia: Museum of Art, 1979.

Fogarty, Anne. *Wife-Dressing.* New York: Julian Messner Inc., 1959.

Fortuny. New York: Fashion Institute of Technology, 1981.

Fortuny nella Belle Epoque. Milan: Electa, 1984.

Forty Years of Italian Fashion, 1940-1980. (organized by Bonizza Giordani Aragno). Rome: Fidevrart, 1983.

Fraser, Kennedy. *The Fashionable Mind.* Boston: David R. Godine, 1985.

Gaines, S. *Simply Halston.* New York: Putnam Publishing Group, 1991.

Galante, Pierre. *Mademoiselle Chanel.* Chicago, 1973.

Garland, Madge. *Fashion.* London: Penguin Books, 1962.

_____. *The Changing Form of Fashion.* London: J.M. Dent & Sons, 1970.

Giroud, Francois. *Dior.* New York: Rizzoli International Publications, 1987.

Glynn, Prudence. *In Fashion: Dress in the Twentieth Century.* New York: Oxford University Press, 1978.

_____. *Skin to Skin.* New York: Oxford University Press, 1982.

Gold, Annalee. *75 Years of Fashion.* New York: Fairchild Publications, 1975.

_____. *One World of Fashion,* 4th edition. New York: Fairchild Publications, 1986.

Gorsline, Douglas Warner. *What People Wore: A Visual History of Dress from Ancient Times to 20th Century America.* New York: Viking Press, 1952.

Haedrich, Marcel. *Coco Chanel: Her Life, Her Secrets.* Boston: Little, Brown & Co., 1971.

Hartnell, Norman. *Silver and Gold* (autobiography). London: Evans Brothers, 1955.

_____. *Royal Courts of Fashion.* London: Cassell & Co. Ltd., 1971.

Haute Couture: Notes on Designers and Their Clothes in the Collection of the Royal Ontario Museum. Toronto: Royal Ontario Museum, 1969.

Hawes, Elizabeth. *Fashion is Spinach.* New York: Random House, 1938.

_____. *It's Still Spinach.* Boston: Little, Brown and Co., 1954.

Head, Edith. *The Dress Doctor.* Boston: Little, Brown and Co., 1959.

A History of Fashion. London: House of Worth.

Hommage à Schiaparelli. Paris: Musée de la Mode et du Costume, 1984.

Horst. *Salute to the Thirties.* New York: Viking Press, 1971.

Houck, Catherine. *The Fashion Encyclopedia.* New York: St. Martin's Press, 1982.

The House of Worth: The Gilded Age, 1860-1918. New York: Museum of the City of New York, 1982.

Howell, Georgina. *In Vogue: Six Decades of Fashion.* London: Allen Lane, 1975.

Hulanicki, Barbara. *From A to Biba.* London: Hutchinson, 1983.

Immagini e Materiali del Laboratorio Fortuny. Venice: Comune di Venezia Marsilio Edition, 1978.

Jachimowicz, Elizabeth. *Eight Chicago Women and Their Fashion. 1860-1926.* Chicago: Chicago Historical Society, 1978.

Jouve, M. and J. Demornex. *Balenciaga.* New York: Rizzoli International Publications, 1989.

Karan, Donna. *An American Woman Observed.* 1987.

Kawakubo, Rei. *Comme des Garcons.* Japan: Chikuma Shobo, 1987.

Keenan, Brigid. *Dior in Vogue.* New York: Harmony Books, 1981.

Kennedy, Shirley. *Pucci: A Rennaissance in Fashion.* New York: Abbeville Press, 1991.

Kennett, Frances. *The Collector's Book of Fashion.* New York: Crown Publishers, Inc., 1983.

Khornak, Lucille. *Fashion 2001.* New York: Viking Press, 1982.

Kybalova, Ludmila, Olga Herbenova and Milena Lamorova. *The Pictoral Encyclopedia of Fashion,* 2nd Edition. Translated by Claudia Rosoux. England: Hamlyn Publishers, 1968. New York: Crown Publishers, Inc., 1969.

Lagerfeld, Karl. *Lagerfeld's Sketchbook: Karl Lagerfeld's Illustrated Fashion Journal of Anna Piaggi.* London: Weidenfeld & Nicolson, 1986.

Lambert, Eleanor. *World of Fashion: People, Places and Resources.* New York: R.R. Bowker Company, 1976.

Langlade, Emile. *Rose Bertin: The Creator of Fashion at the Court of Marie-Antoinette.* Adapted from the French by Dr. Angelo S. Rappoport. New York: Charles Scribner's Sons, 1913.

Latour, Anny. *Kings of Fashion.* Translated by Mervyn Saville. London: Weidenfeld & Nicolson, 1958.

_____. *Paris Fashion.* London: Michael Joseph, 1972.

Laver, James. *Taste and Fashion.* London: George G. Harrap & Co. Ltd., 1937.

_____. *A Concise History of Costume.* London: Thames and Hudson, 1969.

_____. *Fashion, Art and Beauty.* New York: Costume Institute, Metropolitan Museum of Art, 1967.

Lavine, W. Robert. *In a Glamorous Fashion.* New York: Charles Scribner's Sons, 1980.

Lee, Sarah Tomerlin, editor. *American Fashion: The Life and Lines of Adrian, Mainbocher, McCardell, Norell & Trigère.* New York: Quadrangle/The NY Times Book Co., 1975.

Leese, Elizabeth. *Costume Design in the Movies.* New York: Frederick Ungar Publishing Co., 1977.

Levin, Phyllis Lee. *The Wheels of Fashion.* New York: Doubleday & Company, Inc., 1965.

Ley, S. *Fashion for Everyone: The Story of Ready-to-Wear.* New York: Charles Scribner's Sons, 1975.

Leymarie, Jean. *Chanel.* New York: Rizzoli International Publications, 1987.

Lynam, Ruth, editor. *Couture.* New York: Doubleday & Company, Inc., 1972.

Madsen, Axel. *Living for Design: Yves Saint Laurent Story.* New York, 1979.

_____. *Chanel, A Woman of Her Own.* New York: Henry Holt Co., 1990.

Martin, R. and H. Koda. *Giorgio Armani: Images of Man.* New York: Rizzoli International Publications, 1990.

Maxwell, Elsa. *R.S.V.P. Elsa Maxwell's Own Story.* Boston: Little, Brown & Co., 1954.

McCardell, Claire. *What Shall I Wear?*. New York: Simon & Schuster, 1956.

McConathy, D. with D. Vreeland. *Hollywood Costume.* New York: Harry N. Abrams, 1976.

McDowell, Colin. *McDowell's Directory of Twentieth Century Fashion.* New Jersey: Prentice-Hall, Inc., 1985.

Mendes, Valerie D. *Twentieth Century Fashion: An Introduction to Women's Fashionable Dress, 1900-1980.* London: Victoria and Albert Museum, 1981.

Milbank, Caroline Rennolds. *Couture: The Great Designers.* New York: Stewart, Tabori & Chang, Inc., 1985.

_____. *New York Fashion: The Evolution of American Style.* New York: Harry N. Abrams, 1989.

Milinaire, Caterine and Carol Troy. *Cheap Chic.* New York: Harmony Books, 1975.

Miyake, Issey. *Issey Miyake East Meets West.* Tokyo: Shogaku Kan Publishing Co. Ltd., 1978.

_____. Issey Miyake *Bodyworks.* Tokyo: Shogaku Kan Publishing Co. Ltd., 1983.

Moffitt, P. et al. *The Rudi Gernreich Book.* New York: Rizzoli International Publications, 1990.

Mohrt, Francoise. *30 Ans D'Elegance et de Créations Rochas Mode, 1925-1955.* Paris: Jacques Damase, 1983.

Morand, Paul. *Lewis and Irene.* New York: Boni & Liveright, 1925.

Morris, Bernadine. *The Fashion Makers: An Inside Look at America's Leading Designers.* New York: Random House, 1978.

Mugler, Thierry. *Thierry Mugler.* New York: Rizzoli International Publications, 1988.

Nicolson, Nigel. *Mary Curzon.* New York: Harper & Row, 1977.

O'Hara, Georgina. *The Encyclopedia of Fashion.* New York: Harry N. Abrams, Inc., 1986.

Osma, G. *Fortuny. His Life and Work.* New York: Rizzoli International Publications, 1980.

Payne, Blanche. *History of Costume: From the Ancient Egyptians to the Twentieth Century.* New York: Harper & Row, 1965.

Pelle, M. Valentino: *Thirty Years of Magic.* New York: Abbeville Press, 1991.

Perkins, Alice K. Paris *Couturiers & Milliners.* New York: Fairchild Publications, 1949.

Picken, Mary Brooks. *The Fashion Dictionary.* New York: Funk & Wagnalls, 1957.

_____ and Dora Loves Miller. *Dressmakers of France: The Who, How and Why of French Couture.* New York: Harper & Brothers Publishers, 1956.

Poiret, Paul. *En Habillant l'Epoque.* Paris: Grasset, 1930.

Polan, Brenda, editor. *The Fashion Year, 1938.* London: Zomba Books, 1983.

Prichard, S. *Film Costume: An Annotated Bibliography.* Metuchen, NJ: Scarecrow, 1981.

_____. *King of Fashion* (autobiography). Translated by Stephen Haden Guest. Philadelphia: J.B. Lippincott Company, 1931.

_____. *Revenez-Y.* Paris: Lutetia, 1934.

Quant, Mary. *Quant by Quant.* London: Cassell & Co. Ltd., 1966.

_____. *Colour by Quant.*

Rhodes, Zandra and Anne Knight. *The Art of Zandra Rhodes.* Boston: Houghton Mifflin Company, 1985.

Riley, Robert. *Givenchy: 30 Years.* New York: Fashion Institute of Technology, 1982.

Robinson, Julian. *Fashion in the Forties.* New York: Harcourt Brace Jovanovich, 1976.

_____. *Fashion in the Thirties.* London: Oresko Books, 1978.

Rochas, Marcel. *Twenty-Five Years of Parisian Elegance, 1925-1950.* Paris: Pierre Tisne, 1951.

Roshco, Bernard. *The Rag Race.* New York: Funk & Wagnalls, 1963.

Ross, Josephine. *Beaton in Vogue.* New York: Clarkson N. Potter Inc., 1986.

Rykiel, Sonia. *And I Would Like Her Naked.* Paris: Bernard Grasset, 1979.

Salomon, Rosalie Kolodny. *Fashion Design for Moderns.* New York: Fairchild Publications, 1976.

Saunders, Edith. *The Age of Worth: Couturier to the Empress Eugenie.* Bloomington, IN: Indiana University Press, 1955.

Schiaparelli, Elsa. *Shocking Life.* New York: E.P. Dutton & Co., Inc.,1954.

_____. *Elsa Schiaparelli: Empress of Paris Fashion.* New York: Rizzoli International Publications, Inc., 1986.

Schreier, Barbara. *Mystique and Identity: Women's Fashions in the 1950s.* Norfolk, VA: Chrysler Museum, 1984.

Seebohm, Caroline. *The Man Who Was Vogue.* New York: Viking Press, 1982.

Snow, Carmel and Mary Louise Aswell. *The World of Carmel Snow.* New York: McGraw-Hill Book Co., 1962.

Spencer, Charles. *Erté.* New York: Clarkson N. Potter, Inc., 1970.

Steele, Valerie. *Women of Fashion.* New York: Rizzoli Books International, 1991.

Thornton, N. *Poiret.* New York: Rizzoli International Publications, 1979.

Tice, Bill (with Sheila Weller). *Enticements: How to Look Fabulous in Lingerie.* New York: The MacMillan Company, 1985.

Toklas, Alice B. *A New French Style.* Paris: J.F. Verly, 1946.

Tolstoy, Mary Koutouzov. *Charlemagne to Dior: The Story of French Fashion.* New York: Michael Slains, 1967.

Trachtenberg, J. *Ralph Lauren—Image-maker. The Man Behind the Mystique.* New York: Little, Brown and Co., 1988.

Trahey, Jane, editor. *Harper's Bazaar: 100 Years of the American Female.* New York: Random House, 1967.

Vanderbilt, Gloria. *Woman to Woman.* New York: Doubleday, 1979.

Vecchio, Walter and Robert Riley. *The Fashion Makers: A Photographic Record.* New York: Crown Publishers, Inc., 1968.

Von Furstenberg, Diane. *Book of Beauty.* New York: Simon & Schuster, Inc., 1976.

Vreeland, Diana. *Allure.* New York: Doubleday, 1980.

_____. *D.V.* New York: Knopf, 1984.

"W": The Designing Life. Staff of *W,* edited by Lois Perschetz. New York: Clarkson N. Potter, Inc., 1987.

Walkley, C. *The Way to Wear 'Em: One Hundred Fifty Years of Punch on Fashion.* Chester Springs, PA: Dufour (P. Owen Ltd.), 1985.

Weitz, John. *Man in Charge.* New York: The MacMillan Company, 1974.

_____. *Sports Clothes for Your Sports Car.* New York: Arco Publishing Co., Inc., 1958.

White, Emily, editor. *Fashion 85.* New York: St. Martin's Press, 1985.

White, Palmer. *Poiret.* New York: Clarkson N. Potter, Inc., 1973.

Whiteman, Von. *Looking Back at Fashion, 1901-1939.* West Yorkshire, England: EP Publishing, 1978.

Williams, Beryl Epstein. *Fashion Is Our Business.* Philadelphia: J.B. Lippincott Co., 1945.

_____. *Young Faces in Fashion.* Philadelphia: J.B. Lippincott Co., 1957.

Wilcox, R. Turner. *The Mode in Costume.* New York: Charles Scribner's Sons, 1958.

The World of Balenciaga. New York: Costume Institute, Metropolitan Museum of Art, 1972.

Worsley-Gough, Barbara. *Fashions in London.* London: Allan Wingate, 1952.

Worth, Jean Philippe. *A Century of Fashion.* Translated by Ruth Scott Miller. Boston: Little, Brown & Co., 1928.

Yarwood, Doreen. *The Encyclopaedia of World Costume.* London: Anchor Press, 1978.

Yoxall, H.W. *A Fashion of Life.* New York: Taplinger, 1967.

Yves Saint Laurent. New York: Costume Institute, Metropolitan Museum of Art, 1983.

Index of Designers

Index